GIFTS AND GRACES

Prayer, Poetry, and Polemic from Lancelot Andrewes to John Bunyan

DAVID GAY

Gifts and Graces

Prayer, Poetry, and Polemic from Lancelot Andrewes to John Bunyan

UNIVERSITY OF TORONTO PRESS
Toronto Buffalo London

ISBN 978-1-4875-0528-8 (cloth)   ISBN 978-1-4875-3192-8 (EPUB)
ISBN 978-1-4875-3191-1 (PDF)

Library and Archives Canada Cataloguing in Publication

Title: Gifts and graces : prayer, poetry, and polemic from Lancelot Andrewes
    to John Bunyan / David Gay.
Names: Gay, David, 1955– author.
Description: Includes bibliographical references and index.
Identifiers: Canadiana (print) 2020041643X | Canadiana (ebook)
    20200416588 | ISBN 9781487505288 (cloth) | ISBN 9781487531928 (EPUB) |
    ISBN 9781487531911 (PDF)
Subjects: LCSH: English literature – Early modern, 1500–1700 – History and
    criticism. | LCSH: Christian poetry, English – Early modern, 1500–1700 –
    History and criticism. | LCSH: Prayer – England – History – 17th century. |
    LCSH: Religion and literature – England – History – 17th century. | LCSH:
    Polemics in literature. | LCSH: Prayer in literature. | LCSH: Andrewes,
    Lancelot, 1555–1626 – Criticism and interpretation. | LCSH: Herbert, George,
    1593–1633 – Criticism and interpretation. | LCSH: Vaughan, Henry, 1621–
    1695 – Criticism and interpretation. | LCSH: Taylor, Jeremy, 1613–1667 –
    Criticism and interpretation. | LCSH: Milton, John, 1608–1674 – Criticism
    and interpretation. | LCSH: Bunyan, John, 1628–1688 – Criticism and
    interpretation.
Classification: LCC PR428.R46 G39 2021 | DDC 820.9/3823–dc23

University of Toronto Press acknowledges the financial assistance to its
publishing program of the Canada Council for the Arts and the Ontario Arts
Council, an agency of the Government of Ontario.

 Canada Council   Conseil des Arts
for the Arts   du Canada

ONTARIO ARTS COUNCIL
CONSEIL DES ARTS DE L'ONTARIO
an Ontario government agency
un organisme du gouvernement de l'Ontario

Funded by the   Financé par le
Government   gouvernement
of Canada   du Canada

Canadä

In Memoriam
James F. Forrest

Contents

List of Illustrations   ix

Abbreviations   xi

Acknowledgments   xiii

Introduction   3

1 Lancelot Andrewes and George Herbert: The Word
   of Charity   14

2 Jeremy Taylor and Henry Vaughan: The Stock of Nature
   and Art   49

3 John Milton (1634–1650): The Spirit of Utterance   83

4 John Milton (1650–1674): The Spirit of Prayer   101

5 John Bunyan: The Nameless Terrible Instrument   129

Afterword   163

Notes   167

Bibliography   189

Index   203

List of Illustrations

1   Frontispiece: Book of Common Prayer (1700)   4
2   1611 Title page: Lancelot Andrewes's *Nineteen Sermons Concerning Prayer* (1611)   27
3   Title page: Andrewes's *Institutiones Piae or Directions to Pray* (1630)   28
4   Frontispiece for Richard Drake, *A manual of the private devotions and meditations of The Right Reverend Father in God Lancelot Andrews* (1648)   34
5   Title page and frontispiece: Jeremy Taylor's *A Collection of Offices* (1658)   65
6   Frontispiece: *Eikon Basilike,* engraved by William Marshall (1649)   93
7   Illustration by Jean-Baptiste de Medina. *Paradise Lost; A Poem in Twelve Books* 1688)   105
8   Frontispiece: *The Holy War* by John Bunyan (1682)   155

Abbreviations

Apology	Jeremy Taylor, *Apology for Authorized and Set Forms of Liturgy* (London, 1649).
CPW	John Milton, *Complete Prose Works of John Milton.* 8 vols., ed. Don Wolfe et al. New Haven: Yale University Press, 1953–82.
GA	*Grace Abounding to the Chief of Sinners*, in *Grace Abounding with other Spiritual Autobiographies*, ed. John Stachniewski with Anita Pacheco. Oxford: Oxford University Press, 1998.
HW	John Bunyan, *The Holy War*, ed. James F. Forrest and Roger Sharrock. Oxford: Clarendon Press, 1982.
MW	*The Miscellaneous Works of John Bunyan*, 13 volumes, general editor Roger Sharrock. Oxford: Clarendon Press, 1976–94.
NS	Lancelot Andrewes, *Nineteen Sermons Concerning Prayer.* Cambridge, 1641.
PP	John Bunyan, *Pilgrim's Progress*, ed. W.R. Owens. Oxford: Oxford University Press, 2003.
XCVI Sermons	*XCVI Sermons by the Right Honorable and Reverend Father in God, Lancelot Andrewes, late Lord Bishop of Winchester.* London: 1629.

Acknowledgments

I have many people to thank for their support, encouragement, and criticism of my work. I express my deep appreciation to Suzanne Rancourt of the University of Toronto Press for directing the publication process. I thank the anonymous readers engaged by the Press. Their comments brought significant improvements in style and argument. I am grateful to the Faculty of Arts at the University of Alberta and the Office of the Vice-President (Research) for providing financial support for this publication. I thank Steve Patten, Associate Dean of Research in the Faculty of Arts, for offering timely guidance and direction for this support. I thank the Social Sciences and Humanities Council of Canada for a research grant that allowed me to read extensively at the British Library in London and to share my ideas at national and international conferences. Dennis Danielson, one of Canada's most distinguished Miltonists, revealed his role as an adjudicator for the grant application to me at a later date and offered valuable ideas and suggestions that I hope I have fulfilled. Any errors or oversights in this book are mine alone.

SSHRC also allowed me to work with Dr Darrel Bargen and Dr Amie Shirkie, two outstanding Research Assistants whose brilliant doctoral dissertations I was privileged to read. Master's student Kirsten Fast also produced valuable research work. I appreciate the care and knowledge offered by support staff members in the Department of English and Film Studies who manage our research grants. I salute the staff of the British Library. There is no happier moment for a researcher than lining up at the desk in the Rare Books and Manuscripts room to pick up another stack of books. Staff members are unfailingly cheerful, knowledgeable, and professional. I take this moment also to thank Donald Mell, Director of the University of Delaware Press (retired) and his staff for encouraging this project at an early stage and for their support in the past.

I thank scholars who took time to comment on sections of this book: Bob Owens, David Walker, Roger Pooley, Paul Dyck, and Alan Rudrum. I also thank Edward Jones, editor of *Milton Quarterly*; Bob Owens and David Walker, editors of *Bunyan Studies A Journal of Reformation and Nonconformist Culture*; and Peter Lang, publishers of *Milton, Rights and Liberties* (ed. Neil Forsyth and Christophe Tournu) for permission to use some previously published material. I thank Dr Cecily Devereux, Chair of English and Film Studies, and her advisory council for the invitation to deliver the 2019 Edmund Kemper Broadus Lectures. This was an honour and writing the lectures helped me to improve and develop some key points in this study. I salute my early modern colleagues past and present, and thank the University of Alberta for giving me a place to learn, teach, and encourage others. I note especially Sylvia Brown of my department and Arlette Zinck of The King's University who have been fellow travellers in the International John Bunyan Society for many years, and with whom I had the pleasure of organizing the 2019 triennial conference: *Networks of Dissent*. My hope is that the IJBS will remain a supportive academic extended family for emerging scholars in the field. That it has been in the past is due to the hard work and generosity of its members.

As always, I owe a great debt to my debt to my wife Anne for her constant patience, wisdom, and encouragement. Finally, I dedicate this book to the memory of Professor James F. Forrest of the University of Alberta. Dr Forrest was an inspiring teacher and mentor, a prime mover in the formation of the IJBS, and a scholar whose early article on prayer in Milton's "Lycidas" stirred my broader reflections on this subject. He is remembered with great fondness and gratitude by the many students he taught so well.

GIFTS AND GRACES

Prayer, Poetry, and Polemic from Lancelot Andrewes
to John Bunyan

Introduction

i. The Scope of This Study

I begin with the terms in my title. Prayer, poetry, and polemic are broad by any measure and need both definition and limitation. By prayer, I mean two distinct modes of prayer that come into conflict in the early modern period. One is extemporaneous prayer, meaning prayers spoken spontaneously but never written down due to the practices or principles of groups who favoured this mode in public worship. The other is scripted prayer, meaning printed and prescribed prayers, particularly those found in the Book of Common Prayer. First produced by Archbishop Thomas Cranmer during the brief reign of Edward VI, the Book of Common Prayer radically reformed public worship by presenting it in English rather than Latin. The Catholic Queen Mary, who reigned from 1553 to 1558, restored the Latin Mass and condemned Cranmer to be burned at the stake in 1556, making both him and his prayer book martyrs. Elizabeth I revised and restored the Book of Common Prayer in 1559. It remained the official liturgy of the Church of England until a Puritan Parliament abolished it in 1645, replacing it with a simple manual, known as the *Directory of Public Worship*, that promoted extemporaneous prayer. Though proscribed, the prayer book remained in use in Anglican homes and communities during the Interregnum. When monarchy returned to England in 1660, so did the Book of Common Prayer in a new revision published in 1662. Its frontispiece asserted stability with an architectural image of the *Domus Orationis* or "House of Prayer" (Figure 1).[1] But 1662 also witnessed the mass ejection of nonconforming ministers and new laws of religious uniformity. Each of these stages of history provoked sharp polemical attacks either defending or rejecting the Prayer Book. The choice between free prayer and scripted prayer made for a cultural divide in and beyond the seventeenth century.

Figure 1. Frontispiece: Book of Common Prayer (1700), an image first used in 1662. ©Trustees of the British Museum.

Second, I define poetry broadly. The seventeenth century is an extraordinary period for devotional poets, and many scholarly books, whether on single authors or religious topics, explore these works. My focus, however, is on the affirmation or suspicion of poetic invention as a component of religious expression; groups that defended the Book of Common Prayer defend it as poetry working in collaboration with the inspired texts of the Bible. Those who opposed the prayer book were suspicious of "human invention" out of a sense that the book is a vestige of a past Catholic tradition or a present instrument of government coercion. The idea of divine inspiration emerges from this tension. Scripted prayers require the art and effort of natural imagination seen as a gift or talent God expects us to exercise. For others, scripted prayers are by definition external forces that can supplant the operation of the Holy Spirit within each believer. By poetry, then, I mean any kind of imaginative writing including narrative and allegory as well as verse and also polemical prose writings that use patterns of poetic imagery as vehicles of argument.

Third, I see polemic as a broad concept. Polemic comes from the Greek word for warfare, and we usually understand it as a harsh attack on an idea or opinion. As Jesse Lander demonstrates, "the Reformation and the printing press produced polemic, a new form of writing, that animated the literary culture of the mid-sixteenth- to late seventeenth-century England."[2] Arguing that print technology is not a neutral agent, Lander further observes that print and the Reformation together "created a culture that formed not homogeneously but continuously in debate, a culture that can itself be seen as polemical."[3] Polemic, as I describe it, is specific to its context and occasion and not a function of its tone. Poems that seem purely devotional in isolation reveal their polemical traces when viewed in the larger culture Lander describes. In conjunction with prayer and poetry, polemic is often but not always harsh: it can be fiercely partisan but also charitably persuasive, satirically sarcastic but also plainly logical, sharply divisive but radically inclusive, scornful of liturgical poetry as human invention, or richly poetic to scorn the abusers of liturgy. Prayer, poetry, and polemic refract and reflect each other in dynamic ways that merit attention. My main argument is that any work of imaginative literature that addresses or represents prayer in the seventeenth century is partly if not wholly polemical.

ii. Gifts and Graces Defined

Seventeenth-century England was a divided nation, and prayer reveals that division in detail. The Book of Common Prayer includes invented prayers (composed by writers) and biblical prayers (inspired by the Holy Spirit and transcribed by writers). Both kinds are "set forms" of prayer used uniformly throughout the nation. Set forms, such as the blessing of the bread and wine of communion, often use passages of scripture to inspire the listener: "the Lord Jesus the same might in which he was betrayed took bread" is 1 Corinthians 11:23 grafted into the prayer of consecration. The *Venite* in the service of Morning Prayer is Psalm 95: "O come, let us sing unto the Lord." The *Benedictus* is Luke 1:68: "Blessed be the Lord God of Israel for he hath visited and redeemed his people." Prayers not taken from scripture define points in liturgy, such as confessions: "We acknowledge and bewail our manifold sins and wickedness, Which we, from time to time, most grievously have committed,

By thought, word and deed, Against thy Divine Majesty, Provoking most justly thy wrath and indignation against us." Puritan reformers and Dissenters found these "stinted" prayers lifeless, confining, and, above all, controlling.[4] They preferred the inward movement of the Spirit and considered biblical prayers to be models more than scripts. Some found the indwelling Holy Spirit in the familiar words of the prayer book; others felt state coercion of conscience. In consequence, set forms and extemporaneous prayers provoked intense debates.

The early modern period was also a time when defending poetry was a constant occupation. This is a commonplace of sixteenth-century literature, as seen in Edmund Spenser's letter to Sir Walter Raleigh presenting *The Faerie Queene* as a poem in which truth is "clowdily enwrapped" rather than "sermoned abroad." Sir Philip Sidney's *Defence of Poetry* (1595) is an eloquent and extensive treatise that acknowledges the poetry of the Hebrew Bible and the Gospel parable before focusing entirely on the moral and social value of what we might call "secular" literature. The effort continues in the seventeenth century in writings by Jonson, Herbert, and Milton. This is not an ironic coincidence since the Reformation, as a flow of revolutionary intellectual energy, was certain, as all revolutions are, to engender some level of intolerance. Thus, the conflicted attitude to art and literature in the period is a defining condition for the polemics of prayer. Conception and expression are two problematic points. How do prayers edify if we do not supply the words? Can there really be a wordless interior space prior to speaking? Are biblical poems not set forms, as when the ancient Psalms speak our sufferings better than we can? These questions exercised poets and polemicists throughout the seventeenth century. A main issue in each question is the role of the natural imagination.

"Imagination" was starting to take on its modern sense of human creative power. "Imaginings," in contrast, meant misleading and even dangerous images. The benefits and hazards of images found in defences of poetry influenced defences of prayer. In his *Defence of Poetry* (1595), Sir Philip Sidney distinguishes the "eikastic" from the "phantastick" imagination: the former instills virtues, the latter illusions.[5] Jeremy Taylor, a main figure in this study, emulates Sidney to defend common prayer. His *Apology for Authorized and Set Forms of Liturgie: against the pretence of the Spirit*, published in 1649, is extensive and persuasive and certainly indebted to Sidney. As an Anglican priest, Taylor defended the Book of Common Prayer. He saw extemporaneous prayer in public worship as a religious imagining run wild. This passage gives us an overview of the conflict:

It is one of the Priviledges of the Gospel, and the benefit of Christ's ascension, that the Holy Ghost is given unto the Church, and is become to us the fountain of gifts and graces. But these gifts and graces are improvements and helps of our naturall faculties, of our art and industry, not extraordinary, miraculous, and immediate infusions of habits and gifts. That without Gods spirit we cannot pray aright, that our infirmities need his help, that we know not what to aske of our selves is most true: and if ever any Heretick was more confident of his owne naturalls, or did ever more undervalue Gods grace, than the Pelagian did, yet he denies not this; but what then? therefore without study, without art, without premeditation, without learning, the Spirit gives the gift of prayer, and it is his grace that without any naturall or artificiall help makes us pray *ex tempore?* no such thing. (*Apology* 8)

The two terms in my main title – gifts and graces – are prominent in this passage. All parties agreed that the Holy Spirit is the Spirit of prayer. The dividing point is over the relation of these gifts and graces to natural imagination and human invention, or in one word, art. Taylor insists on the necessity of human art and human invention. Art exercises the natural talents in the production of prayers and frames them in a coherent tradition accessible to all. In contrast, the immediate infusion of inspiration in prayer is impermanent, undisciplined, delusional. The opposing argument resists the intrusion of "other men's words" that rival rather than complement the Holy Spirit. "Gifts and graces" refer to the fruits of the Spirit. The phrase sounds benign and harmonious rather than polemical in its familiar sense, but polemic is broader than the familiar. Gifts and graces are points of contention when prayer meets poetry. The stark divide in seventeenth-century prayer polemics is between gift and art, and between grace and nature.

"Gifts and graces" was a familiar phrase in the early modern period because it is a common theme in Paul's letters. Paul asserts the unity of the Church as a necessary condition for the exercise of diverse gifts: "So we, being many, are one body in Christ, and every one members one of another. Having then gifts differing according to the grace that is given to us, whether prophecy, let us prophesy according to the proportion of faith; Or ministry, let us wait on our ministering: or he that teacheth, on teaching" (Rom. 12:5–7).[6] The Holy Spirit itself is a gift received in baptism (Acts 2:38). Taylor seeks a right understanding of "inspiration," which cannot be "immediate" in public prayer. The Book of Common Prayer caringly supports worshippers as a printed record of inspiration and invention. He concedes the arguments of his opponents who rely on Romans 8:26: "Likewise the Spirit also helpeth our infirmities: for we know not what we should pray for as we ought: but the Spirit itself maketh intercession for us with groanings which cannot be uttered." Without "Gods spirit we cannot pray aright" may be true, but to claim this disposes of poetry is false. Inspiration and art must collaborate.

The paragraph follows Taylor's narrative of early church history. The Holy Ghost was "given unto the Church" on the Day of Pentecost:

> And suddenly there came a sound from heaven as of a rushing mighty wind, and it filled all the house where they were sitting. And there appeared unto them cloven tongues like as of fire, and it sat upon each of them. And they were all filled with the Holy Ghost, and began to speak with other tongues, as the Spirit gave them utterance. (Acts 2:2–4)

The variety of "tongues" might vindicate immediate inspiration. Peter, however, explains the phenomenon to the crowd (Acts 2:14–40). He acknowledges the Holy Spirit: "And it shall come to pass in the last days saith God, I will pour out of my Spirit upon all flesh: and your sons and your daughters shall prophesy, and your young men shall see visions, and your old men shall dream dreams" (Acts 2:17). But Peter is also the rock upon which Christ builds his Church (Matt. 16:18). He links the outpouring of the Spirit to the larger narrative of redemption to exhort his audience to repentance and baptism. Eventually, "they, continuing daily with one accord in the temple, and breaking bread from house to house, did eat their meat with gladness and singleness of heart" (Acts 2: 26). The Church is the main beneficiary of the Spirit, and its unity is the main sign of the Spirit's work. It is significant that Taylor affirms gifts *and* graces. His mind is characteristically relational, conjunctive, and incorporating. Some have the gifts of speech or writing; all have the grace of the Holy Spirit. Gifts and graces carry Taylor's thesis of essential collaboration.

Milton became a strong opponent of the Book of Common Prayer over time. His view of the relation of prayer and poetry is at first similar to Taylor's but ultimately different. Milton compared the vocations of priest and poet in "Lycidas" (1638), a pastoral elegy memorializing the death of Edward King, a Cambridge classmate and an ideal future priest. Any notion that Milton might have taken orders, a notion perhaps still held by his father, ended there. The poem divides rather than blends the two vocations, with Milton embracing poetry. Announcing his poetic vocation in *The Reason of Church Government* in 1642, he sees poetry as a calling separate but equal to priesthood:

These abilities, wheresoever they be found, are the inspired gift of God rarely bestowed, but yet to some (though most abuse) in every Nation and are of power beside the office of a pulpit, to inbreed and cherish in a great people the seeds of virtue, and public civility, to allay the perturbations of the mind, and set the affections in right tune. (*CPW* 1: 816–17)

The poet worships "in glorious and lofty Hymns the throne and equipage of Gods Almightinesse, and what he works, and what he suffers to be wrought with high providence in his Church." The poet also worships in "devout prayer to that eternall Spirit who can enrich with all utterance and knowledge, and sends out his Seraphim with the hallow'd fire of his Altar to touch and purify the lips of whom he pleases" (*CPW* 1: 820–1). The "hallow'd fire" alludes to Isaiah's anointing as a prophet (Isaiah 6:6). Where Taylor firmly connects the gifts of the Spirit to the continuity of Church tradition, Milton ultimately connects prayer to prophecy since the Church is a work in progress needing endless reformation. Prophecy, the most potent and polemical of biblical modes, is the regenerating energy of reformation that preserves its vision and counters its prejudices.

The amalgam of prayer, poetry, and reformation was present from the inception of the Book of Common Prayer. The prayer book is a poetic invention thanks to its originator, Archbishop Thomas Cranmer (1489–1556). As Ian Robinson explains, Cranmer knew that poetry "is not restricted to verse; *poesis* is making (from the same root as the first verb in the Septuagint, when God created heaven and earth), and much of the prayer book prose is poetry."[7] And as David Curry observes, "Cranmer drew upon many, many sources, both ancient and modern. It was not a one-man production, nor could it be. Yet his was the dominant hand in terms of editorship and translation into English of a variety of liturgical sources that has resulted in the Book of Common Prayer and, especially, in terms of its Reformed emphasis."[8] Stella Brook remarks on Cranmer's "ability to assimilate elements from different liturgies into a homogeneous whole" in his Litany, a precursor of his work on the Book of Common Prayer. She calls this the power of "creative translation."[9] Just as William Tyndale transformed English with simple phrases like "light of the world," "twinkling of an eye," "salt of the earth," and "powers that be," so did Cranmer move worshippers with non-scriptural phrases such as "devices and desires," "peace in our time," and "a pure heart and humble voice." As P.D. James remarks, "the words of the Prayer Book echo in the mind. And not only in the individual mind, but in the corporate mind of the church, indeed in the mind of the nation."[10] The English Bible and Prayer Book demonstrate the powerful formative influence of poetic language.

Elizabeth I, as Daniel Gibbons argues, "needed to produce a convincing vision of the English nation as unified by Christian faith."[11] So she issued a revision of the Book of Common Prayer in 1559. Some traditionalists "maintained the usefulness and beauty of the Latin prayers" in the Catholic Mass.[12] Nevertheless, the shift from Latin to English was inevitable from the moment Tyndale began to create enduring modern English phrases. English was not a weaker language, as Anne Ferry points out: "[N]ot only the sacred and (to the unlearned) mysterious power of language of the Latin Mass, but also the vernacular was thought to be charged with power even in its most elemental features. This conception may have contributed to its acceptance in place of Latin in the ritual of the English church."[13] English common prayer would prove momentous and divisive for the national unity Elizabeth wanted to instill (and Charles II would later impose).[14]

The Bible also permeates the Book of Common Prayer. As Curry remarks, Cranmer's long "Litany," a prayer of contrition and his short prayers or "Collects" for each Sunday of the year illustrate his "incorporation of the language of Scripture into the language of prayer. Not only is the Prayer Book 80 per cent Scripture; it is a way of praying the Scriptures."[15] His Litany (1549) echoes James 1:27: "Pure religion and undefiled before God and the Father is this, To visit the fatherless and widows in their affliction, and to keep himself unspotted from the world" in "defende and provide for the fatherless children and wyddowes, and all that be desolate and oppressed."[16] He invokes the fruits of the Spirit as well: *"We beseche thee to heare us good lorde. That it may please thee to geve all thy people increase of grace, and to heare mekely thy worde, and to receyve it with pure affeccion, and to bring forth the fruits of the spirite."*[17] Despite this history, the prayer book came over time to mean spiritual lethargy, vestigial Catholicism, and unfinished reformation to its adversaries. By the mid-seventeenth century, Parliamentarians were claiming that Cranmer would have consented to the abolition of his own prayer book. By the later century, it was poised to make a permanent division in English society. How this came to be is the subject of the following chapters.

iii. Chapter Previews

My first chapter focuses on the writings of Bishop Lancelot Andrewes (1555–1626) and the poetry of George Herbert. Born one year before Cranmer's martyrdom, Andrewes illustrates what Peter Lake calls "avant-garde conformity" in the Elizabethan and Jacobean Church. In the minority as an anti-Calvinist divine, Andrewes mentored a younger generation that included William Laud, King Charles I's Archbishop of Canterbury. As P.E. McCullough has shown, Andrewes's influence requires consideration of his literary afterlife. Laud edited and published many of his works in the 1630's when he imposed provocative ceremonial reforms. I examine Andrewes in three areas: his sermons claim the Lord's Prayer as a set form; his private devotions show his poetic skill and gave him a saintly image of prayerful piety after his death; his sermons influence George Herbert. While Herbert's theology is much debated, we know that Andrewes influenced him as his childhood teacher and as a model for his priesthood. Herbert internalizes conflicts over prayer as he meditates on divine grace. His sincerity shows in his willingness to undercut his own art in deference to the power of the Spirit even as he affirms the texts and traditions of Anglicanism. This quality made him popular with leading reformers such as Richard Baxter and Dissenters in the later seventeenth century.

My second chapter examines Jeremy Taylor (1613–67), a writer who deserves more attention in literary studies. Born when Andrewes was an influential preacher and Bible translator, Taylor entered the Church under Laud's mentorship. He lived through Parliament's abolition of his church and prayer book in 1645, and the execution of the king in 1649. His *Psalter* of 1644 shows how he read the Psalms as an ancient prayer book against the recent backdrop of proscription. His *Apology for Authorized and Set Forms of Liturgie against the Pretence of the Spirit*, published in 1649 is an expansion of *A discourse concerning prayer ex tempore*, published in 1646. His target is Parliament's *Directory of Public Worship*, which replaced the Book of Common Prayer in 1645. I include the English Roman Catholic writings of Augustine Baker and Serenus Cressy to compare the Catholic critique of extemporaneous prayer with Taylor's. I explore Henry Vaughan's *The Mount of Olives: or, Solitary Devotions*, published in 1652 and selected poems from *Silex Scintillans* to present Taylor and Vaughan as the major writers of Anglican exile. Finally, I examine Taylor's devotional and liturgical writings from the 1650s, showing his conservation of conformist tradition and his increasingly sharp polemical tone.

The third chapter focuses on Milton up to the execution of King Charles I. The later Milton – radical, republican, unorthodox – was hostile to the Book of Common Prayer, but this view took time to develop. Milton's earlier Anglican conservatism, illustrated in the first performance of his *Mask presented at Ludlow Castle*, shows the influence of Andrewes's view of imagination and religion. Unlike Herbert, Milton turns conflict outward in polemical exchanges between the central characters. I explore Milton's development from *Comus* (1634, 1637) to *Eikonoklastes* (1649) to show how a more radical Milton emerges out of his early phase. Laud's authoritarian pressure, which Herbert did not live to see, is one factor in Milton's development. We eventually see how Milton reframes his early poems, including *Comus*, in his 1645 poems, published in the year Parliament abolished the prayer book. Taylor and Milton stand in opposition over the *Eikon Basilike*, also published in 1649 shortly after the king's execution. This influential book vindicates King Charles I as a royal martyr. Taylor participated in its production and coined its title. Milton's attack on the book in *Eikonoklastes* seeks to distinguish prayer from the voice of the suffering monarch. Milton emerges as a polemicist of intensity and erudition hostile to the coercion of conscience. The stage for the Restoration was set.

The fourth chapter considers Milton's three major poems, all published after 1660. I argue that Satan's soliloquy in Book 4 is modelled on formal prayer and meditation and affected by *Eikonoklastes*, which mocks the prayerful soliloquies of King Charles I. I examine intercessory prayer in the poem, and show how Milton uses zeal, blasphemy, and temptation to distinguish sacred and profane speech. Andrewes's sermons on Christ's temptation in the desert again influence Milton's concept of temptation in *Paradise Regained*, but his Jesus is a Dissenter tempted to conform. In the Athenian temptation, Jesus asserts the primacy of the Psalms over classical literature to assert the Lord's Prayer as a model for extemporaneous prayer.

In 1662, the restored regime reinstated the Book of Common Prayer as the only legal liturgy, with the Acts of Uniformity as its preface. These laws produced a literary culture of dissent and nonconformity under the glittering world of the Restoration Court, the culture of John Bunyan and Margaret Fell and George Fox, and of Milton despite his distance from these figures in class and education. Samson has been called a drama of dissent by Sharon Achinstein. I take this further by calling it a liturgy of dissent, using liturgy to highlight the complex amalgam of prayer and meditation that transforms cognitive dissonance into catharsis through a powerful mimetic imagining of the hero's chaotic life. In its layering of biblical poetry and narrative through meditative remembering, it also has the qualities of a liturgy of dissent that counters, by virtue of its scriptural complexity, the more facile liturgies of conformity, or forms of prayer the restored Church produced and published to narrate the Restoration as a providential event. This point of conflict engages with the discourse of monarchy the *Eikon Basilike* had sustained since its appearance in 1649. Milton uses tragedy to rise above this propaganda, and to critique the unification of church and state and the malleability of history and memory state liturgies assume.

The fifth chapter examines John Bunyan (1628–88). Bunyan was formed by the criminalization of dissent after 1660. Prayer was a main topic of debate between Bunyan and his judges at his trial. His first prison writing was *I Will Pray with the Spirit*, which opposes the Book of Common Prayer. It is perhaps the most detailed discourse we have on the experience of prayer from a Calvinist Dissenter. It anticipates the depiction of prayer in his spiritual autobiography, *Grace Abounding*, his best-known work, *The Pilgrim's Progress*, and his battle allegory, *The Holy War*. Like Milton, Bunyan saw the dissenting conscience as subject to verbal invasion. *Grace Abounding* examines the discernment of right prayer and genuine voices in a subjectivity that evolves in conjunction with internal vocal doubts and temptations, and external pressures of conformity. *Pilgrim's Progress* converts this experience into allegory, as readers watch the central character distinguish prayer from blasphemy and truth from error.

I examine Bunyan's opposition to Quaker teachings through the writings of George Fox, the founder of the Quaker movement, and the blasphemy trial of James Nayler. Fox made inner light available for all people, discarding the exclusionary categories of reprobate and elect in Bunyan's Calvinism. In 1682, the conflict touched on prayer when women members of his congregation asked to hold separate prayer meetings, evoking the gender equality practiced by Quakers. Bunyan refused in *A Case of Conscience Resolved*. I conclude with *The Holy War*. Never as popular as *The Pilgrim's Progress*, this work shows the challenge of representing prayer by an artist skeptical of set forms. I offer a new interpretation of a major critical crux in Bunyan's allegory – the "nameless terrible instrument in Mansoul" – as a fitting end to this study. Bunyan's riddling emblem highlights the role of enigma in Dissenting literature, since a riddle can be overt to a godly readership and obscure to persecutors. The division of readers in this poetic representation of prayer is a culmination of decades of polemical debate.

Chapter One

Lancelot Andrewes and George Herbert: The Word of Charity

In no part of this prayer is found either the word Mine, or I. Our, is a word of Charitie and Unitie. Let every one therefore, not only pray for himselfe, but for others also; considering, that in so doing, hee prayeth for him, whom Charitie hath made as himself.

Lancelot Andrewes, *Institutiones Piae or Directions to Pray* (1640)

In this chapter, I examine Andrewes's sermons on prayer as defences of common prayer. Viewed in light of his cautionary sermon on religious "imaginings," and his private prayers intended for the clergy, we can see how and why Andrewes argued for the Lord's Prayer as a set form prescribed by Christ. George Herbert's poems can be read in light of Andrewes's sermons on prayer. Both writers use pastoral guidance in affirming set forms of prayer. Andrewes argues for charity as the virtue of public prayer by based on the plural pronoun that begins the Lord's Prayer" "our." Collective charity is greater than personal zeal, the virtue of Puritan fervency. In "Love (2)" Herbert shows his debt to Andrewes by calling charity the "greater flame" of correction, and the virtue of Christ as "the way."

i. Lancelot Andrewes and Religious Imaginings

Labels often show general differences across the religious spectrum of early modern England. In her study of confessions of faith as autobiographical products of early modern polemical culture, Brooke Conti argues that the binaries of Anglican and Puritan have given way to a more fluid view of religious identity: "[T]hose whose beliefs and practices we might label as Catholic or Puritan did not necessarily see themselves or their neighbours that way."[1] The "Anglican" Church was "anything but homogeneous."[2] It included Calvinists, who, like most Puritans, embraced predestination and also proto-Arminians, like Andrewes, who did not. And Bunyan was deeply hostile to Quakers who might otherwise share his view of the prayer book. Anthony Milton sees that the "problem for the historian of the period is of how to do justice to this range of opinion without losing sight of the dualistic terminology with which contemporaries portrayed and understood (and therefore ultimately shaped) their situation, and the polarizations of opinion which social and political upheavals could so easily provoke."[3] Prayer polemics reveal fissures within the fluidity of the religious spectrum: set forms of prayer and extemporaneous prayers move from natural complements to stark alternatives. For my purpose, there is a clear line between Conformist Anglicans who maintained the book of Common Prayer and Puritan Reformers and later Dissenters who did not.

Foundational narratives of English Protestantism appealed to both sides. John Foxe published his massive national martyrology in 1563. Bunyan would read it in prison one hundred years later. As Patrick Collinson remarks, *Actes and Monuments* makes "fifteen hundred years of church history a coherent and meaningful plot, its ground bass the unrelenting warfare between the false church, visible, commanding, and apparently flourishing, and the true church, depressed almost out of sight, a 'secret multitude of true professors.'"[4] The image of true and false churches, starkly polarized on Foxe's title page, is an apocalyptic pitting of Catholic Rome against Protestant England. Biblical apocalypse is a genre of crisis. Crisis is both the cause and effect of polarization. Revelation unfolds polarized symbols and figures in a guided reading of scripture: Christ and Anti-Christ, Jerusalem and Babylon, the Woman Clothed with the Sun and the Whore of Babylon. Popular belief then and now yields naive rather than literary readings of the text.[5] Collinson sees an absence of apocalyptic references in Foxe's text, seeing it as closer to Augustine's *City of God*, a work of patristic historiography.[6] It offers a dualistic view of history predicated on Abel and Cain, one a type of the Kingdom of Heaven and the other the Kingdoms of Earth. Earthly kingdoms and empires wax and wane, as Rome was waning while Augustine was writing. The godly community is on pilgrimage through the cycles of time that consist of six "days" generations from Adam to the end with a seventh or sabbath vision. Milton masters the literary apocalypse by blending Revelation and the *City of God* in the final two books of *Paradise Lost*, which mark out Augustine's seven days precisely. Adam foresees the downfall of the Antichrist before starting his life in exile. Polarities, whether apocalyptic, Augustinian, or Calvinist, served religious polemic.

The connection of church and state, established in Henry VIII's claim to be head of the Church, was another defining condition for prayer polemics. Crises of religious proscription and regulation from the Civil War to the Restoration came from state-enacted laws. As Charles Prior notes, early conformists "argued that the English church was both a spiritual and a political association: a state church founded on a mingling of doctrine and law, and hence able to enjoin conformity among its members."[7] Richard Hooker (1554–1600) defended the connection of church and state in his *Laws of Ecclesiastical Polity*. Hooker's task was to "establish a usable account of the mingling of sacred and human history, and therefore the mingling of sacred and human authority."[8] As Lake notes, Hooker "can be seen almost to have invented the style of piety associated with the rise of English Arminianism and the ecclesiastical policies pursued by Charles I, Laud and their supporters during the personal rule."[9] Elements of this style include a "broadly based vision of the Christian community" that rejects the Calvinist division of the elect (those predestined for Heaven) and the reprobate (those predestined for Hell), a focus "more on the sacrament and public worship than on preaching," and an effective view of "the rituals and observances of the church."[10] Hooker's values were not overly popular in the 1590s or in the early reign of James I, who deftly mediated tensions between conformists and reformers.

Lancelot Andrewes conveyed Hooker's ideas from the Jacobean Church to the church of Laud and added some of his own. Andrewes mentored a circle that included Laud, the future Archbishop of Canterbury under Charles I. Acting as Andrewes's literary executor after his death in 1626, Laud, along with John Buckeridge, Matthew Wren, John Cosin, and others, edited Andrewes's sermons. Andrewes served their plan for an Anglican counter-Reformation committed to ceremony. Encouraged by James's successor, King Charles I, the group set policies of decency and decorum for the Church, provoking backlashes in England and, with the imposition of the Book of Common Prayer in 1637, a riot in Scotland.

There are differences between Andrewes and Hooker. Hooker died in 1600 near the end of Elizabeth I's reign, and was the most prominent apologist for church polity to that point. Hooker countered Cartwright's arguments for Presbyterian church government. As Diarmaid MacCulloch observes, Hooker's massive *Laws of Ecclesiastical Polity* opposed the "mind-set behind the sermon based 'Bible alone' style of English Reformed Protestantism," instead emphasizing "a philosophy of human action, motivation, and discipline, analyzed as expressing God's laws for his creation."[11] Hooker relies on reason, making no claims to a divine or exclusively scriptural warrant for tradition: he "chose not to echo fellow conformist English polemicists who in the 1590's were beginning to emphasize divine-right claims for episcopacy."[12] He did not argue for the divine right of monarchs, an idea that aggravated the conflict over prayer in the mid-seventeenth century. Deborah Shuger argues, "Hooker virtually never thinks of royal power as participation in the divine," although power comes indirectly from God.[13] The Church is a mystical body, but Hooker does not mystify the relation of Church and King. Andrewes did. Sacramental time enacted in ceremonies could enhance the divine-right image. Sermons supported James as a type of David or Solomon. The "energy behind these sermons is the longing for mystification," Shuger suggests.[14]

Andrewes had limited influence under James I, becoming chief translator of the Authorized Version of the Bible, and Bishop of Ely and Winchester, but not Canterbury, which went to the Calvinist George Abbott in 1611. James was a deft mediator between Puritan and Anglican positions, but Charles I lacked tact and skill, bringing a top-down authority to a restive nation. In consequence, MacCulloch notes, the rise of Laud and other protégés of Andrewes in the 1630s "destabilized the English Church and brought it crashing down in ruin."[15] In their hands, Andrewes's well-intentioned sense of sacred majesty would bring what Patrick Collinson calls the "unexpected provocation of Arminianism and Laudianism" in the 1630s.[16]

Andrewes detested puritanism. He considered predestination presumptuous in its separation of elect and reprobate. In fairness, as Collinson suggests, Calvinists "did not presume to know who were the members of Christ's true, invisible Church, which was a mystery known only to God."[17] Calvin himself affirmed the importance of mystery. Nevertheless, the level of anxious self-analysis Calvinism produced is evident in many writers up to and including Bunyan. For Andrewes, self-analysis courts presumption: "[W]e are not curiously to enquire and search out of God's secret touching election or reprobation, but to adore it."[18] As Lake comments, "such speculative flights of fancy represent a clear infringement on the majesty of God."[19] Fancy is prone to vain imaginings; it must be regulated by reason.

Andrewes preached on "imaginings" at St Giles' Cripplegate on 9 January 1592. The sermon is in the 1629 Andrewes folio collection edited by Laud and Buckeridge, who titled it "Of Imaginings." The sermon covers imaginings in philosophy, law, and religion. The final three imaginings concern fellowship, communion, and prayers. "Imaginations touching the Apostle's fellowship" incorporates the individual into the Christian community, "called the fellowship, or corporation of the Gospell" (*XCVI Sermons*, IX, 32). Andrewes then addresses the second commandment: "Thou shalt not make unto thee any graven image." The text equates religious idolatry with vain imaginings. Andrewes declares his additional text to be Acts 2:42: "And they continued in the Apostle's Doctrine, and Fellowship, and breaking of bread & Praiers." The text represents the fellowship of the Holy Spirit in the early Church as the right safeguard against idolatry and speculative fancy. It asserts the gravity of orthodoxy, the charity of community, and the vitality of prayer and sacrament.

In "Imaginings touching prayers," Andrewes views the conflict between set forms and extemporaneous prayers. Rejecting the Lord's Prayer as a set form is "an idle conceit" that "never came into the heads of any of the old haeretiques, though never so brain-sicke once to imagine." Those who "strive by diverse other forms" cannot "come neere the high art, and most excellent spirit of perfection in that pattern" (*XCVI Sermons*, IX, 36). Its profundity and perfection are evident from its first word of charity. Andrewes sets out the role of art that would later motivate Laud's protégé Jeremy Taylor.

Opponents of set forms "erre in their imaginations." Those "finding fault with a sett Liturgie (which they call stinted prayers)" give themselves "to imagine prayers at the same instant." Instantaneous inspiration is a false imagining, or what Taylor would later call a pretense. Andrewes sees long extemporaneous prayers as pharisaical. They even parody Catholic prayers: "[I]nstead of Rosaries and a number of prayers, they bring in the Pharisee's imagination of long prayers (that is) a prayer as long as a whole Rosarie. And this they take to be a great part of holynesse; but indeed it is nothing but the former superstition drawen in backward" (*XCVI Sermons*, IX, 37). It would be hard to imagine a worse insult to a Puritan than this.

On public worship, Andrewes denies that common prayer conceals the ungodly. Andrewes makes "an implicit distinction," Lake remarks, "between the works of charity, piety and worship enjoined by God and those merely formal marks of apparent zeal, devised by hypocrites like Pharisees and the puritans, in order to mark themselves off from their contemporaries."[20] In his sermons on prayer, Andrewes develops the twofold nature of his anti-puritan polemic. Zeal with presumption is the target of his warnings against religious imaginings. He needed a different virtue to conserve tradition: charity. "Imaginations touching the breaking of bread" asserts the inseparability of "Doctrines and Prayers" in the bond of collective charity: "except he be in Charitie, Matt. 6.14. he is no more fit to pray, than to communicate" (*XCVI Sermons*, IX, 37).

Imaginings generate multiple heresies. Charity embraces one orthodox communion.

ii. Andrewes and the Lord's Prayer

Christ's intentions for the Lord's Prayer divided Conformists and Puritans. Did Jesus authorize set forms of prayer when he invented the prayer? Or is the prayer a model for extemporaneity? The Bible is ambiguous. Matthew's version appealed to Puritans:

> And when thou prayest, thou shalt not be as the hypocrites are: for they love to pray standing in the synagogues and in the corners of the streets, that they may be seen of men. Verily I say unto you, they have their reward. But thou, when thou prayest, enter into thy closet, and when thou hast shut thy door, pray to thy Father which is in secret; and thy Father which seeth in secret shall reward thee openly. But when ye pray, use not vain repetitions, as the heathen do: for they think that they shall be heard for their much speaking. Be not ye therefore like unto them: for your Father knoweth what things ye have need of, before ye ask him. After this manner therefore pray ye: Our Father which art in heaven, Hallowed be thy name. Thy kingdom come. Thy will be done in earth, as it is in heaven. Give us this day our daily bread. And forgive us our debts, as we forgive our debtors. And lead us not into temptation, but deliver us from evil: For thine is the kingdom, and the power, and the glory, for ever. Amen. For if ye forgive men their trespasses, your heavenly Father will also forgive you: But if ye forgive not men their trespasses, neither will your Father forgive your trespasses. (Matt. 6:5–15)

Luke appealed to Conformists:

> And it came to pass, that, as he was praying in a certain place, when he ceased, one of his disciples said unto him, Lord, teach us to pray, as John also taught his disciples. And he said unto them, When ye pray, say, Our Father which art in heaven, Hallowed be thy name. Thy kingdom come. Thy will be done, as in heaven, so in earth. Give us day by day our daily bread. And forgive us our sins; for we also forgive every one that is indebted to us. And lead us not into temptation; but deliver us from evil. And he said unto them, Which of you shall have a friend, and shall go unto him at midnight, and say unto him, Friend, lend me three loaves; For a friend of mine in his journey is come to me, and I have nothing to set before him? And he from within shall answer and say, Trouble me not: the

door is now shut, and my children are with me in bed; I cannot rise and give thee. I say unto you, Though he will not rise and give him, because he is his friend, yet because of his importunity he will rise and give him as many as he needeth. And I say unto you, Ask, and it shall be given you; seek, and ye shall find; knock, and it shall be opened unto you. For every one that asketh receiveth; and he that seeketh findeth; and to him that knocketh it shall be opened. (Luke 11:1–10)

In Matthew, Christ tells his disciples to avoid "heathens" known for their "vain repetitions." God knows the heart behind artful speech. "Closet prayer" is sincere, but public prayer can be hypocritical. Luke is less polarizing. Prayer is not seclusion in a closet. There is no us and them. Everyone who seeks will find; everyone who knocks will have an answer.[21] Matthew's Christ says "pray after his manner"; Luke's says, "pray thus." "Manner" may mean a sketch, not a script; "pray thus" sounds prescriptive. Thomas Manton, who resigned his living following the Act of Uniformity in 1662, shares Matthew's ideals: "God's command to pray, first falls upon single Persons, before it falls upon Families or Churches, which are made up of single persons."[22] The plural "Our" Father should mean the "general interest of all the Elect in Christ."[23] Andrewes preferred Luke, arguing that "Our" means the whole Church.

Christ's other prayers add controversy. Was his cry from the cross – "My God, my God, why hast thou forsaken me?" – extemporaneous or a recitation of Psalm 22? Henry Hammond, vindicating "ancient liturgy," argued that Christ prayed Psalm 22 as a set form.[24] Did Christ draw from Jewish tradition at the Last Supper, or did he bless the bread and wine extemporaneously? Christ used "words which were usuall in the Jewish feasts" according to Abrahamus Scultetus, professor of divinity at Heidelberg.[25] Thomas Long argued that both the Eucharistic prayer and the Lord's Prayer adapt human invention: "Now if our Saviour did accommodate the Jewish Forms (some of which were merely of humane invention) to the solemne administration of that most blessed Sacrament, which is to continue in his Church until his coming again; we may not think it strange that he should prescribe a form of prayer of his own composure, and enjoyn his Disciples to the frequent use of it in their solemn devotions."[26] Supporters of set forms found continuity with Jewish examples.[27]

The Roman patristic writer Septimus Tertullian (160–220 AD) wrote the earliest known commentary on the Lord's Prayer.[28] His treatise *De Oratione*, "On the Prayer," may have evolved out of a sermon for newly baptized Christians, revealing the Lord's Prayer as part of early

Christian liturgy.[29] The first ten sections of *De Oratione* address parts of the prayer; the remaining nineteen explain the occasions and properties of prayer; the ending is a peroration on the power of prayer. Two features of Tertullian's analysis influence seventeenth-century writers: his view of the Lord's Prayer as a compression or epitome (at times called summary or abridgement) of the entire gospel and his view of the prayer's structure. The Trinity, as the unity of God, Christ, and Holy Spirit, underlies his view of the prayer:

> God's Spirit and God's Word and God's Reason, the Word of the Reason and the Reason of the Word, and both of these Spirit, Jesus Christ our Lord, has marked out for the new disciples of the new covenant a new plan of prayer. For it was right that in this case, too, new wine should be stored in new bottles and a new patch be stitched on to a new garment.[30]

The Latin is "novam orationis formam determinavit" or "has marked out for the new disciples of the new covenant a new plan of prayer." Tertullian's Latin does not settle the question; "praescribere," to prescribe, is stronger than "determinavit." He insists, wrongly, that the prayer has no Jewish precursors; it is a new plan, not an old form. He appealed to Puritan reformers like the Smectymnuus group: "[W]e shew you in Tertullian, where there were prayers that were not stinted or prescribed forms, shew us if you can in Tertullian, any such there were."[31]

In Luke, the disciples ask Jesus to teach them to pray as "John also taught his disciples." If John the Baptist provided a prayer, there is no record of it. Tertullian, who had a polarizing temperament, says this is fitting, since the Lord's Prayer contains everything in the Gospel. There should be no precedent:

> Consequently it is not even on record according to what formula John taught them to pray, because earthly things have given way to heavenly (He that is from the earth, he says, speaketh earthly things, and he who is come from heaven, what things he hath seen, those he speaketh), and everything which belongs to the Lord Christ is heavenly, as is also this science of praying.[32]

Tertullian highlights the prayer's Trinitarian elements: "[I]n it our Lord Jesus Christ is approved as God's Spirit and God's Word and God's Reason – Spirit in view of his power, Word in view of his teaching, Reason in view of his intervention."[33] Tertullian's perception of this theological deep structure reinforces the prayer as epitome. Epitome rebukes long-windedness: "[T]hat brevity (and let this serve for a third degree of wisdom) rests upon the foundation of a great and fruitful interpretation, and in proportion as it is restrained in wording, so is it copious in meaning."[34] Andrewes echoes Tertullian's precept: "Prayer is a summary of faith, an interpreter of hope."[35] The prayer as doctrinal "summary" was central to the Anglican ideal.

Andrewes examines the Lord's Prayer in his writings on private prayer and his sermons. His *Institutiones Piae, or Directions to Pray* was a private text first published in 1630 and in five augmented editions from 1633 to 1684. The source for this text was Andrewes's *Preces Privatae*, his private devotions in Greek and Latin circulated among his associates, including Laud, Andrewes's literary executor. The *Institutiones Piae* is an anthology of excerpts from the *Preces Privatae* edited and translated by Henry Isaacson.[36] The second work is *Nineteen Sermons Concerning Prayer*, first published in Andrewes's lifetime as *Scala Coeli: Nineteen Sermons Concerning Prayer* and under the English title alone in 1641.

Institutiones Piae offers a "short exposition" of the Lord's Prayer and analyses of the Apostle's Creed, the Ten Commandments, seven penitential Psalms, and seven Psalms of thanksgiving. *Nineteen Sermons* is an extensive exposition of the Lord's Prayer, with six sermons on the nature of prayer and thirteen more on the parts of the Lord's Prayer. In both works, Andrewes addresses connections between language and Spirit.

Institutiones Piae is conciliatory to Reformers. Fervency, for example, is better than eloquence:

> For it is not a chill and cold Perseverance, or expectation, that will serve our turnes, to prevaile with God, but a fervent Spirit to pursue the same. For God heareth not, at least regardeth not, cold, faint, and drowzie prayers, nor loud crying, long babling, or many tautologies or repetitions; (not intending or minding what wee pray for) which proceede onely from the lips: but it is the affection, and zealous desires of the devout, mixed with sighes, teares, and grones, not to bee uttered, which moove, and prevaile with him. For God (being a Spirit) looketh to bee worshiped in Spirit.[37]

Tautologies belong to "imaginings." Pharisees who like to be heard are vain. Andrewes's marginal gloss is Romans 8:26, a key text for extemporaneous prayer. Andrewes sees "closet prayer" as the place for fervency: "[T]hese retired Soliloquies, and private meditations and conferences, betweene God and our soules, and betweene our selves and our soules, have ever beene much approved by the Ancients."[38] The authority of the "Ancients" links Matthew's closet prayer to centuries of tradition.

Andrewes shifts to charity when he turns to the Lord's Prayer. The plural "Our Father" signifies collective charity: "In no part of this prayer is found either the word Mine, or I. Our, is a word of Charitie and Unitie. Let every one therefore, not only pray for himselfe, but for others also; considering, that in so doing, hee prayeth for him, whom Charitie hath made as himselfe."[39] "Our Father" signifies the Church as Body of Christ. Andrewes defers the question of whether the Lord's Prayer is a set form, instead summarizing its attributes. It is:

> ... the Abridgement of the Gospell and our Faith.
> The Interpretation of our desires and hope.
> The very Bond of Charity.
> And an inexhaustible Treasury.[40]

The prayer is compressed rather than verbose, but inexhaustible for commentary and meditation. It is always unifying through the charity of "our."

Nineteen Sermons begins with 2 Cor. 3:5: "Not that we are sufficient of ourselves to think any thing as of ourselves; but our sufficiency is of God." The text again draws a line between disciplined invention and insubstantial imaginings. Despite his concessions to fervency, Andrewes cautions reformers against idolizing their utterances:

> Both heathen and holy writings do commend to us this saying, γνῶθι σεαυτόν [know thyself], but in a divers sense. The Heathen use it as a means to puff up our nature, that in regard of the excellency which God hath vouchsafed us above other creatures, we should be proud thereof; but Christian religion laboureth by the knowledge of ourselves and of our misery to *cast down every high thing that exalteth it self against the knowledge of God, and to bring into captivity all imagination to the obedience of Christ,* 2 Cor. X.5. (*NS* 4–5)

Much depends on how Andrewes reads Paul's word "imagination." Heathens use imagination to rival God, Christians to obey him. Andrewes recommends humility as another prayer book virtue. Humility subdues pride for Christians who feel superior. The persons Paul "chargeth with this want of ability are not the common sort of naturall men, that are not yet regenerate by Gods Spirit, 1 Cor. ii, but he speaketh of himself and his fellow-apostles" (*NS* 13). Behind this argument lies Andrewes's rejection of Calvinist predestination. All Christians must rely on grace, and the "means to find grace is prayer."

Sermon 2 explores nature and grace further. "To supply the defect that is in nature," Andrewes teaches, "grace is added; that grace might make that perfect which is imperfect" (*NS* 36). Sermon 3 emphasizes the "negative condition" of dependence on grace: "[I]t now followeth by good order that we repair to God for that power which we have not of our selves" (*NS* 50–1). Sermon 4 addresses Romans 8:26. Andrewes rejects the vanity of rhetoric: "It is not fine phrases and goodly sentences that commend our prayer, but the fervency of the Spirit from whom it proceedeth" (*NS* 99). "Every prayer," he concedes, "is lukewarm, which is not prevented with inspiration" (*NS* 92). If "our prayers do draw out sighes and gronings from our hearts, it is the better; for then it appeareth that our prayer is not a breath coming from the lungs, but from the very depth of the heart" (*NS* 99). The absence of these qualities makes prayer seem futile to some. Andrewes draws them to the corporate Church rather than leaving them in isolation:

> [W]hen we most faint in prayer, there are of Gods Saints that pray for us with all instancy; by which it cometh to passe, that being all but one body, their prayers tend to our good as well as their own: For the faithfull, howsoever they be many, and dispersed into divers corners of the world, yet they are but one dough; and as they are the members of one body, so they pray not privately for themselves but for the whole body of the Church, so that the weaknesse of one member is supplied by the fervent and earnest prayer of the other. (*NS* 95–6)

Prayer cannot isolate the self from God or exclude the "the other." His preaching shows real psychological insight and builds up the Church as a body in which members find solace with others.

The text for Sermon 5 text is Luke 11:1: "And so it was, that, as he was praying in a certain place, when he ceased, one of his Disciples said unto him, Master, teach us to pray, as John also taught his Disciples." The subject pivots towards set forms. The "Spirit of God maketh intercession for us" by moving "the Disciples to seek for a form of Prayer of Christ" (*NS* 104). He reconciles Romans 8:26 with the Lord's Prayer as a set form: "[S]eeing God both commandeth us to pray, and promiseth to grant us what we pray for; seeing he doth not onely by his example teach us that Prayer is requisite, but prescribeth us also a Form of Prayer, we ought not to be negligent in this duty" (*NS* 108–9). The disciples "therefore being privy to their own infirmities in this case, are stirred up by Gods Spirit to seek for a perfect form of prayer of Christ" (*NS* 114–15). The Disciples "received a platform of prayer from Christ" to use "as a pattern and complement of all their petitions" (*NS* 115). This "pattern and complement" contains both "matter and manner." Since the Lord's Prayer is an order of words "free from all imperfection, because it was penned from him that was from above," it follows that the prayer must not only be thought (*cogitate*) but spoken (*dicite*)" (*NS* 122). He reinforces the plural pronoun: our "prayer must have a body: Our tongue must be the pen of a ready writer, Psal. xlv." Eyes and hands as well as hearts and minds must be uplifted: "As David sayeth, Psal. cxxxv, all our bones must be exercised in prayer" (*NS* 123). "Our" means the Church.

Sermon 6 sets times for prayer. Prayer without ceasing needs some structure: "[W]hen we are commanded to praye always, the meaning is, that it is our duty to appoint certaine howres for prayer" (*NS* 135). Set times "appointed to the service of God in the Law" are morning and evening (*NS* 136). Prayer is not only the general duty of every Christian but "more particularly and specially to those that have any Ecclesiasticall authority over others" (*NS* 137). Andrewes strengthens the role of priests by comparing them to angels who "not onely descend to the people to teach them the will of God, but ascend to the presence of God to make intercession for the people (*NS* 139–40). Priests are the "Lords Remembrancers"; God has "a greater respect to the prayers of those that have a spirituall charge, then to those that are of the common sort" (*NS* 140). Private prayer is beneficial, but is "not enough, unlesse at times appointed we meet together to pray publickly" (*NS* 144). Confessions of sin lead to expressions of praise in the Eucharist. Petitions, whether "deprecations" (to ward off or avoid evil) or "comprecations" (to join together in prayer) proceed from faith, whereas intercessions proceed from charity, or concern for others. Christ asked that the cup of suffering might pass from him (deprecation), but interceded for others from the cross. All scriptural prayers find a home in Andrewes's taxonomy. The priority of public intercession over private petition demonstrates Andrewes's corporate ecclesiology.

Sermon 6 diagrams the prayer:

> The petitions, being seven, are divided thus: the first concerneth God himself, the other six concern us. They concern us in a threefold estate: first, of Glory; secondly, of Grace; thirdly, of Nature. In these petitions that concern us, the evil that we would have removed from us, is first, sinne; secondly, temptation; thirdly, evil. The good we desire to be granted to us, is first, that Gods kingdome may be in our hearts, secondly, that his wille may be performed of us; thirdly, that he will give us things necessary for this present life. (*NS* 154–5)

The divine takes precedence in the first petition: "hallowed be thy name." The remaining six are three triads mirroring our "threefold estate." The triads repeat the precedence of the divine as glory first, grace second, and nature third. Glory corresponds to forgiveness and the indwelling kingdom; grace corresponds to the prevention of temptation and the performance of God's will; nature corresponds to deliverance from evil (the random calamities of life) and the nourishment of daily bread. Configuring the six petitions inculcates the Trinity and explicates the deep structure of the divine-human relationship within the prayer. As a Trinitarian construct, the prayer proclaims the Incarnation as a descent of glory and grace into the midst of human existence. As a pattern of relationships, it affirms the Church as the Body of Christ in time.

Andrewes goes on to connect the prayer to the components of formal liturgy such as confession and creed. Sermon 18, for example, compares the prayer to public confession: "[A]ll Prayer and Invocation is nothing else but a testimony, and confession. The petitions that are severally made in this prayer, are confession of our weaknesse, want, need, and unableness to any thing that may please God."[41] Confession brings assurance that God, "is inclined to supply our wants," which he is willing to do "as a Father, but able as a King" (NS 410–11). Andrewes argues that the Spirit prefers set forms; in *Institutiones Piae*, relationships between heaven and earth, grace and nature, anticipate the creed. Taken together, the two works incorporate the reader into a church of order and tradition.

Whether this incorporation was more persuasive than coercive brought conflict after Andrewes's death. As P.E. McCullough has shown, Laud used the late Bishop Andrewes to speak to his goals for the English Church. Laud is often vilified for authoritarianism, but he must surely have appreciated Andrewes's persuasive approach. Nevertheless, his style differed from Andrewes's. McCullough observes how the "design and the contents of *XCVI Sermons* underwrote a Laudian style of churchmanship." The sermons were "literally inscribed or arranged into a larger liturgical whole" marked by major festivals such as the Nativity or Pentecost.[42] Title pages from different decades also illustrate the change of style. The 1611 title page of *Scala Coeli, Nineteen Sermons Concerning Prayer* is plain and simple with no visual adornment. The subtitle guides the reader "to the true Doore," with the remainder teaching "how soe to knocke thereat that wee may enter." (See Figure 2.)

The 1641 full title, in contrast, summarizes the contents: "The first six shewing the nature of Prayer, as a preparative thereunto; the residue a large and full exposition upon the Lord's Prayer." (See Figure 3.)

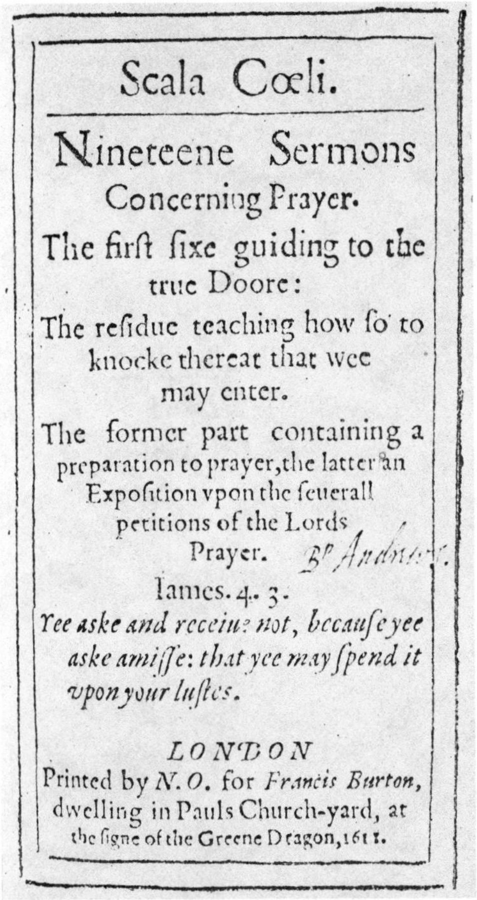

Scala Cœli.

Nineteene Sermons
Concerning Prayer.
The firſt ſixe guiding to the
true Doore:
The reſidue teaching how ſo to
knocke thereat that wee
may enter.
The former part containing a
preparation to prayer, the latter an
Expoſition vpon the ſeuerall
petitions of the Lords
Prayer.   Bp Andrewes

Iames. 4. 3.
Yee aske and receiue not, becauſe yee
aske amiſſe: that yee may ſpend it
vpon your luſtes.

LONDON
Printed by N. O. for Francis Burton,
dwelling in Pauls Church-yard, at
the ſigne of the Greene Dragon, 1611.

Figure 2. Title page: Lancelot Andrewes's *Nineteen Sermons Concerning Prayer* (1611). Courtesy of the Huntington Library.

Andrewes's name does not appear on the 1611 title page; on the 1641 page, which includes Andrewes's portrait, we read, "By that learned Divine, Lancelot Andrewes, Doctour of Divinitie and late Bishop of Winchester." This version asserts Andrewes' scholarly and ecclesiastical authority in a growing polemical climate.

One year after Laud's 1629 edition of *XCVI Sermons*, Henry Isaacson, Andrewes's secretary, published the *Institutiones Piae*, "a rough compilation of extracts from Andrewes's devotional and catechetical writings."[43] Andrewes's name did not appear on this work until

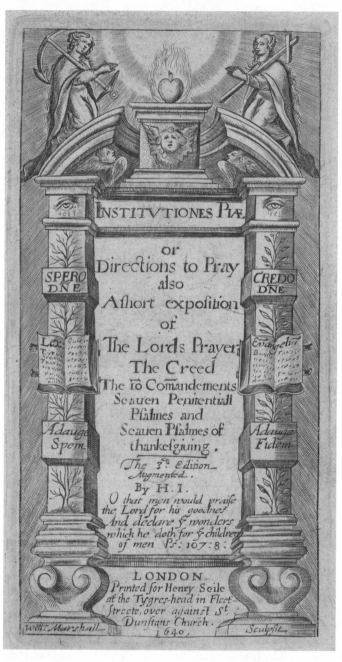

Figure 3. Title page: Andrewes's *Institutiones Piae or Directions to Pray* (1640).
Courtesy of the Huntington Library.

after Isaacson's death in 1654. As McCullough speculates, the editions were "probably not assigned to their true author in deference to William Laud's exclusive copyright to Andrewes's works."[44] The volume includes a title page produced by William Marshall, who later engraved the image of Charles I at prayer for the *Eikon Basilike*. This page shows two pillars of hope and faith leading upwards from heart-shaped bases to converge in a flaming heart at the top. Allegorical figures of hope (holding an anchor) and faith (holding a cross) kneel in prayer on either side of the flaming heart, indicating the value of bodily postures in prayer. Charity, central to Andrewes's reading of "Our Father," is the flaming heart at the top. In comparison to Laud's use of the church calendar to structure Andrewes's sermons, Isaacson is attentive to the significance of the virtues of faith, hope, and charity in Andrewes's exposition of the Lord's Prayer. Architectural emblems, moreover, imply the Church as a structure animated by the gifts and graces of the Spirit. The emblem also promises that Andrewes's work will edify (a word meaning to build) the spirits of readers.

iii. Andrewes the Devotional Writer

Andrewes's piety affirms the beauty of holiness in material worship, the authority of bishops as stewards of tradition, and the recognition of what Diarmaid MacCulloch calls the "liturgical splendor in Cranmer's prayer book," a splendour he believes Cranmer would have rejected.[45] Graham Parry shows that the promotion of "more ceremonious forms of worship" by Andrewes and his circle called for "devotional manuals that would help to create a more harmonious shape to personal prayer."[46] Andrewes had a reputation for fervent personal piety, spending as much as five hours a day in private prayer. *Preces Privatae*, his manual of private devotions, was written in Latin and Greek with occasional Hebrew, and circulated only among his followers. It would not remain private for long. Defenders of the prayer book translated and published it in whole or in part when the Church was under siege. The first translation appeared in 1648.

Private Devotions is a poetic work. As Elizabeth McCutcheon suggests, the prayers are built "out of the most traditional devotional materials – the Bible and other ancient and meditative prayer forms." They "could have been, and in less artistic hands would have been, an eclectic miscellany of prayers and meditations. They are, instead, singular prose-poems" comparable in their intensity to Herbert.[47] The unity of the collection consists in its expression of the unity of time: human and natural, cosmic and divine: the "pattern is initially shaped by Genesis and the original seven days of creation; Andrewes begins the prayers for each day by commemorating the work of creation on the day it was created: light on Sunday, the firmament on Monday, and so on through Saturday, when God rested."[48] Genesis endorses the art of prayer as the art of God in creation.

Second, the collection shows Andrewes's interest in sources. The Greek, Latin, and Hebrew languages he employs are, as Brightman notes, "the three tongues consecrated on the Cross"[49] that appeared in the sign Pilate ordered placed on the Cross (John 19:20). These languages are also the sources for the English translation of Andrewes's main source, the Bible. The prayers are a "mosaic" of scriptural citation, quotation, and typology, a characteristic of the Book of Common Prayer. Additionally, Brightman identifies Andrewes's use of rabbinical, patristic, and medieval sources and Greek and Latin service books. Embracing tradition, the *Preces Privatae* "are for private devotion, only even more comprehensively in respect of their sources, what the Book of Common Prayer is in its way for the Church."[50]

The prayer sequence shapes daily life. "Points of Meditation Before Prayer" encourages readers to pray incessantly (Luke 21:36), while noting patristic sources in the margins for precepts such as "More is done by groanings than by words" or "Prayer goeth up, pity cometh down" (St Augustine, sermon 236). "Circumstances of Prayer" asserts times and places for prayer. Andrewes recommends evening and morning and a structure of seven hours, evoking medieval breviaries while citing scriptural supports for set times. Places are public (the congregation) and private (the closet). "Accompaniments" affirms the value of bodily positions such as kneeling, bowing, smiting the breast, and lifting up the eyes.

Andrewes's artistry is evident in genres and occasions. The prayer of penitence in his "Form of Morning Prayer" situates the praying subject in divine creation while encouraging kneeling and the lifting of hands:

> Superessential essence, nature uncreate,
>   Framer of the universe,
> I set Thee, Lord, before me,
>   And to Thee I lift up my soul:
> I worship Thee kneeling upon my knees
>   And I humble myself under thy mighty hand:
> I stretch forth my hands,
>   My soul gaspeth unto Thee as a thirsty land.[51]

The opening is theological: "Essentia superessentialis, natura increata, universi creatrix."[52] This implies his target audience: priests. The vast frame of God's superessential and uncreated nature also frames the local sufferings of the psalmist. The final simile of the "thirsty land" paraphrases Psalm 143:6. The Geneva and the Authorized Versions read: "my soul thirsteth." Brightman's translation is "gaspeth," the word used in the bishop's bible. Andrewes's original is an exact quotation of the Vulgate: "anima mea sicut terra sine aqua tibi" (Ps. 142:6).[53] In fact, the passage contains three references to the Psalms (16:9, 29:1; 143:5–6) and one to 1 Peter 5:6, illustrating a dense network of scriptural citations. Brightman's "gaspeth" is more auditory and intense than "thirsteth." A gasp is a rudiment of prayer, like breath.

The prayer of penitence alludes to the Parable of the Pharisee and the Publican (Luke 18:9–14). The parable contrasts two men at prayer, one presumptuous, the other humble. Andrewes is against presumptuous Puritans:

> I smite upon my breast,
>   And I say with the publican
> God be merciful to me the mere sinner,
>   The chief of sinners
>   To the sinner beyond the publican
>   Be merciful as to the publican.[54]

This passage also shows Andrewes interweaving scriptural allusions. The "chief of sinners" is taken from 1 Timothy 1:15. He repeats "sinner" three times and "publican" three times, reinforcing penitence as an auditory pattern in the reader's mind. He repeats words to intensify private devotion.

A comparison of prayers for Sunday and Friday and Saturday reveals more of Andrewes's art. Sunday evokes both the creation of light in Genesis 1 and Christ's Resurrection. Friday is both the creation of man and woman and the Crucifixion. He links these temporal typologies to the Book of Common Prayer. He begins by echoing the Benedictus (Luke 1:68–79): "Through the tender compassions of our God,/The Dayspring from on high hath visited us."[55] Brightman uses "tender compassions" rather than the "tender mercie" found in both the 1559 prayer book and the Bishop's Bible.[56] In the "Commemoration," he asserts the creation of light using the technique of parallel structure or structural repetition central to Hebrew poetics: "Glory be to thee, O Lord, glory be to Thee,/which didst create the light and lighten the world" (Ps. 118:27). He links the Resurrection to this event: "By thy resurrection raise us up to newness of life" (Rom. 6:4) and also Pentecost, the day of the gift of the Spirit: "renew It day by day in us who supplicate Thee."[57]

The sixth day meditates on the Crucifixion:

Blessed art Thou, O Lord, for the holy sufferings of this day.
  By thy saving sufferings on this day
    save us, O Lord.[58]

The artistry is plain and powerful. It begins and ends with God. Echoes and repetitions of "holy sufferings" and "saving sufferings" impress a redemptive sequence. The grace of salvation is extended in the long opening line and compressed in the final line. In patterns of preparation, penitence, and thanksgiving within the six-day's work, Andrewes inserts gems of poetic meditation that reward close reading.

Saturday is the day Christ lay in his tomb. Andrewes shows artistic skill in a change of mood, which McCutcheon describes: "In contrast to Friday's throbbing, passionate cries, these prayers are gentle .... His journey ended, he turns to Revelation's vision of the end of all time, meditating upon, hoping for, and celebrating the rest, the peace, and the joy which the saints have already inherited, for which he still thirsts."[59] Andrewes shares the meditative power of Donne and Herbert in imagining the Passion and a Sabbath vision in the close of the week.

Following the seven days are evening prayers, prayers of penitence, prayers of confession and thanksgiving, deprecations and comprecations, and intercessions. Significantly, Andrewes ends with a paraphrase of the Lord's Prayer. The section is in three parts. The first is a verse preface, which works as a preparation for prayer. It makes the reader bold to say the Lord's Prayer. The second is a paraphrase. It elaborates on the seven petitions of the prayer, offering scriptural and patristic citations to support each part. The third is a list of Old Testament passages that parallel each part of the Lord's Prayer. Andrewes places the Lord's Prayer in private devotion while affirming its role in public worship and revealing its biblical precursors.

The *Preces Privatae* became polemical twenty-two years after Andrewes's death. In 1648, the clergyman Richard Drake published *A manual of the private devotions and meditations of The Right Reverend Father in God Lancelot Andrews*, the first full English translation of Andrewes's *Preces Privatae*. As McCullough notes, Drake's publication remedies the omission of this text by Laud and Buckeridge in their 1629 folio. Drake sees it as a polemical antidote "to extempore prayer and preaching." The frontispiece shows Andrewes as pious and authoritative. The motto beneath his image names him the "universall bishop" even after the abolition of episcopacy; his prayers are "pious dropps" of "the purest kind," a dig at those who longed to purify the Church. (See Figure 4.)

His hands show the book in use, his right gesturing to the book as a whole, his left marking a place. This image of Andrewes using his own book suggests how translators used his works. Drake calls his 1648 edition a "sacred Relique." He recalls tear-stained pages: "Had you seen the Originall Manuscript, happy in the glorious deformity thereof, being slubber'd with His pious hands, and water'd with his penitential tears, you would have been forced to confesse That Book belonged to no other then pure and Primitive Devotion."[60] This use of emotion is polemical: Andrewes exceeds the fervency Puritans claim for their prayers.

Drake draws on the Parable of the Pharisee and the Publican to attack Puritans. Like the presumptuous Pharisee, extemporaneous prayer affronts the "Majesty of Heaven":

> There is too much of a Pharisee in him that dares trust to his Memory, his Phancy, or Invention, before the Majesty of Heaven; when even his most premeditated and weighted thoughts, though cloathed in the best attire of language, would be esteemed by himselfe too unworthy to be offered to his Prince. And yet, such is the irreligion of this Age, the most High God must take up and be content with that homely entertainment, which my Lord or Lady, forsooth, would not receive from their most faithfull servant, without great scorn and indignation.[61]

Drake's attack on "phancy" and "invention" deploys Andrewes's statement in Sermon 1: the Christian religion works "to bring into captivity all imagination to the obedience of Christ, 2 Cor. X.5." In short, Drake taps into an iconoclastic energy latent in Andrewes's conciliatory analysis of the Lord's Prayer. In the 1640s, the idol that needs toppling is vanity, not formality. Drake's adaptation of Andrewes's prayers illustrates the twofold purpose of polemic. He attacks the errors of his adversaries and supports Anglican communities in need of books and even reliquaries to preserve memory and tradition.

iv. George Herbert and Andrewes's Sermons

As Graham Parry suggests, "Andrewes was a powerful influence on Herbert from his youth."[62] He taught Herbert at Westminster school when Herbert was nine. Herbert complimented Andrewes in a Latin epigram, calling him a "watchman of heaven" who "matches holiness."[63] When Parry contends that Herbert is "best understood as the poetic exponent of the churchmanship of Lancelot Andrewes,"[64] he is contrasting Andrewes and Laud. Rowan Williams also cautions against

Figure 4. Frontispiece for Richard Drake, *A manual of the private devotions and meditations of The Right Reverend Father in God Lancelot Andrews* (1648). Courtesy of the Huntington Library.

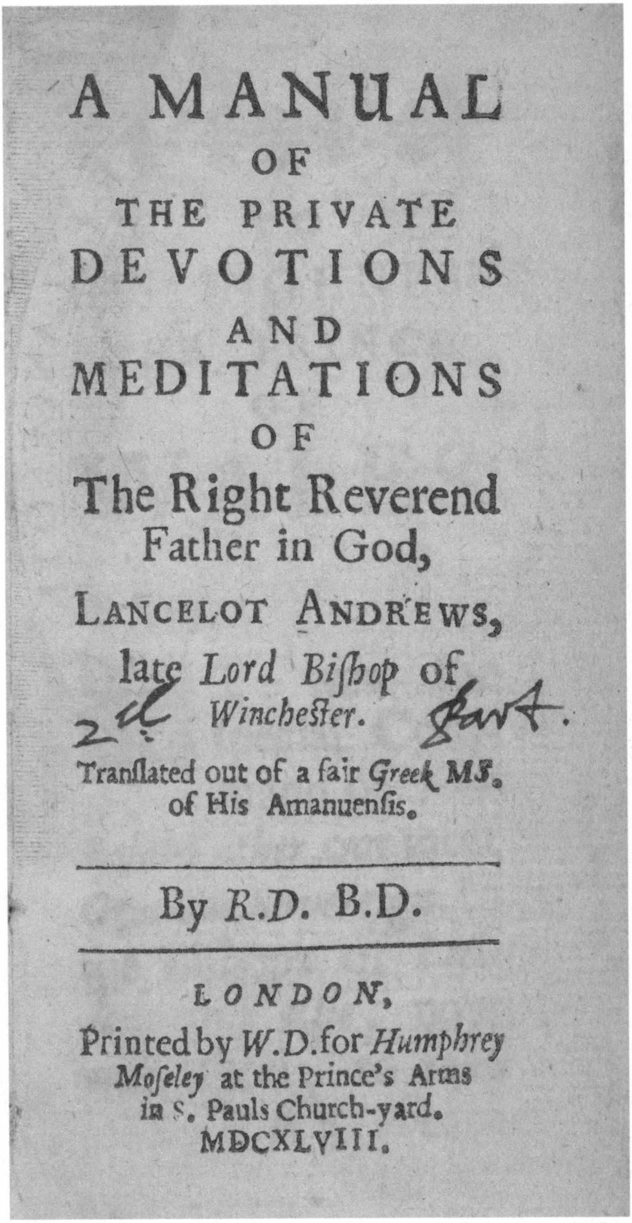

A MANUAL

OF

THE PRIVATE

DEVOTIONS

AND

MEDITATIONS

OF

The Right Reverend
Father in God,

LANCELOT ANDREWS,

late *Lord Bishop of*
Winchester.

Translated out of a fair *Greek* MS.
of His Amanuensis.

By *R.D.* B.D.

LONDON,

Printed by *W.D.* for *Humphrey*
Moseley at the Prince's Arms
in S. Pauls Church-yard.
MDCXLVIII.

Figure 4. (Continued)

conflating Andrewes and Laud: "Herbert died before Laud had become Primate, and so experienced nothing of the fierce conflicts around Laud's policies. We cannot know how he would have reacted; but it is certainly a mistake to see Herbert and Laud as part of some unified 'Caroline' ethos."[65]

As with Andrewes, a challenge in characterizing Herbert lies in his literary afterlife. The representation of Andrewes as an Anglican saint by his literary executors affirms his status as a proto-Laudian. Similarly, as Sharon Achinstein observes, "George Herbert, the 'Anglican Saint,' was enshrined by Izaak Walton. As a country parson of moderate ecclesiology, with abundant concern for practical piety and noble obscurity, Walton's Herbert became a focal point for writing the history of Anglicanism across the turbulent seventeenth century."[66] Yet, as Achinstein reveals, Herbert appealed to post-Restoration Nonconformists, who found in him an "authentic spiritual communion with the Divine" and even a "potent critique of ceremonial worship" (430–1).

Herbert writes with the pastoral concern of a priest who affirms the prayers and sacraments of the official Church in richly didactic meditative poems. Echoes and allusions to the Book of Common Prayer in his poetry have the quality of a spiritual exercise rather than a dogmatic prescription. He probes religious experience through his inward conflicts rather than in quarrels with others. Readers follow his personal exploration of vocation, sacraments, and prayer because he speaks to their inner conflicts as well as his own. Poet and priest are inseparable in his voice.

Andrewes's work on the King James Bible suggests his influence on Herbert. Gary Kuchar observes Andrewes's conciliatory nature in his supervision of the translation of the King James Bible, noting the degree of exegetical openness in the translation.[67] The Temple is "an exquisite expression of the same flexibility that gave rise to the Authorized Version and the climate of synthesis and compromise in which its translators worked. Like the Authorized Version, The Temple was written out of an intellectually vigorous belief in the virtues of wise ignorance and the complex simplicity that follows from it." Moreover, Herbert's years as Andrewes's student (1604–8) coincided with Andrewes's work on Genesis through 2 Kings, making Andrewes a daunting figure in Herbert's formative years.[68] Andrewes's influence on Herbert "should not be underestimated, particularly when it comes to biblical hermeneutics and the edifying power of liturgy."[69] Both men knew the power of language in spiritual formation, and Herbert saw spirituality as a self-critical and questioning process.

Herbert's appeal across the religious spectrum owes much to two major liturgical texts of the period: the Book of Common Prayer and the Psalms. There are two because Puritan Reformers who rejected the Prayer Book embraced the Psalms as a biblical model for prayer. Herbert draws deeply from the Psalms to voice to inner conflict, intense questioning, and transformative suffering. At the same time, many of his poems explore the sacraments of communion and baptism and draw from the Prayer Book. Herbert can "transcend parties and factions" in his spirituality.[70]

Is there a clear interface between private and public prayer in Herbert? Targoff's Herbert illustrates the poetics of common prayer. She suggests critics have "identified literary debts to Scripture, particularly the wealth of his allusions to the Psalms, but have done very little to disclose the ways in which Herbert employed the devotional models of the Prayer Book."[71] Kate Narveson, in contrast, sharpens the border between private and public prayer by placing Herbert in early modern Psalmic culture: "Private devotion was voluntaristic and involved scripture reading, meditation, application of doctrine to the heart, and affective address to God." Public worship "is the act of the community performing its duty to worship God – it is the act of the citizen in the public sphere."[72] For Narveson, Herbert's use of the Psalms manifests his pastoral concern for his readers. Paul Dyck argues that Herbert transcends the distinction between private and public as a biblical-liturgical poet: "Herbert's poetry operates within a biblical discursive space that has been significantly formed by Prayer Book worship." Poetry "can be an inspired act, but only when it works liturgically – that is, as a work to receive the Word."[73] "Aaron" illustrates this view. The priest examines his dependence on grace privately before entering the public worship space: "Come people, Aaron's dressed." Herbert is not a conventional polemicist because he turns conflict inward, not outward; nevertheless, his analysis of vestments and the fitness of the clergy were polemical subjects in the period.[74] The speaker's call to the people in these final four words asserts the second purpose of polemic: community formation.

Andrewes emphasized the power of "Our" in his analysis of the Lord's Prayer. Herbert uses the solitary "I" in many of his poems of affliction. This "I" appeared when he commended his manuscript to Nicholas Ferrar as "a picture of the many spiritual Conflicts that have past betwixt God and my Soul, before I could subject mine to the will of Jesus my Master, in whose service I have now found perfect freedom."[75] The shaped poem "The Altar" is visually both altar and "I." He shifts to "we" in poems that meditate on preaching, sacraments, and sacred space, as he teaches meditative practice to his readers. Finally, Andrewes is a consummate rhetorician as he persuades people to embrace common prayer. Herbert, Rowan Williams reminds us, was a rhetorician who served as university orator at Cambridge. In keeping with his Calvinist tendencies, he subverts pleasure in poetic and rhetorical invention through irony, which Williams sees as Herbert's leading trait: "[I]rony is essentially the tool of the rhetorician – someone whose primary skill is to use language in such a way that a listener or reader is changed by it." Prayer may be the "Church's banquet," but beyond metaphor it is "something understood."

Terry Sherwood offers a key word to explain Herbert's broad appeal: "spiritual." The "constant interplay between prayer and praise in *The Temple* has deep roots in Christian spirituality."[76] Far more of the lyrics in *The Temple* are prayers than we might think. Herbert's prayerful art "assumes, more generally, that the many practices of prayer are themselves artful."[77] Herbert's sense of self affirms his joint vocation as poet and priest. This affirmation is in turn consistent with the central conflict this book explores: in the debate between unpremeditated spontaneity authored by the Holy Spirit and the need for human art and invention to complement the Spirit, Herbert affirms the role of art. God is "delighted with man's efforts," as Sherwood maintains: "Herbert's notion of the self expresses his conviction that it is inseparable from its artistic powers."[78] As prayers, they undertake a poetic process marked by inward self-analysis in conjunction with outward rituals and symbols. This process gives Herbert's poetry a deep sincerity that further explains his appeal to early modern readers of different convictions.[79]

Herbert declares the importance of public prayer in "The Church Porch," a poem of seventy-seven stanzas offering plain advice for those entering the Church:

> Though private prayer be a brave design,
> Yet public hath more promises, more love:
> And love's a weight to hearts, to eyes a sign.
> We all are but cold suitors; let us move
> Where it is warmest. Leave thy six and seven;
> Pray with the most: for where most pray, is heaven.[80] (st. 67)

Herbert elevates public over private prayer; moreover, he identifies public prayer with the heart, contradicting the notion that set forms are mere "lip-labour," as Bunyan later called them. Whether the "brave design" of private prayer is a devotional manual or a mental conception by a praying subject, the stanza attributes more "weight" to public prayer. This is a striking reversal of assumptions over invention and inspiration that define prayer controversies. The design implies artifice; the heart conveys plain sincerity. Fervency is hot, but here the individual suitor is cold. Warmth lies in the public assembly. The gamble of "six and seven" opposes the certainty of order and decency. Herbert exhorts the reader to move to "Where it is warmest." Love is a word of charity, like the *our* in "Our Father." This remarkable stanza makes both the preparation and performance of public prayer a standard for the poems that follow.

"The Altar," the first poem in the church proper, replicates the pattern of stanza 67. Representing a classical altar in shaped verse, it is among Herbert's best-known poems.

THE ALTAR

A broken A L T A R, Lord, thy servant rears,
Made of a heart, and cemented with tears:
Whose parts are as thy hand did frame;
No workman's tool hath touched the same.
A H E A R T alone
Is such a stone,
As nothing but
Thy power doth cut.
Wherefore each part
Of my hard heart
Meets in this frame,
To praise thy Name;
That, if I chance to hold my peace,
These stones to praise thee may not cease.
O let thy blessed S A C R I F I C E be mine,
And sanctify this A L T A R to be thine.

The poem turns the practical advice of stanza 67 into a meditation on sacrifice. Its focus is the worthiness of the priest who presides at the material altar and seeks the sanctification of his own heart. The artificiality of shaped verse constructs the basic tension between human invention and divine inspiration that runs through early modern prayer polemics. As Michael Schoenfeldt has shown, the poem "aspires to show God's power by relinquishing all claims for its artful shape to the provenance of God."[81] Art itself must be sacrificed to grace, a point made visually in the final couplet, where the capitalized "SACRIFICE" rests artfully on the capitalized "ALTAR." And yet Herbert opens the questions human invention raises: "Should one only rearrange the biblical phrases that God's power has already shaped?"[82] The Book of

Common Prayer is just such a rearrangement. The first four lines of the poem combine allusions to Exodus 20:25 and Psalm 51:7. The final four lines allude to Luke 19:40. Thus, the top and bottom of this textual altar construct a typology of Old and New Testament stones. Daniel Doerksen reads the final prayer for sanctification as Calvinist: the "place for sacrifice, the human heart, has been broken and framed by God" but "its real significance will be lacking if the final prayer is not answered."[83] Consecration would evoke a material altar; sanctification is a life process for the elect person. I argue that the prayer is not only for the altar of the individual heart: it also asks a blessing on poetry itself as prayer. Sanctification confesses a dependence on grace rather than complacency over material externals such as altars, windows, and vestments, all subjects of poems in *The Temple,* all points of contention in religious polemic. Herein lies his broad appeal to readers across the religious spectrum of the time: Herbert is meticulous in describing the conditions of grace as the sine qua non of worship. His poems offer a broad invitation into his Church through his personal and exemplary heartwork, yet that work is accessible to all readers.

Importantly, "The Altar" follows "Superliminare," the poetic threshold of the church. Readers approach the altar as textual communicants seeking sanctification:

Thou, whom the former precepts have
Sprinkled and taught, how to behave
Thy self in church; approach, and taste
The church's mystical repast.

Avoid profaneness; come not here:
Nothing but holy, pure, and clear,
Or that which groaneth to be so,
May at his peril further go.

Echoes of the prayer book make public prayer, as in the priest's invitation to the "mystical repast" of communion, a prior condition for private self-reflection: "Take and Eat this in remembrance that Christ died for you and feed on him in your hearts by faith with thanksgiving." "The Altar" applies equally to priest or communicant by ascribing sanctification to the grace of God.

Andrewes, we recall, contrasts zeal and charity as virtues of private and public prayer. As Cynthia Garrett argues, Andrewes's descriptions of fervency "forcefully express what both Anglican and Puritan accept, despite philosophical declarations of God's unchangeability: that God responds to fervency and that fervency shows itself not in frequency of prayer alone, but in the expression of powerful emotion."[84] He places scriptural precepts that support extemporaneous prayer in the service of private prayer as Matthew's Gospel does. Andrewes pivots from private fervency to public charity through the Lord's Prayer, offering persuasion, not coercion. This is Herbert's approach too. He writes of flames and fire, but inverts the virtues readers might expect. Stanza 67 of "The Church Porch" invites readers to gather at the warm fire of public prayer and forgo their cold suits. The greater flame is charity, not zeal.

Charity is the strong foundation of the Church in "The Church Floor."

> Mark you the floor? that square and speckled stone,
> > Which looks so firm and strong,
> > > Is *Patience*:
> And th' other black and grave, wherewith each one
> > Is checkered all along,
> > > *Humility*:
> The gentle rising, which on either hand
> > Leads to the quire above,
> > > Is *Confidence*:
> But the sweet cement, which in one sure band
> > Ties the whole frame, is *Love*
> > > And *Charity*.

Sin and death facilitate the cleansing and sweeping of the room. The lyric concludes with yet another metaphor of heart architecture: "Blessed be the *Architect* whose art/Could build so strong in a weak heart."

Herbert writes of the "greater flame" of the Holy Spirit under the title of love. "Love (2)" begins by preferring the fire of the Spirit to the fires of lust:

> Immortal Heat, let Thy greater flame
> Attract the lesser to it; let those fires
> Which shall consume the world first make it tame,
> And kindle in our hearts such true desires,
> As may consume our lusts, and make thee way

It is appealing to think that Herbert might have read "Holy Sonnet 5" years before writing "Love (2)." Herbert's mother Magdalen Herbert was Donne's patron and friend. Donne is resigned to the burning of the world:

> But oh it must be burnt; alas the fire
> Of lust and envy have burnt it heretofore,
> And made it fouler; let their flames retire,

> And burn me O Lord, with a fiery zeal
> Of thee and thy house, which doth in eating heal.[85]

Herbert defers that conflagration to kindle chaste desires with the charity of "our." Zeal is a virtue of desired sanctity, but the greater flame is love. If love and time permit this pause, change can happen:

> Then shall our hearts pant thee, then shall our brain
> All her invention on thine Altar lay,
> And there in hymns send back thy fire again.

Herbert casts this poem in plural pronouns that are words of charity. Hearts will "pant," as in Psalm 42:1: "so panteth my soul after thee, O God." Panting conveys the more formless, wordless rudiments of praying in the Spirit described by Paul. Panting is also vocal and auditory, as is Andrewes's "gaspeth." Human invention, capable of producing artificial prayers, will lie on God's altar. Sanctified fire effects a reversal: the Spirit descends on people, and sanctified voices can send prayers back. The poem ends with an image of collective worship:

> Our eyes shall see Thee, which before saw dust
> Dust blown by wit, till that they both were blind:
> Thou shalt recover all thy goods in kind,
> Who wert disseised by usurping lust:
> All knees shall bow to thee; all wits shall rise,
> And praise Him Who did make and mend our eyes.

The sense of sight elevates charity over zeal. He alludes to 1 Corinthians 13:12: "For now we see through a glass, darkly; but then face to face." This passage occurs in Paul's affirmation of charity as a unifying bond for a community splintered by differing claims to gifts and graces: "Charity never faileth: but whether there be prophecies, they shall fail; whether there be tongues, they shall cease; whether there be knowledge, it shall vanish away" (13:8). "And now abideth faith, hope, charity, these three; but the greatest of these is charity" (13:13). "Love (2)" concludes with an exhortation to kneel, but it too is entirely scriptural: "[A]t the name of Jesus every knee should bow, of those in heaven, and of those on earth, and of those under the earth, and that every tongue should confess that Jesus Christ is Lord, to the glory of God the Father" (Phil. 2:10–11). "Love (2)" is a powerful orchestration of charity over zeal, making it an adaptation of Andrewes's main argument in his sermons on prayer.

We turn now to Herbert's poems on prayer. In "Prayer I," Herbert includes Tertullian as interpreted by Andrewes. Tertullian, we recall, summarizes the Lord's Prayer: "[I]n proportion as it is restrained in wording, so is it copious in meaning." Andrewes broadens this to all prayer in *Preces Privatae*: "Prayer is a summary of faith, an interpreter of hope."[86] Herbert develops both parts of this precept in "Prayer I." The Lord's Prayer is the epitome of prayer and summary of faith. Copia, in contrast, proliferates metaphors:

Prayer the Churches banquet, Angels age,
   Gods breath in man returning to his birth,
   The soul in paraphrase, heart in pilgrimage,
The Christian plummet sounding heav'n and earth;
Engine against th'Almightie, sinners towre,
   Reversed thunder, Christ-side-piercing spear,
   The six-daies world transposing in an houre,
A kinde of tune, which all things heare and fear;
Softnesse, and peace, and joy, and love, and blisse,
   Exalted Manna, gladnesse of the best,
   Heaven in ordinary, man well drest,
The milkie way, the bird of Paradise,
   Church-bels beyond the starres heard, the souls bloud,
     The land of spices; something understood.

This is an excess of answers to the question: what is prayer? Similarly, God's answers to prayer can exceed the petitioner's hopes. Copiousness is both temporal – the "six-daies world transposing in an houre" – and spatial: the "Christian plummet sounding heav'n and earth." Herbert includes Tertullian's idea of prayer as spiritual weapon – "Prayer alone it is that conquers God"[87] – since it is an "Engine against th'Almightie" and "sinners towre." Prayer both assaults heaven and protects the sinner. "Christ-side-piercing spear" is surprising. It recalls the Roman soldier who pierced Christ's side with his spear after his death, "and forthwith came there out blood and water" (John 19:34). This image combines with "Exalted manna" to typify the Eucharist, extending the theme of prayerful sacrifice that begins with "The Altar."

Man "well drest" alludes to Romans 13:14: "But put ye on the Lord Jesus Christ, and make not provision for the flesh, to fulfil the lusts thereof." The passage recurs in "Aaron" in the disparity between the speaker's inner self and his vestments: "Come people; Aaron's drest." In both poems, inward dress signifies sanctification through grace. "Prayer I" exhibits wit and invention to instruct and delight the reader.

There is a transition, however, from the art of human invention to the art of God. The "milkie way" exceeds the power of human sight, and church bells heard beyond "the starres" exceed human hearing. Divine art exceeds human speech. Herbert's metaphors for prayer are natural, scriptural, or traditional, but all are products of wit. We should expect the human invention to be undercut at some stage in the poem, just as "The Altar" sacrifices the poet's manifest wit on God's altar. The undercutting happens in the final two words of "Prayer (I)": "something understood." These words make us aware of the artificiality of the comparisons that come before. Images support prayer and worship, but no image is comprehensive. Poetic invention must remain grounded in scriptural precepts of prayer to avoid the dangers of what Andrewes calls "imaginings," or invention as an end in itself.

The source of "something understood" is 1 Corinthians 14:15: "I will pray with the spirit, and I will pray with the understanding also." In Herbert's sonnet, Paul's text composes the *topos* of art and grace. Metaphors are artful, but the Spirit alone animates, validates, and generates prayer. Metaphor dissolves into the amorphous "something." Art is a means, not an end. In addition, the referent is ambiguous: prayer is "something understood," but by whom? Is it understandable to God or the praying subject or both? In his sermons on prayer, Andrewes used these texts to pivot from private zeal to public charity. Herbert follows this pattern, but the inexpressibility of human understanding humbles poet and reader before God's infinite understanding. We can see now why Herbert was important to people on all sides of this controversy, but he is partial to conformity since he folds Tertullian's trope of weaponry into a charitable polemic that claims Pauline precepts for the prayer book and for Puritans.

The unity of Herbert's poetic and religious vocations is also evident in *The Country Parson,* which includes sections on the parson at prayer. We can see Andrewes's example in Herbert's prose prayers. These passages convey a strong sense of extemporaneous prayer in print, as also happens in Donne's *Devotions on Emergent Occasions.* Herbert's prayerful perorations graft private prayers into the life of the Church.

"The Author's Prayer before Sermon" rehearses creation and fall: "O Almighty and ever-living Lord God! Majesty, and Power, and Brightnesse, and Glory! How shall we dare to appear before thy face, who are contrary to thee, in all we call thee? for we are darknesse, and weaknesse, and filthinesse, and shame."[88] Rhetorically, this echoes the prayer book's "Almighty and everlasting God." It also maintains the "we" of public prayer. It then narrates the remedy of Christian redemption: "[W]hen we had sinned beyond any help in heaven or earth, then thou saidest, Lo, I come! then did the Lord of life, unable of himselfe to die, contrive to do it. He took flesh, he wept, he died; for his enemies he died; even for those that derided him then, and still despise him. Blessed Saviour!"[89] He "took flesh" echoes the Eucharistic prayer, "he took bread," and broke it and blessed it. Like Andrewes, Herbert applies prayer to sacrament.

Herbert then invokes the power of art to shape prayer and praise: "Blessed be the God of Heaven and Earth! who onely doth wondrous things. Awake therefore, my Lute, and my Viol! awake all my powers to glorifie thee! We praise thee! we blesse thee! we magnifie thee for ever!"[90] Herbert invokes art symbolized by musical instruments. He echoes the "Gloria" following communion: "We prayse thee, we blesse thee, we worshyppe thee, we glorifye thee."[91] The passage illustrates the collaboration of art and grace.

The passage is a preparation for the Lord's Prayer: "O make thy word a swift word, passing from the ear to the heart, from the heart to the life and conversation: that as the rain returns not empty, so neither may thy word, but accomplish that for which it is given. O Lord hear, O Lord forgive! O Lord, hearken. and do so for thy blessed Son's sake, in whose sweet and pleasing words, we say, *Our Father*, &c." Herbert insists that Christ's "sweet and pleasing words" are a set form of prayer. This section of *The Country Parson* emulates Andrewes's sermons on prayer: fervency should proceed to the charity epitomized in the Lord's Prayer. The process folds the reader into a communion of prayer; congregants beseech God "to blesse thy word, wherever spoken this day throughout the universall Church."[92]

"Prayer (II)" follows Andrewes's use of the creed as an antitype of prayer. Herbert affirms the role of the body in the speaker's uplifted eyes:

Of what an easie quick accesse,
My blessed Lord, art thou! how suddenly
    May our requests thine eare invade!
To shew that state dislikes not easinesse,
If I but lift mine eyes, my suit is made:
Thou canst no more not heare, then thou canst die.

The poem unfolds the Trinity. Prayer can "invade" God's ear faster than language. This is the Holy Spirit by whom prayer is understood (Rom. 8:26). The second stanza shows the Father as the wisdom of God manifest in creation. The third meditates on the Son in the Incarnation as "unmeasurable" love. In the final stanza, the speaker considers his loss of "Wealth, fame, endowments, virtues"; yet, this emptiness deepens his prayer and his meditation on the Trinity. He names the three persons as *"Ease, Power,* and *Love"*: the Spirit as comforter; the Father as creator; the Son as redeemer.

"The Collar" may seem a surprising choice for this study. It is a poem of venting, not praying. The speaker raves against his calling, showing the professional exhaustion we call "burnout." What does that have to do with prayer? Herbert calls prayer "Reversed thunder" in "Prayer (1)." "The Collar" illustrates the paradox of reversed thunder as the agency of God rather than the willfulness of a speaker imagining escape:

> I struck the board, and cried, "No more;
> I will abroad!
> What? shall I ever sigh and pine?
> My lines and life are free, free as the road,
> Loose as the wind, as large as store.
> Shall I be still in suit?

Schoenfeldt captures the reversal: "The power of prayer circulates from the God it wounds; he loads the cannon and fires it at himself."[93] This is the extreme redirection of Tertullian's spiritual weapon. Herbert juxtaposes this reversed thunder to the "Christ-side-piercing spear" that also wounds God in "Prayer (1)." In comparison, "The Collar" reveals God as suffering in and with his creature. It is a reverse prayer that wounds the self, just as God accepts the wound of real prayer.

"The Collar" also parodies prayer by combining extemporaneous speech with sacramental images. It begins with aural violence: "I struck the board, and cried, 'No more.'" The "I" separates the priest from the "our" of public prayer. The "No" forecloses the process of conflict and resolution, but the imagery foregrounds the Eucharist.

> Have I no harvest but a thorn
> To let me blood, and not restore
> What I have lost with cordial fruit?
> Sure there was wine
> Before my sighs did dry it; there was corn
> Before my tears did drown it.
> Is the year only lost to me?

Sighs and tears suggest the wordless "groanings" of Romans 8:26, as the Spirit helps the speaker in his weakness. Wine is an element of communion, but "cordial fruit" touches the heart (from the Latin *cordialis*, belonging to the heart). Sacramental time empties itself kenotically when the speaker asks, is "the year only lost to me?" A priest's year consists of liturgical seasons and holy days, not simple duration. He marks time as his "sigh-blown age," but sighs always carry the second meaning of prayer. It is a spontaneous effusion that can reject but not escape his calling.

The speaker plans a future without his vocation. His "I will" contradicts "Thy will be done."

> Away! take heed;
>   I will abroad.
> Call in thy death's-head there; tie up thy fears;
>   He that forbears
> To suit and serve his need
>   Deserves his load.

The long rant ends; the reversal finds room in the conclusion:

> But as I raved and grew more fierce and wild
>   At every word,
> Methought I heard one calling, *Child!*
>   And I replied *My Lord.*

The ending reverses Romans 8:15: "For ye have not received the spirit of bondage again to fear; but ye have received the Spirit of adoption, whereby we cry, Abba, Father." To cry "Abba, Father" is to pray sincerely, particularly in Puritan polemics justifying extemporaneous prayer. Here, God calls the speaker "child," and the speaker answers much as God might answer a human prayer. Why does Herbert change "Father" to "Lord"? "Lord" means a restored priestly vocation. It emphasizes discipleship, not simply filial obedience. The entire poem is about vocation, and vocation is inseparable from Herbert's poetic art. The end of "The Collar" shows that sincere prayer is deeper than sighs, tears, or words, as Paul said. But the poem is about the return to a calling, and the wildness of words without one. Like Andrewes, Herbert shows how the Church can harmonize private and public devotion and connect both modes of prayer through ceremony and tradition even at the extremes of dissonance.

"Prayer I" and "Prayer II" demonstrate controlled imagination. Both yield human art to grace. "The Collar" complements both poems as a reverse prayer. "The Collar" is ironic because the speaker is praying without realizing it. "Prayer I" is a spontaneous array of prayer metaphors grounded in church tradition. "The Collar" is a sequence of disordered Eucharistic and vocational images imagined in separation from God. It dramatizes extemporaneous speech that places divine and human wills in conflict. God treats it as a prayer, undercutting even the art of a spontaneous rant.

Like Andrewes, Herbert shows the capacity of the Church to harmonize private and public devotion and to ground both modes of prayer in sacramental images. The spontaneous proliferation of metaphors for prayer includes the "Church's banquet," an image of social and sacramental order that incorporates the altar as a place of sacrifice. As Herbert attests in stanza 67 of "The Church Porch," the collective banquet offers warmth that can go missing in private prayer. Similarly, Andrewes argued that the cold perseverance of the individual should lead to the "zealous desires" of the community. "The Collar" proliferates images as anxious "imaginings" in monologue. God's voice restores the poet inwardly and intimately, but to a vocation of public prayer. In reading Herbert, we do not need to calibrate the private and public at every turn, but rather to consider the pastoral dedication with which Herbert reveals his private conflicts with empathy as he guides readers towards public prayer with words of charity.

Chapter Two

Jeremy Taylor and Henry Vaughan: The Stock of Nature and Art

His aides are not inspirations of the habit, or infusions of a perfect gift, but a subliming of what God gave us in the stock of nature and art to make it in a sufficient order to an end supernaturall and divine.

Jeremy Taylor, *Apology for authorized and set forms of liturgie against the pretence of the spirit* (1649)

In this chapter, I examine Jeremy Taylor's extensive writings on prayer. Taylor responded to the crisis facing his Church by defending the Book of Common Prayer in theory and producing devotional manuals in practice. He followed this course in the face of the movement to abolish episcopacy in 1642 to the regicide and abolition of monarchy in 1649 and through the Interregnum. His polemic is adversarial but always constructive. His thesis is clear: poetry and prayer join in an "ingeminate expression," reflecting collaboration. If prayer is charitable, poetry is civilizing: the "first civilizing of people used to be by Poetry, and their Divinity was conveyed by Songs and Verses, and the Apostle exhorted the Christians, to exhort one another in Psalmes and Hymnes, for he knew the excellent advantages were likely to accrue to Religion by such an insinuation of the mysteries."[1] God expects people to make art in the sphere of prayer and devotion. Taylor's prose style is rich and various in poetic imagery and equivalent to Milton's from the opposing side of the debate. As it is for Milton in *Areopagitica* with its waves of imagery, Taylor's poetical style is itself polemical in asserting the vital power of poetry in open debate in a free society.

i. Taylor's Tolerant Polemic

Taylor (1613–67) marks the fourth generation of Anglican divines following Cranmer (1489–1556), Hooker (1554–1600), Andrewes (1555–1626), and Laud (1573–1645).[2] He studied at Cambridge and became a priest at the age of twenty. He impressed Laud, who appointed him one of his chaplains. Bishop William Juxon offered Taylor a parish in Uppingham in the East Midlands. Taylor served there until 1641. In 1642, at the outbreak of civil war, he joined the Royal Court at Oxford. Taylor wrote steadily through the turbulent 1640s. In 1646, he went to Wales where he became family chaplain and tutor to the Earl of Carbery at Golden Grove. King Charles I, who was impressed by Taylor's 1646 defence of the prayer book, *A discourse concerning prayer ex tempore,* brought him into the clerical circle that would produce the *Eikon Basilike.* Once poised to become an influential Churchman and preacher, he instead witnessed the destruction of his king and Church and the exile of Anglican society. With Church and monarchy restored in 1660, Taylor ended his career as Bishop of Down and Connor in Ireland, overseeing the construction of Dromore Cathedral. The heart of his writing is found in the tumult of the 1640s and 1650s. As happened with Andrewes, a posthumous collection of Taylor's works appeared in 1674 under the title, *Symbolon theologikon, or, A collection of polemicall discourses wherein the Church of England, in its worst as well as more flourishing condition, is defended in many material points, against the attempts of the papists on one hand, and the fanaticks on the other.* It contains some of his finest works, including his *Apology for Authorized and Set Forms of Liturgy* (1649); and it includes *The Liberty of Prophesying* (1646), a treatise of toleration. The full title is not in Taylor's more tolerant polemical tone, and was likely the choice of the publisher, Richard Royston, the King's Printer.

"Taylor had a poet's mentality."[3] This observation by C.J. Stranks is crucial to understanding the man. Like Andrewes, Taylor set some prayers and meditations in verse, but he is a prose writer. His prose reveals his poetic depth. His style is characterized by rich images, copious analogies, and high energy. For example, in his sermon "The Return of Prayers" he considers the challenges of praying:

> We bring unhallowed censers, our hearts send up to God an unholy smoke, a cloud from the fires of lust; and either the flames of lust or rage, of wine or revenge, kindle the breast that is laid upon the altar; or we bring swine's flesh, or a dog's neck; whereas God never accepts or delights in a prayer, unless it be for a holy thing, to a lawful end, presented to him on the wings of zeal and love, of religious sorrow, or religious joy; by sanctified lips and pure hands, and a sincere heart.[4]

We can read this long sentence as a "found poem." Setting it in lines shows Taylor's poetic mind:

We bring unhallowed censers
Our hearts send up to God an unholy smoke
A cloud from the fires of lust;
And either the flames of lust or rage,
Of wine or revenge,
Kindle the breast that is laid upon the altar;
Or we bring swine's flesh, or a dog's neck;

Whereas God never accepts or delights in a prayer,
Unless it be for a holy thing, to a lawful end,
Presented to him on the wings of zeal and love,
Of religious sorrow, or religious joy;
By sanctified lips and pure hands, and a sincere heart.

The passage links vivid images mainly from scripture that sound the depths of sin and the heights of grace. Taylor prefers the pronoun "our" to uphold common prayer, but not as complacent recitation. The pronoun tells readers they are not alone when prayer is difficult. The poetry itself lifts such readers out of spiritual lethargy, which is precisely Taylor's point. He recognizes a divide between people and God, then unites zeal and charity in wings that carry prayers to heaven. This prose poem is polemical because it asserts the need for poetic invention in prayer.

The sermon calls for charity in the face of hostility: some Christians "think God is tied to their sect, and bound to be of their side and the interest of their opinion."[5] This echoes *The Liberty of Prophesying*, which called for toleration in 1646 by distinguishing the different opinions of sects from the core doctrines of the Apostle's Creed. He frames prayer controversy succinctly, as he does in a prefatory epistle to a treatise on prayer by Henry Leslie, whom Taylor succeeded as bishop of Connor and Down: "My Lord, I have often considered concerning the pretensions of those persons, who think no prayer is good if it be studied; and none spiritual, unlesse it be extempore."[6] The point of this attack is not extemporaneous prayer per se, which simply exists and should exist; it is the attitude that nothing else is valid, spiritual, or simply good. The confrontational tone in his polemic increased over the course of the Interregnum as exile tested his patience.

Taylor's first polemical work, *Of the sacred order and offices of episcopacy*, appeared in 1642. Laud was a prisoner in the Tower of London, and debates over church government and episcopacy were raging. This work shows the ideals that inform his view of prayer. The full title affirms episcopacy, or the government of the Church by bishops according to "divine institution, apostolicall succession & catholike practice." The divine institution occurs when Christ gives his disciples the keys of the kingdom: "Verily I say unto you, whatsoever ye shall bind on earth shall be bound in heaven: and whatsoever ye shall loose on earth shall be loosed in heaven" (Matt. 18:18). Apostolic succession cannot simply shift to priests or presbyters, making bishops redundant. Christ commissioned his disciples first, and afterwards made the "great commission" to seventy-two new disciples, distinguishing the two groups. Thus, the "office and ministry of the Apostolate is distinct, and superior to that of Presbyters; and this distinction must be so continued to all ages of the Church." It is "as perpetuall as the Clergy, as the Church itself."[7] Moreover, he binds church to state: "[I]t is one of the main excellencies in Christianity that it advances the State and well-being of Monarchies and Bodies Politique." Bishops are "bound to promote the Honour and Dignity of Kings, whom Christianity would have so much honour'd, as to establish the just subordination of people to their Prince upon better principles than ever."[8] Taylor supports the political partnership of bishops and kings, not to maintain the status quo of honour, but to realize "just subordination" and "better principles" as Christian ideals.

Taylor was more tolerant than many Royalists. His approach to toleration appears in his *Liberty of Prophesying*, published the same year as his *Discourse concerning prayer ex tempore*, his first defence of the prayer book. The full title unveils his thesis: "Shewing the unreasonableness of prescribing to other mens Faith, and the iniquity of persecuting differing opinions." No part of Taylor's treatise "encourages variety of Sects, and contradictions in opinion, but supposes them already in being," as indeed they were.[9] Taylor presents the Apostle's Creed as the foundation of faith. Beyond that, there are only "superstructures" of ideas and opinions that are not articles of faith. Taylor argues that persecution, which is the opposite of toleration, is not a valid response to diverse opinions.

Tolerationist thinking gained prominence in 1644 with the publication of Milton's *Areopagitica*, though Milton excludes Catholics, and Roger Williams's *The Bloudy Tenent of Persecution*, a radically inclusive view, along with works by William Walwyn and John Goodwin. Taylor places Anabaptists (believers in adult baptism and, in some cases, pacifism) and Catholics at opposite ends of a socio-religious spectrum: "[I]t is a hard case that we shall think all Papists and Anabaptists and Sacramentaries to be fooles, and wicked persons, certainly among all these sects there are very many wise men and good men."[10] Problems arise with "men who will endure none but their own Sect."[11] Such men can be tolerated if they do not threaten the peace of the state.

The treatise was too liberal for the king's taste, and his opinion mattered.[12] Taylor's tolerant stance may seem inconsistent with his commitment to a state Church, but his argument does not, in fact, compromise episcopacy or the king's authority. His case is elementary: to tolerate is not to persecute. Sects already exist and cannot be wished away. Heresy and error exist, but prayer and charity can overcome them better than persecution. He distinguishes faith from opinion, warning that too many are in love with their own opinions. Taylor was confident in the long-term power of charity to maintain tradition. He saw the problems of imposing an official prayer book but was appalled at those who made it illegal. Much of our story is driven by the imposition and prescription of prayer practices. Taylor preferred to bend when others wished to break. His polemic elevates persuasion over fear.

ii. Taylor's *Psalter* of 1644

Taylor published his *Psalter of David* in 1644, reissuing it in 1647, 1650, and 1655. He added it to his *A Collection of Offices or Forms of Prayer* published in 1657. Paula Loscocco sets Taylor's *Psalter* in the vanguard of what would become, after the trauma of the regicide, a recovery for the Royalist ecclesiastical cause in the 1650s. The Psalms were a preserve of Puritan devotion; yet, Loscocco argues, if "the Puritan impulse to 'sing or say' the psalms is an essentially 'devotional' one that turns excerpted sections of scriptural text into 'set formes of prayer,'" then there is "little difference between the Puritan psalter and the Church's prayer book."[13] Beyond the confutation of Puritan opponents lies Taylor's hope for unforced unity. Once again, polemic is twofold in its critical and constructive functions.

The threat to the prayer book in 1644 and its proscription in January 1645 marked a crisis and set a new context for the Psalms. Taylor republished his *Psalter* to present the Psalms as an ancient common prayer book. As H. Boone Porter argues, the *Psalter* was "Taylor's first venture into the production of devotional manuals, and it was to be the threshold into his later compilations of both private and public prayers." If the polemical force of the book became clear as the situation worsened, the "potential ecumenical character" of the Psalms was always apparent to Taylor.[14] Like the Lord's Prayer, the Psalms did not belong to any one party, and Taylor was not about to cede them to Puritans.

Psalms are deeply ingrained in the texture of early modern art and literature. Calvin and Luther convey the affective power of the Psalms, elevating their already high standing for Reformation Protestants. Importantly, Calvin sees the Holy Spirit as an artist: there is "not an emotion of which anyone can be conscious that is not here represented as in a mirror. Or rather, the Holy Spirit has here drawn to the life all the griefs, sorrows, fears, doubts, hopes, cares, perplexities, in short, all the distracting emotions with which the minds of men are wont to be agitated."[15] Luther saw the Spirit as a teacher giving voice to storm-tossed souls: these "storm winds teach us to speak with earnestness, to open the heart and pour out what lies at the bottom of it."[16] The Book of Psalms is an encyclopedia of spiritual experience. Its dialectic of praise and lamentation, exile and deliverance, joy and sadness, stimulates empathy with the human condition.

Taylor's title page shows King David with crown and robes. He constructs the typology of King David and King Charles I in his preface: "In this most unnatural Warre commenced against the greatest solemnities of Christianity, and all that is called, God, I have been put to it to run somewhither to Sanctuary."[17] King David, like King Charles, experienced civil war, and took refuge in devotion: "[A]mongst all the great examples of trouble and confidence, I reckon'd King David one of the biggest, and of greatest consideration. For considering that he was a King, vexed with a Civill-Warre, his case had so much of ours in it, that it was likely the devotions he used might fit our turne, and his comforts sustain us."[18] Taylor finds "very many Prayers against the enemies of the King and Church, and the miseries of Warre" in the Psalms.[19] He is confident "God will defend his Church and his Anoynted."[20] With the link between king and Church preserved, he orders the Psalms as a prayer book: [S]ome "are historicall, many Eucharisticall, many Propheticall, and the rest Prayers for several occasions."[21] Church Fathers found the Psalms "the most profitable of books," even superior to "the monuments of Learning in any Library."[22] Like Sidney, Taylor sees the Psalms as both divinely inspired speech and unsurpassed human invention.[23] Sidney performed this principle by paraphrasing the Psalms in collaboration with his sister Mary, who completed the project after her brother's death in 1586. Taylor emulates Sidney by valuing the "stock of nature and art" that is essential to the expression of gifts and graces.

The Psalms' purpose as a common prayer book is the "secondary intention" of the Spirit: "The Prayers which I have collected out of the Psalmes are nothing else, but the matter of the Psalmes put into another mood, and fitted to the necessities of Christendome, and of our selves in particular, according to the first designation or secondary intention of the blessed Spirit." The secondary intention persists through the centuries:

[T]he use of them could not expire in David, though first occasioned (many of them) by his personal necessities: for all Scripture was written for our learning upon who the ends of the world are come, (saith the Apostle) & Christ, & his Apostles, and the Church of all ages, hath taught us by their example and precepts, that the purposes of the Holy Ghost were of great extent.[24]

David's first intention was to pray privately. The Spirit's "secondary intention" is public worship made possible by hand copying and later the printing press.

The Psalms also support different traditions, a view that shows Taylor's tolerance and curiosity. Writers of "the old Liturgies of the Eastern and Western Churches" drew "their waters from the fountains of our Blessed Saviour, but through the limbecks of David."[25] He even reaches out to Catholic tradition: "[D]evout men of severall ages drew them into Collects, Antiphonaries, Responsories, and all other part of their devotions. They made their Prayers out of the Psalmes, their confessions, their doxologies, their ejaculations were for the most part clauses or periods of the Psalter."[26] Porter sees the influence of John Cosin, a member of Laud's circle and author of the controversial *A Collection of Private Devotions* (1627), in Taylor's "Antiphonaries" and "Reponsories."[27] Taylor asks readers to consider the scriptural roots of these prayer practices.

The Psalms are also a map of human salvation: "[W]e may easily beleeve that Christ with a Key of David in his hand, is nothing else but Christ fully open'd and manifested to us in the Psalmes in the whole mystery of our Redemption."[28] By opening "many mysteries of Religion," specifically Christ's birth, priesthood, kingdom, passion and death, the Psalms convey the sacramental and sacrificial values Andrewes passed down to Laud and his circle. Taylor is an optimistic ecumenist: "I have had a meditation that this manner of devotion might be a good Symbol and instrument of Communion betweene Christians of different perswasion. For if we all would communicate in the same private devotion, it were a great degree of Peace and Charity."[29] The word "symbol" signifies common ground among divided Christians, just as the Apostle's Creed was a "symbolum fidei" for the early Church.

iii. Taylor's *Apology* and the *Directory of Public Worship*

Taylor is to liturgy as Sidney is to "secular" literature. His *Apology for authorized and set forms of liturgie against the pretence of the spirit* (1649) has many similarities to Sidney's famous *Defence of Poetry* (1595). Sidney championed imaginative literature, particularly classical works, as a moral complement to sacred truths. He first affirms biblical poetry: "And may not I presume a little farther to show the reasonableness of this word 'vates,' and say, that the holy David's Psalms are a divine poem? If I do, I shall not do it without the testimony of great learned men, both ancient and modern."[30] He concedes the central place of the Bible, but argues for poetry as a vital complement that moves readers to virtue. Sidney also distinguishes imaginative literature from divine inspiration. As Timothy Rosendale argues, "[A]lthough he adduces poetry's long vatic tradition and the Psalms of David as evidence of its high cultural position, he distances himself from Neoplatonic claims about the divine inspiration of poetry, upholding instead a poetic process entirely contained within the human sphere."[31] The Bible is a sacred text. Its readers identify the "divine poem" of the Psalms with the Holy Spirit. But Sidney's David is first a human poet.

Taylor makes the same distinctions in the *Apology*. Claims to immediate inspiration are pretentious. Liturgical writing exercises human poetic talents in relationship with God. Poetry was vital to the earliest teaching of holy mysteries, and therefore a sign of collaboration between art and the Spirit. Extemporaneous prayer is at best a variable individual performance, whereas formal liturgy is constant but not static. The Spirit works through set forms of prayer, connecting "all Christians in succession" (*Apology* 10), making common prayer a source of charity.

The *Apology* is both a defence of Anglican prayer practice and an attack on the *Directory of Public Worship*, also called the *Westminster Directory*. The Directory appeared by order of Parliament in 1645. Earlier, the imposition of a prayer book on Scotland in 1637 sparked civil unrest and two short wars between England and Scotland. Not all Puritan Reformers rejected prayer books. Presbyterians could have accepted William Whittingham's 1556 translation of Calvin's prayers, *The Forme and ministration of the Sacraments*, used by the English Congregation at Geneva. Presbyterians could have pressed for a national liturgy on these lines. Instead, they compromised with Independents who favoured congregational autonomy. Independents wanted scope for unscripted prayer. Some Independents "were unalterably opposed to liturgies in any shape or form as a quenching of the inspiration of the Holy Spirit."[32] Geoffrey Nuttall traces the emergence of the *Directory of Public Worship* to a "sudden uprush of Independency" emerging from the internal politics of the Westminster Assembly, a body of ministers summoned by Parliament to settle questions of religious practice.[33] Independents, though a minority, prevailed.

The Directory is in large part a polemic against the Book of Common Prayer. Its authors contend that the prayer book served "to make and increase an idle and unedifying Ministry, which contented itself with set Forms made to their hands by others, without putting forth themselves to exercise the gift of Prayer, with which our Lord Jesus Christ pleaseth to furnish all his Servants whom he calls to that office."[34] This is a summary of the typical complaints: in other words, set forms induce complacency.

The Directory is a practical manual, not a work of art. It wisely makes no claims to inspire its readers. In keeping with political compromise, it supports ministers to pray extemporaneously with some brief guidelines. In reminding the people of their sinful natures, or in petitions for rulers, the minister should "call upon the Lord to this effect." The Directory considers scripted prayer as confining, since supporters of the Book of Common Prayer see no other "way of Worship of God amongst us."[35] Habitual readings discourage knowledge of true doctrine and the practice of piety, making the service book "no better then an Idol by many Ignorant and Superstitious people, who pleasing themselves in their presence at that Service, and their Lip-Labour in bearing a part in it, have thereby hardened themselves in their ignorance, and carelessnesse of saving knowledge and true piety."[36] Paul Dyck offers a brilliant rejoinder to this claim: "While the Prayer Book, as with every other form of worship, can become an empty habit, it *offers* not only an experience with scripture but an encounter with God, and this encounter is precisely not stable and unchanging."[37] The key word is "offers." The life of prayer is not consistent; it varies in sickness and health, and in youth and age. Nor is God static because eternal. Deprived of the prayer book, the faithful risk idolizing their variable "imaginings," as Andrewes argued. Andrewes's negative idea of imaginings is implicit throughout Taylor's *Apology*. Poetic scripts prevent vain imaginings, a point that informs Taylor's polemic.

The Directory is also sensitive to continental perceptions of the English Reformation. If "Papists" boast that the prayer book "was a compliance with them in a great part of their Service," while "Reformed Churches abroad" dislike it, then it is not advancing the Reformation.[38] The authors respect the prayer book in its historical moment. Cranmer and others were "Excellent Instruments raised by God to bring the purging and building of his House." If they were still alive, they would surely "joyne with us in this work" of expelling the Book of Common Prayer.[39] Making the dead speak is going to some lengths.

The Directory had defenders. William Dell, a Congregationalist minister, served as a chaplain to parliamentary forces during the Civil War. He published *The Power of the Holy Ghost Dispersed through the Whole Body of Christ* in 1645. A Calvinist, Dell distinguishes the elect from "reprobates and devils."[40] He raises the same question as Taylor: how can an individual be certain of the Spirit's presence? By the Spirit is Dell's answer: "[W]e cannot by any acts of our owne prepare our selves to receive the Spirit; but only by the Spirit we prepare our selves to receive the Spirit."[41] If the Spirit is at work, it will subdue the sinful self and support the regenerate self: "He emptyes us. And this emptying is the first and chief worke of the Spirit upon the Elect, whereby he prepares them to receive himself. For the more empty a man is of other things, the more capable he is of the Spirit."[42] Dell traces the Spirit to a place where there is no language and no human art and "other things." The emptying of the self and its inventions makes extemporaneous prayer more individual. Dell does use plural pronouns, however, to signify a church: "For we have not the Spirit immediately in it selfe, but in the flesh of Christ. And when we by faith are made the flesh of Christ, then wee partake of that Spirit that dwells in the flesh of Christ."[43] For Dell, that "flesh" manifests a new visible church. Taylor's *Apology*, in contrast, offers a church enriched by continuous tradition.

Taylor witnessed the rift Nuttall sees between Presbyterians receptive to an alternative liturgy and Independents who were not. He exploits this early in the *Apology*: "The *Directory* takes away that Forme of Prayer which by the authority and consent of all the obliging power of the Kingdome, hath been used and enjoyned ever since the Reformation. But this was done by men of differing spirits, and of disagreeing interests" (*Apology* 3). This wittily exposes Presbyterians and Independents divided by conflicting attitudes to "authority" or tradition and "deliberation" or premeditation.

Taylor calls for deliberation in the human sphere. He recommends thinking before speaking. He cites Solomon – "Be not rash with thy mouth, and let not thy heart be hasty to utter any thing before God, for God is in Heaven and thou upon Earth, therefore let thy words be few" (Ecclesiastes 5:2) – and Quintilian, "A wise mans speech should be like his life, and actions; composed, studied, and considered" (*Apology* 4). He then addresses the texts the Directory cites for extemporaneous prayer, including Zechariah 12:10 and Romans 8:26. Taylor calls this selection "somewhat wild." Baiting Independents, he quips, "there is great independency in the severall parts" (*Apology* 8). The wild assembly of proof texts is like a congregation in chaos. Divisions make the Directory a force for fragmentation, which is anti-Eucharistic: "I will not say into how many Churches, but into how many innumerable atomes, and minutes of Churches those Christians must needes be scattered, who alter their Formes according to the number of persons, and the number of their meetings, every company having a new Forme of

Prayer at every convention" (*Apology* 69). If extemporaneous prayer is an individual phenomenon, then religion will disintegrate into individual atoms. The dissociation of the Church works against the unifying power of the Eucharist.

Unity requires the support of "all the arts in the world" (*Apology* 69). The spirit works with human "industry" to connect prayer and poetry: its "gifts and graces are improvements and helps of our naturall faculties, of our art and industry, not extraordinary, miraculous, and immediate infusions of habits and gifts" (*Apology* 8). Taylor invokes the Parable of the Talents to stir human effort: "[S]omething must be done on our part, we must improve the talents, and swell the bank; for if either we lay them up in a napkin, or spend them, suppresse the Spirit, or extinguish it, we shall dearly account for it." The same parable defines Milton's poetic vocation in his Sonnet 19, but with a difference. Milton is anxious to use "that one Talent which is death to hide" first out of personal obligation. Taylor, in contrast, uses the "we" of the corporate Church throughout. *We* "must improve the talents." The helps of the Spirit, therefore, "are not inspirations of the habit, or infusions of a perfect gift, but a subliming of what God gave us in the stock of nature and art to make it in a sufficient order to an end supernaturall and divine" (*Apology* 13). The Church should exercise the gifts of its members.

Taylor challenges Puritan interpretations of Romans 8:26:

> But it is pretended that there is such a thing as the gift of prayer, a praying with the spirit; *Et nescit tarda molimina spiritus sancti gratia,* Gods Spirit (if he pleases) can doe his worke as well in an instant, as in long premeditation. And to this purpose are pretended those places of Scripture which speak of the assistance of Gods spirit in our prayers.... especially Rom. 8. 26. *likewise the Spirit also helpeth our infirmities, for we know not what we should pray for as we ought, but the Spirit it selfe maketh intercession for us with groanings that cannot be uttered,* &c. From whence the Conclusion that is inferred is in the words of Saint Paul, that we must pray with the Spirit, therefore not with set formes, therefore ex tempore.[44]

Pretense rebuffs the Puritan charge of hypocritical formalism with a reasonable skepticism towards claims of inspiration. Rejecting pretense, Taylor sees the Spirit's role as instructive, not possessive:

> Thus the Holy Ghost brought to their memory all things which Jesus spake and did, and by that means we come to know all that the Spirit knew to be necessary for us, the Holy Ghost being author of our knowledge by being

the fountain of revelation; and we are therefore *theodidaktoi*, "taught by God," because the Spirit of God revealed the articles of our religion that they might be known to all ages of the church .... we need no other immediate inspiration or extraordinary assistance than that we derive from the Holy Ghost by the conveyance of the apostolical sermons and writings. (*Apology* 9)

Theodidaktoi (Θεὀδίδακτοι) – to be taught by God – comes from 1 Thessalonians 4:9: "But as touching brotherly love ye need not that I write unto you: for ye yourselves are taught of God to love one another." The message is love but the act of translation is polemical: it debunks the notion of "an idle and unedifying" Anglican ministry described in the Directory. Some argued that set forms allow ministers to avoid thinking about translation. Taylor sets a high scholarly standard to refute any notion that printed texts are easy. He goes on to translate Romans 8:26 – "the Spirit also helpeth our infirmities" – in original Greek: συναντιλαμβανεται (*syn-anti-lambanetai*: jointly helps). He adds a Latin phrase of his own to emphasize collaboration, reinforcing it with the rhetorical term ingemination: "[I]t is in the Greek, *collaborantem adjuvat:* it is an ingeminate expression of our labours; and that supposes us to have faculties capable of improvement and an obligation to labour, and that the effect of having the gift of prayer depends upon the mutual concourse, that is, upon God blessing our powers and our endeavours." Even the inspired "penmen" of scripture chose words: "[C]ertainly they were moved by a more immediate motion, and a motion neerer to an Enthusiasme, then now adaies in the gift and spirit of Prayer. And yet in the midst of those great assistances and motions they did use study, art, industry, and humane abilities. This is more than probable in the different stiles of the several books, some being of admirable art, others lower and plaine. The words were their owne, at least sometimes, not the Holy Ghosts" (*Apology* 19). Taylor models the human effort he advocates. His erudite and poetic polemic is the expression of his talent and the gifts and graces of the Spirit.

Ironically, extemporaneous prayer competes with scripture: "[I]f these who pray *ex tempore,* say that the assistance they receive from the Spirit is the inspiration of words and powers without the operations of art and naturall abilities and humane industry, then besides that it is more then the Pen men of Scripture sometime had (because they needed no extraordinary assistances to what they could of themselves doe upon the stock of other abilities)" (*Apology* 21). He challenges ministers suspicious of print to record their inspired prayers: "If his first conceptions were of God, and Gods Spirit then they are so still, even when they are written. Or is the Spirit departed from him, upon the sight of a Pen and Inkhorne?" (*Apology* 20). The Spirit is not a "spirit of utterance" according to Romans 8:26. To suppose otherwise is to indulge in the vain "imaginings" Andrewes warns against. A minister who demands immediate inspiration asks God to "multiply and continue miracles to justify his fancy."[45]

Taylor uses Andrewes's idea of fancy. Reid Barbour argues, if "as Lancelot Andrewes puts it, the essence of profanity is the replacement of God's law with one's 'own fancy and affection,' it is widely recognized in the period that fancy or imagination is powerfully instrumental in the maximization of devotion."[46] Spiritual exercises of meditation discipline these faculties, for example. Barbour equates fancy and imagination; Andrewes uses "imaginings" as a cautionary word. Taylor marks the distinction with Sidney's concept of the "phantastick imagination."[47] With extemporaneous prayer, "it is nothing but the fantastique and imaginative part that is pleased, which for ought appears, may be disturbed with curiosity, peevishnesse, pride, spirit of novelty, lightnesse, and impertinencie: and that to satisfie such spirits, and fantastique persons, may be as dangerous and uselesse to them, as it is trouble some in it selfe" (*Apology* 40). Andrewes and Taylor regard set forms as authentic supports for both fancy and imagination.

Taylor's deconstruction of the Directory's inconsistencies is masterful. Forgoing an isolated, defensive persona, he creates a "Eucharistic" consciousness that insists on prayer as a linking, connecting, unifying expression. From this position, he seeks both to oppose and reunite the "differing spirits" that produced the Directory.

iv. The Interregnum: Taylor the Devotional and Liturgical Writer

The Book of Common Prayer remained in covert use despite punishing fines.[48] Taylor used it during his chaplaincy at the Golden Grove estate in Wales. Between 1649 and 1653, Taylor published his best-known devotional works, *The Rules and Exercises of Holy Living* (1650) and *The Rules and Exercises of Holy Dying* (1651), and he reissued *The Great Exemplar*, a narrative of the life of Christ. He continued his liturgical scholarship, examining "eastern and medieval western liturgical sources."[49] Porter notes that "Taylor's writings contain thousands of citations of ancient and foreign writers."[50] His manuals "take care that Religion may be convey'd in all its material parts the same as it was, but by new and permitted instruments."[51] He augmented the prayer book to produce a liturgy not subject to fines, and to enrich a tradition he believed could disappear in England.

In 1654, Taylor published twenty-eight sermons delivered at Golden Grove. He delivered the first of these – "Of the Spirit of Grace" – on Whitsunday or the day of Pentecost when the Holy Spirit descends on the Apostles (Acts 2). His text was Romans 8:9–10: "But ye are not in the flesh, but in the Spirit, if so be that the Spirit of God dwell in you. Now if any man have not the Spirit of Christ, he is none of his. And if Christ be in you, the body is dead because of sin; but the Spirit is life because of righteousness." The sermon reveals a new polemical tone honed by exile. For example, it contrasts Jews and Christians with condescension: Jews "had the infancy of knowledge; and revelations to them were given as a Catechisme is taught to our children." Although "the Psalms of David was their Great office, and the treasury of devotion to the Nation (and very worthily) yet it was full of wishes for temporals, invocations of God the Avenger, on God the Lord of Hosts, on God the Enemy of their Enemies; and they desired their Nation to be prospered, and themselves blessed, and distinguished from all the world, by the effects of such desires."[52] The supersessionist view is polemical: he compares his vindictive Puritan contemporaries to Pharisees who seek a public reputation for holiness.

Taylor sharpens Andrewes's attack on Puritan "imaginings." Prayer should not produce a "sensible or phantastick pleasure," but "conversation" with God and "holy living."[53] The pretense of the Spirit serves "a hypochondriacall religion." Taylor invokes Andrewes's idea of idolatry: "Jews in the declensions to folly and idolatry did worship the stone of imagination," but "we have also taken up this folly, and worship the stone of imagination: we beget imperfect phantasms and speculative images in our phansy, and we fall down and worship them."[54] Remarkably, Taylor still maintains the pronoun "we," refusing to give up on the constructive potential of his polemic.

Taylor is provocative in *The golden grove, or, A manuall of daily prayers and letanies, fitted to the dayes of the week. Containing a short summary of what is to be believed, practised, desired* (1654). He restores hours and days found in medieval manuals and John Cosin's controversial *Book of Hours*. The design emulates Andrewes's *Preces Privatae*. A "credenda" establishes doctrine and beliefs. An "agenda" describes daily and hourly duties in prayer. A sharper polemical tone also rolls through the prefaces. He surveys the ruined landscape of church and state in the preface to *Golden Grove*.[55] The faithful are the "Watchmen of the Church." Cromwell, on the other hand, leads "Supplanters and Underminers" who "are digging down the foundations" having "destroy'd all publick Forms of Ecclesiastical Government, discountenanc'd an excellent Liturgie, taken off the hinges of Unity, disgrac'd the Articles of Religion, polluted publick Assemblies, taken away all cognizance of Schism, by mingling all Sects, and giving countenance to that against which all Power ought to stand upon their guard."[56] He compares Anglicans to Israel in exile: "[W]e must now take care that the young men who were born in Captivity may be taught how to worship the God of Israel after the manner of their fore-fathers, till it shall please God that Religions shall return into the Land, and dwell safely, and grow prosperously."[57] His conclusion is simple: "There is now nothing left, but that we take care that men be Christians."[58] England is now Babylon.

Never designed to inspire, the *Directory of Public Worship* was never very popular. Outlawing the prayer book was a key to its success. As Edward Vallance notes, reluctance "to adopt the new form led in August 1645 to the criminalizing of the use of the old liturgy, even in private services. From the outset, the debate over the liturgy carried clear political overtones."[59] Aware of ongoing use of the prayer book in the Interregnum, Cromwell chose to insult it. On Tuesday, 29 August 1654, he issued an "An Ordinance for the ejecting of Scandalous, Ignorant and Insufficient Ministers and School-Masters." The ordinance empowered commissioners to summon "any publique Preacher, Lecturer, or other persons formerly called Parsons, Vicars or Curats" along with any schoolmasters "who are or shall be ignorant, scandalous, insufficient or negligent in their several and respective places."[60] The ordinance roots out "Blasphemous and Atheistical opinions," to eliminate swearing, adultery, fornication, and drunkenness and to suppress "Whitson-Ales, Wakes, Morris-Dances, May-poles" and "Stage-plays." Parliament enjoyed stirring the Book of Common Prayer into this pool of vice. It condemns "such as have publiquely or frequently read or used the Common-prayer Book."[61] Cromwell knew the prayer book was "the badge of the Royalist Party."[62] As Diarmaid MacCulloch observes, Cromwell knew they were "nursing and honing their grievances against the new Church establishment, and burnishing the memory of the late King Charles as a martyr."[63] At the same time, he tolerated Anglicanism as a "federation of parishes" with "no central structure," allowing Anglicans to function as a quiet sect.

The ordinance teaches a lesson much-repeated but seldom learned: repressive laws generate dissent. We see this in the imposition of the prayer book after 1660. We also see it in defences of the prayer book in the 1650s. Lionel Gatford's *A petition for the vindication of the publique use of the Book of Common-Prayer, from some foul, but undeserved aspersions lately cast upon it* rejects the association of the prayer book with atheism and immorality, arguing that a "faithfully pious" minister would lose his job "to his own and his poor wife and childrens ruine."[64] Conversely, Dissenters like Bunyan were targets of identical aspersion after the Restoration.

In *Euchologia, or, The doctrine of practical praying*, Bishop John Prideaux reminds his daughters Sarah and Elizabeth that they descend on their mother's side from the Marian martyr Rowland Taylor, Jeremy Taylor's direct ancestor. Rowland Taylor left his Book of Common Prayer to his wife, "holding that book (above all other, next the Bible) the most absolute Directory for all his effectual Devotions."[65] "Directory" scorns the *Directory of Public Worship*, illustrating how religious minorities appropriate and invert the language of the state.

John Harwood's *A Plea of the Book of Common Prayer*, published in 1654 and again in 1657, opens with a prayer for vindication: "Lord, open the eyes of the dissenters that they may see what damage accrues the Doctrine of thee, the Lord Jesus, for want of uniformity in Church Service."[66] Harwood chooses to call opponents of the prayer book dissenters even while they are in power.

Anthony Sparrow's *A Rationale Upon the Book of Common Prayer* also answers the ordinance. Sparrow in particular burnishes the memory of the king and earlier Anglican divines. The second edition of 1657 marks festival days in the church calendar. The frontispiece depicts a minister kneeling at a prayer desk reciting the Litany with a citation to "Bishop Andrews Notes." Sparrow also quotes the *Eikon Basilike*, "Meditat. 16. upon the Ordinance against the Book of Common Prayer": "Hardly can the pride of those men that study Novelties, allow former times any share or degree of Wisdom or Godliness."[67] Sparrow enshrines Andrewes and the *Eikon Basilike* in the canon of Anglican devotion. Sparrow would join the team of the Anglicans negotiating the restored liturgy at the Savoy Conference in 1662.

In 1657, Taylor published his service book: *A Collection of Offices or Forms of Prayer In Cases Ordinary and Extraordinary; Taken out of the Scriptures and the Ancient Liturgies of several Churches, especially the Greek, Together with a large Preface in Vindication of the Church of England*. The frontispiece shows Christ kneeling in prayer with hands, bearing his stigmata, outstretched in a cruciform position (see Figure 5).

The Latin caption translates as: "With a strong cry, tears, and prayers, his offerings were heard for their reverence." Visually and linguistically provocative, both image and text polemically reclaim fervency and authenticity for Christ as the mediator of the Church. Once again, the printer was Royston, who commissioned the image of Charles I as a martyr for the *Eikon Basilike*. The Anglican printing network was still functioning.

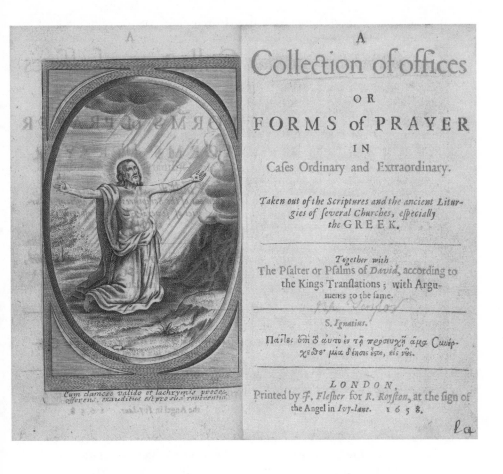

A

Collection of offices

O R

FORMS of PRAYER

I N

Cafes Ordinary and Extraordinary.

Taken out of the Scriptures and the ancient Litur-
gies of feveral Churches, efpecially
the G R E E K.

Together with
The Pfalter or Pfalms of *David,* according to
the Kings Tranflations ; with Arguments to the fame.

S. *Ignatius.*

Πάντες ὅτι ᾖ αὐτὸ ἐν τῇ προσευχῇ ἅμα ζωύέρ-
χεοθε· μία δ'ἐησις ἔτω, εἰς ὑμᾶς.

L O N D O N.
Printed by *J. Flefher* for *R. Royfton,* at the fign of
the Angel in *Ivy-lane.*   1 6 5 8.

Cum clamore valido et lachrymis preces
offerens, exauditus eft pro sua reverentia.

Figure 5. Title page and frontispiece: *A Collection of Offices* (1658). Courtesy of
the Huntington Library.

The *Collection of Offices* uses the church calendar as a template of memory. Taylor includes a list of religious days that were no longer public holidays "by the laws of England"; a calculation of all moveable feasts until 1706, a "Table to find Easter for ever"; and prayers for occasions, including prayers for madmen, prisoners, and heretics. The *Collection* shows that Taylor did not expect the prayer book to return, even at this late stage of the Interregnum. The preface bears this out. It is a history of liturgy in fifty numbered paragraphs. His tone grows more frustrated, but he writes for future generations to fulfill the positive purpose of polemic.

Taylor identifies Interregnum England with the period of the Judges, which falls between the conquest of Canaan by Joshua and the advent of monarchy in Israel when Samuel reluctantly anointed Saul and David as kings. Apostasy is a tragic cycle in Judges. A refrain marks each cycle: "In those days there was no king in Israel. And every man did what was right in his own eyes" (21:25). Suffering for their apostasy, the people pray for deliverance and God raises up a deliverer. Taylor locates England at the nadir of the cycle: "[W]e also have been but too like the sons of *Israel*; for when we sinned as greatly, we also have groaned under as great and sad a calamity. For we have not onely felt the evils of an intestine Warre, but God hath smitten us in our spirit, and laid the scene of his judgments especially in Religion."[68] He indicts the whole nation and its differing parties and factions.

Taylor turns prophet in this jeremiad by urging the nation to turn back. He echoes Psalm 137: "I shall onely crave leave that I may remember *Jerusalem* and call to minde the pleasures of the Temple, the order of her services, the beauty of her buildings, the sweetness of her songs, the decency of her Ministrations."[69] This passage has the qualities of a manifesto reconstituting the Anglican Church:

That we may follow the example, and obey the precept of our blessed Saviour, who appointed a set form of devotion (and certainly they that profess enmity against all Liturgy can in no sense obey the precept given by him who gave command, When ye pray, say, *Our Father*. [3.] That all that come may know the condition of publick Communion, their Religion, and manner of address to God Almighty. [4.] That the truth of the proposition, the piety of the desires, and the honesty of the petitions, the simplicity of our purposes, and the justice of our designs may be secured before-hand, because Whatsoever is not of faith is sin (and it is impossible that we should pray to God in the *extempore* prayers of the Priest, by any faith but unreasonable, unwarranted, insecure and implicit.)[70]

He is out of patience with his opponents who profess "enmity against all Liturgy." Even so, he keeps polemic constructive by writing for a faithful remnant and praying for the future, a convention of the Jeremiad.

Taylor connects Anglican memory to the English Reformation: "[T]o the Churches of the Romane Communion we can say that ours is reformed, to the reformed Churches we can say that ours is orderly and decent; for we were freed from the impositions and lasting errours of a tyrannical spirit, and yet from the extravagancies of a popular spirit too: our reformation was done without tumult, and yet we saw it necessary to reform; we were zealous to cast away the old errours, but our zeal was balanced with consideration and the results of authority."[71] This locates his church between Catholic and Puritan positions. It characterizes the former as tyrannical in its maintenance of "old errours," and the latter as ungovernable in its diverse opinions. He recommends episcopal authority to balance zeal, defending Laud's drive to bring order and decency to worship.

Taylor dismisses the notion that English martyrs would replace the Book of Common Prayer:

> The zeal which Archbishop *Grindal*, Bishop *Ridly*, Dr *Taylor*, and other the holy Martyrs and Confessors in Queen *Maries* time expressed for this excellent Liturgy before and at the time of their death, defending it by their disputations, adorning it by their practice, and sealing it with their blouds, are arguments which ought to recommend it to all the sons of the Church of *England* for ever, infinitely to be valued beyond all the little whispers and murmurs of argument pretended against it: and when it came out of the flame, and was purified in the Martyrs fires, it became a vessell of honour, and used in the house of God in all the days of that long peace which was the effect of Gods blessing.[72]

The zeal of the martyrs sanctifies the prayer book and martyrdom defines national memory in the tradition of Foxe. The Directory, in contrast, induces national amnesia and neglects the Eucharist, a sacrament "in much danger to become invalid, for want of provision of due forms of Ministration."[73] This scathing peroration lists the dangers to Christianity incurred by the Directory's preference for novelty over authority.

The balance of pastoral concern and polemical edge remained constant through the Interregnum, but the edge hardened at times. Taylor defended set forms in times of crisis and defeat. He expected generations of Anglicans to be born in ecclesiastical exile. His twofold polemic exposes the dangers of isolated individualism implied in Puritan standards of inspiration while preserving the Church as an ancient community with a language of devotion ready for future generations. His polemic remains more communal than adversarial, showing that he sometimes felt but never cultivated bitterness.

v. Taylor and Roman Catholic Polemic

Taylor occasionally commends the Roman Catholic Church: "If any man hath a mind to exercise his Gift of Prayer, let him set himself to work, and compose Bookes of Devotion, (we have need of them in the Church of *England*, so apparent need, that some of the Church of *Rome* have made it an objection against us)" (*Apology* 86). He also defines Anglicanism as a properly reformed tradition. His critique of Roman Catholicism in *The Liberty of Prophesying* distinguishes superstructures from foundations of faith. Catholic doctrine consists of "superstructures ill built, and worse manag'd, but yet they keep the foundation, they build upon God in Jesus Christ, they professe the Apostles Creed, they retain faith and Repentance as the supporters of all our hopes of Heaven."[74] His main criticism is Catholicism's "making so great a part of Religion to consist in externals and Ceremonialls," and "indulging Penances so frequently." In the final analysis, however, "[f]alse superstructures doe not always destroy Faith."[75] Their errors "are not faults of their will, but weaknesses and deceptions of understanding."[76] Heresies are acts of will, and so the foundations of Catholicism are not heretical.

In the the reign of Queen Elizabeth I, English Catholics faced fines as recusants for not attending Anglican worship services. Harbouring a Catholic priest was a criminal act, and priests could expect banishment or execution if caught. Catholic citizens could live normally within limits in Protestant England, but the defeat of the Spanish Armada in 1588 and the thwarting of the Gunpowder Plot in 1605 heightened anti-Catholic sentiment. The Gunpowder Plot shaped the collective memory of England throughout the seventeenth century.[77]

Despite decades of suppression, the Catholic Church found strong voices in English converts. David Baker (1575–1641) appears in the early seventeenth century amid the marginalization of Catholics. Baker converted in 1600. Five years later, he took the name Augustine on joining the Benedictine order in 1605, the year of the Gunpowder Plot.

Baker left England for Cambrai in 1623, becoming spiritual advisor to English novices in a Cambrai convent. He translated Catholic mystics and wrote treatises until his death in 1641. As David Rees suggests, his writings on prayer emphasize the inner workings of the Spirit, making him unorthodox but not heretical. The imprimatur ("let it be printed") on Cressy's 1657 translation of Baker's *Sancta Sophia* certifies Baker's orthodoxy.[78]

Hugh Paulinus Cressy (1605–74) met Taylor in the 1630s when both were members of the Great Tew Circle, a heterodox group eager to explore toleration and irenic unity. Cressy converted to Catholicism in disillusionment with the Civil War, taking the name Serenus on entering the Benedictine order in Douai in 1648. He entered the Catholic priesthood in 1651. Serenus may signify Saint Serenus of Marseille, who joined St Augustine's mission to England in 596. Cressy gained standing as a polemicist in the 1670s in his exchanges with Edward Stillingfleet, a defender of the Anglican Church.[79] His translation of Baker's *Sancta Sophia* flowed from his work with Baker's Cambrai community and his desire to make Baker's work known to English Catholics.

Cressy's edition of *Sancta Sophia* is another case of context-defined republication. Cressy's Baker brings Catholic insights to the workings of the Holy Spirit in a troubled moment. While Baker's emphasis on the Spirit could appeal to the Spirit-centred sects emerging in the 1640s, it coheres more with Anglican traditionalists by affirming the unity of the Body of Christ and the discipline of meditation. Cressy's Baker is like Taylor in criticizing extemporaneous prayer, but his idea of contemplative prayer is distinctly Catholic.

The translation of *Sancta Sophia* begins with praise for Baker. The frontispiece to the British Library copy includes a portrait of Baker facing a dedicatory poem titled, "On the Picture and Writings of the late venerable F. Augustine Baker." The poem is by Leander Norminton, another English convert to the Benedictines. The poem defines prayer polemically by describing those who misunderstand prayer. Baker's "secret life and published Writing prove:/To pray is not to talke, or thinke, but love."[80] The emphasis on love as the sine qua non of prayer invites comparison with Richard Crashaw who converted to Catholicism in 1645, the year of Laud's execution.[81] His poem, "A Hymn to the Name and Honor of the Admirable Saint Teresa" celebrates love as "absolute, sole lord/Of life and death."[82] This intense Baroque poem recounts "Love's noble history" through the sixteenth-century saint who examined love in *The Way to Perfection*. The common source for Norminton, Crashaw, and Saint Teresa is the Gospel of John and its Great Commandment: "That ye love one another; as I have loved you, that ye also love one another" (13:34).

The second stanza develops polemic as contrast:

No streame of Words, nor Sparkes of Witt did fill,
His tongue or fancy when he Pray'd: His Will

Through Beames divine, conceivd a chast Desire
And Teares of Joy enlivened the soft Fire.

Extemporaneity is a "streame of Words" born of tongue and fancy, a typical attack on sectarians. Baker's prayer, conversely, is a supernatural conception engendering emotion that animates devotion. Light, fire, and tears present a Baroque Crashavian iconography.

The third stanza contrasts the "sober flame" of devotion with "Wild-fires" of enthusiasm:

Yet some have falsely thought his sober flame
With those Wild-fires that haunt our Isle, the same,
So Idolls to Church-pictures like may be,
And fondest love resemble Charity.

Protestant polemic attacked the Catholic sacraments and the Missal or "Mass Book" as idols. To confuse extemporaneous zeal with deep devotion, however, is to idolize words of fancy. As Taylor argues, "words are not properly capable of being holy; all words are in themselves servants of things."[83] Norminton turns idolatry back on those Puritans who condemned "Church-pictures" as idols. He then restores love as the foundation of prayer. The contrast between spiritual experience and superficial imaginings persists.

The final stanza commends the book to the English nation:

Hayle Booke of life! Temple of Wisedome, hayle
Against the Synagogues of Hell prevaile.
England may now her SAINT-SOPHIA boast:
A fairer too, then that the Grecians lost.

Temple is a key word in various Laudian texts of the 1630s, such as *God's Holy House* by Foulke Robartes, or *De Templis* by "R.T." Ferrar chose the word to house Herbert's poems. Norminton uses the positive associations of "temple." As Graeme Watson observes, with "the eruption of the Civil War and the defeat of the Royalists, the world was turned upside down and with it the assumptions which lay behind the word 'temple' were reversed."[84] The material temple was no longer available for public worship. Taylor preached at his patron's estate, not in a church, a condition familiar to Catholics since the time of the Elizabethan recusants. Baker's book is a temple of wisdom; moreover, it prevails over the Synagogue of Hell (Revelation 3:9), an image that hurls apocalyptic rhetoric back at Puritans.

Baker's emphasis on the inward Spirit interested some later Quakers.[85] Cressy, however, was no friend of sects. His preface complains some "make an ill use and perverse advantage" of "Divine Illuminations, Inspirations, Impulses, and other Secret Operations of Gods Holy Spirit in the Hearts of Internall Livers" for their own purposes.[86] The operation of the Spirit is not without spiritual discipline: the initiate must "give up his Soule and all its Faculties to Gods Internall Guidance and Direction only, relinquishing and renouncing all other Instructours and Instructions as far as they are not subordinately cooperating with this our Divine Maister."[87]

Mental faculties and carnal influences are put off, allowing the Spirit to move contemplative prayer. All instructors other than the Spirit are set aside."[88] Baker's thought is found "Sprinckled every where in almost all Mystick Writers."[89] He follows the negative path of renunciation and self-emptying. It accords with St Augustine's concept of divine love, in which the mind is "cleared of all strange images, and the Will purified from all strange Affections."[90]

Cressy attacks the supposed antinomian contempt for "common Doctrines & Rules of Faith and a good life."[91] Authentic illumination requires "a firmer assent unto them, a greater love to them, an abhorring of all Novelties of Doctrines, and a most fervent zeale to the Unity and peace of the Church, and to the reducing of all Unbelievers misbelievers and Schismaticks into its bosome and Communion."[92] Cressy sees the potential for sects to misappropriate Baker:

> It is to be feared that the fanatick Sectaries which now swarme in England more then ever, will be ready to take advantage from hence to justify all their frenzies and disorders: all which they impute with all confidence to Divine Inspirations, Illuminations and Impulses. For can wee forbid them the practice what wee our selves teach to be a Christian Duty? And yet it is apparent what fearfull and execrable effects the practice of the pretended Duty doth produce among them. It was by Inspiration, say they, that their Progenitours did breake out of the Church: and by Inspiration they doe still by Inspiration that they endanger the ruine of Christianity it selfe by infinite Schismes and pestilent Reformations. It is by Inspiration that they employ the Gospell to destroy the Gospell: from thence preaching Heresies in Churches and Chambers; Sedition in States; Rebellion against Princes and Prelates: So destroying all Order, Unity and Peace every where. These things considered, what can be more reasonable then that wee should take heed how wee furnish them thus with armes to maintaine themselves, and to fight against God & his Church?[93]

The final image repossesses the metaphor of holy war found in Protestant toleration treatises, notably John Goodwin's *Theomachia* (1644), a title that means fighting against God. Cressy's polemic is uncompromising, however, since evidence of the Spirit means obedience to Catholic teachings. There is no compatibility between contemplative prayer and sectarian inspiration: "Thus stands the case between Catholick Inspirations and the pretended inspirations of Sectaries. Such is that Spirit of Charity and Peace, and so divine are the effects of it directing the minds of good, humble, Obedient & devout Catholicks: And such is the Spirit of Disorder, Revenge, Wrath, Rebellion &c. and so dismall the effects of that Spirit wherewith selfe-opinionated, presumptuous, frantick Sectaries are agitated. What resemblance, what agreement can there be betweene these two?"[94] He maps Baker's treatise onto the spiritual landscape of Interregnum England leaving little room for the radical side.

Prayer is "the most perfect & most Divine Action that a rationall soule is capable of; yea it is the only principall Action for the exercising of which the soule was created; since in Prayer alone the soule is united to God. And by consequence, it is of all other Actions & Duties the most indispensably necessary."[95] Prayer alone exercises all of the virtues since it is an action incompatible with sin. Romans 8:26 defines inspiration: "Wee know not how to pray as we ought; And therefore the Spirit of God helps our infirmity; yea (saith he) The Spirit it selfe makes requests in us & for us; & this oft with grones which cannot be expressed, & which the soule it selfe cannot conceive. It is this inspiration only which gives a supernaturality to our Praiers, & makes them fit to be heard & granted by God."[96] Among Baker's scholastic, patristic, and mystical sources, Paul is paramount.

The strong Catholic interpretation of free prayer citations was timely in the Interregnum. Cressy's attack on radical sects was meant to impress on Cromwell that Catholics are not enemies of order or followers of fancies. Following the Restoration of 1660, the imposition of uniformity through religious persecution would bring suffering to sects and Catholics, and provoke new eloquence from every persecuted religious minority.

V. Henry Vaughan: Taylor's Counterpart in Exile

Briefly, do as thou wouldst be done unto,
Love God, and love thy neighbour; watch, and pray.
These are the words and works of life.[97]

The poet who best complements Taylor is Henry Vaughan. Both shared the experience of the exile of the Anglican Church. Both spent much of the 1640s and 1650s in Wales. Taylor compared his arrival in Wales to sheltering from a "great storm which hath dashed the Vessell of the Church all in pieces."[98] Vaughan returned home to Wales from studies in Oxford and London in 1642. His finest devotional poetry is found in *Silex Scintillans*, or "flashing flint," published in 1650 and expanded in 1655. Vaughan credits Herbert, whose "holy life and verse gained many pious Converts (of whom I am the least)."[99] Herbert pervades *Silex Scintillans*, beginning with the subtitle that copies *The Temple*: "sacred hymns and private ejaculations." Vaughan emulates Herbert's prayerful art in a time of exile.

Exile appears in his translations. For example, *The Praise and Happiness of the Country-Life*, written in Spanish by Don Antonio de Guevera, a bishop of the sixteenth century, suggests rural contentment, but also a vantage point on national conflict. Rural retirement was one response to conflict, but Vaughan was not escaping. Pastoral poetry creates a place to criticize the problems of the world. Vaughan's prose and poetry show engagement, not retreat. He is similar to Taylor in this respect; moreover, both were part of a circle surrounding Katherine Philips, who wrote a poem praising *Silex Scintillans*. Taylor dedicated his *Discourse of the nature, offices, and measures of friendship*, published in 1657, to her under her initials M.K.P. Her poem "The Country Life" expresses a theme common to Taylor and Vaughan: the civilizing power of poetry:

> Twas here the poets were inspired
> Here taught the multitude;
> The brave they here with honour fir'd
> And civilised the rude.

The stanza echoes Taylor's claim that the "first civilizing of people used to be by poetry." It also compares with, "To Mr. Henry Vaughan, Silurist, on his poems":

> Thou (fill'd with Joys too great to see or count)
> Descend'st from thence like Moses from the Mount,
> And with a candid, yet unquestion'd awe,
> Restor'st the Golden Age when verse was Law.[100]

Both passages equate scripture with poetry, since Christ taught "the multitude." While Taylor and Vaughan may not have been close, their place in the Philips circle applies the pastoral context to the preservation of Anglican civil society.[101]

Biblical geography and typology infuse Vaughan's pastoral polemic. He published *The Mount of Olives: or, Solitary Devotions* in 1652. This text includes his translation of Anselm's *"discourse of the blessed state of man in glory, written by the most reverend and holy Father Anselm Arch-Bishop of Canterbury."* Vaughan uses Anselm to appeal to Anglican antiquity in response to what Alan Rudrum calls the "special intensity about the suppression of Anglicanism in Wales," manifested in the "Commission for the propagation of the Gospel in Wales," combined with a "vigorous purgation of Royalist clergy."[102] Vaughan's preface laments the destruction of his church in biblical code. Addressing Sir Charles Egerton, Vaughan writes: "I know, Sir, you will be pleased to accept of this poore Olive-leafe presented to you, so that I shall not be driven to put forth my hand to take in my Dove again."[103] The source is Genesis 8:11: "And the dove came in to him in the evening; and, lo, in her mouth was an olive leaf pluckt off: so Noah knew that the waters were abated from off the earth." The sentiment seems peaceful, but it is also polemical: God flooded the earth because of human wickedness.

The ark is the true church that endures tempests. Vaughan writes for its "precious generation" in "the day of trouble": "And indeed (considering how fast and how soone men degenerate), It must be counted for a great blessing, that there is yet any left which dare look upon, and commiserate distressed Religion. Good men in bad times are very scarce."[104] The Mount of Olives is the antitype of the olive branch, as the ark rests on a mountain when the waters recede. The Mount is a vantage point for Christ who "had no place to put his head in," but who retired there to pray each evening during his final week in Jerusalem. For this reason, Vaughan's epigraph counsels prayer: "Watch ye therefore, and pray always, that ye may be accounted worthy to escape all these things that shall come to pass, and to stand before the Son of man. And in the day time he was teaching in the temple; and at night he went out, and abode in the mount that is called the Mount of Olives" (Luke 21:36–7).

Watch and pray is Vaughan's most basic advice for the Church in exile. For example, his poem "Rules and Lessons" ends with this counsel:

> Briefly, do as thou wouldst be done unto,
> Love God, and love thy neighbour; watch, and pray.
> These are the words and works of life.[105]

Vaughan finds foundation in the words of Christ. The first precept is the Great Commandment drawn from the Hebrew Bible; the second is a command to the disciples who slept in the garden before Christ's arrest. Watch and pray conveys a sense of urgency, but also instills a patience for the eventual return of light through resurrection.

The Mount of Olives or Solitary Devotions begins with an epistle to the "Peaceful, humble, and pious Reader." It attacks radical claims to inspiration:

> I know the world abounds with these Manuals, and triumphs over them. It is not then their scarsity that call'd this forth, nor yet a desire to cross the age, nor any in it. I envie not their frequent Extasies, and raptures to the third heaven; I onely wish them real, and that their actions did not tell the world, they are rapt into some other place. Nor should they, who assume to themselves the glorious stile of Saints, be uncharitably moved, if we that are yet in the body, and carry our treasure in earthen vessels, have need of those helps.[106]

Vaughan evokes 2 Corinthians 12:2: "I knew a man in Christ above fourteen years ago, (whether in the body, I cannot tell; or whether out of the body, I cannot tell: God knoweth;) such an one caught up to the third heaven. Whether it was in the body or out of the body I do not know – God knows." The man hears "inexpressible words," but Paul refuses to boast. In 1 and 2 Corinthians, Paul teaches that common gifts build up the Body of Christ more than private ecstasies. His teaching is a corrective to spiritual pride. Vaughan sees this lesson as lost on those who abolished the prayer book, and who, moreover, refuse it to those who are content to be still in the body: "[W]e have this treasure in earthen vessels, that the excellency of the power may be of God, and not of us" (2 Cor. 4:7). In consequence, Vaughan contrasts *The Mount of Olives* with *Silex Scintillans*: "I have purposely avoided to leade thee into this little Book with a large discourse of Devotion, what it is, with the severall Heads, Divisions, and sub-divisions of it, all these being but so many fruitlesse curiosities of Schoole-Divinity.... Besides, thou hast them already as briefly delivered as possibly I could, in my Sacred Poems." The titles of his poems express topics for meditation. *The Mount of Olives* offers meditations within a liturgical framework, including morning and evening prayer, "most times and occasions," and "Meditations before we come to the Lord's Table."[107]

Thomas Calhoun brings perspective to the relationship between Vaughan's *Silex Scintillans* and *The Mount of Olives*: their existence "attests the seriousness with which Vaughan viewed the problems attending the churchman, of any faith, during this period. Both are books of private worship, and they complement one another as demonstration

complements expository instruction."[108] Vaughan's attention to morning and evening prayer challenges the elimination of set times and dates
in Puritan worship. In *Silex Scintillans*, "Isaac's Marriage" shows interest in times for prayer. The poem has received fruitful attention in recent
scholarship. Its scene is set in Genesis 24:63. Isaac, son of the patriarch
Abraham, "went out to pray in the field at the Even-tide, and he lift
up his eyes, and saw, and behold. The Camels were coming." This is
Vaughan's epigraph to the poem. Importantly, as Glyn Pursglove points
out, Vaughan "substitutes the word 'pray' (which is found in the Geneva
translation) for 'meditate' which appears in the Authorized text."[109] The
epigraph follows the Authorized Version in all other respects. As Pursglove argues, the change constructs a link between the text and the first
word of the poem:

> Praying! And to be married? It was rare,
> But now 'tis monstrous; and that pious care
> Though of our selves, is so much out of date,
> That to renew't were to degenerate.[110]

These four lines contrast then and now in a manner typical of Taylor and Philips. Isaac meets his future wife Rebecca beside a well, a
life-giving place in the desert and therefore an answer to the prayers
of travellers, even as Isaac prays to find a wife. As Rudrum observes,
there is far more to this poem than the simplified polemic of then versus
now. He draws from Robert Alter's concept of the biblical type scene
to establish the significance of the setting. A type scene is a recurrent
motif in scripture. Betrothals beside wells are one such motif. Jacob and
Rachel meet at a well (Gen. 29:10), as do Moses and Zipporah (Exod.
2:16). Milton adapts the type scene to the meeting of Adam and Eve in
Paradise Lost (4: 456–91), as Eve awakens beside a pool of water. The
encounter between Christ and the Samaritan woman at Jacob's well
(John 4:6) is a variation on the type, since marriage is not the outcome.
Revelation ends with the marriage supper of the lamb, the symbolic
union of Christ and his Church, with the water of life and tree of life
restored to humanity. As Rudrum demonstrates, Vaughan constructs
a complex typological network based on this type scene to affirm the
symbolic union of Christ and the Church: "Vaughan is recalling a biblical occasion which gives sanction to what was apparently his own
habit: to pray and meditate in the open air, and to do so in the morning
and 'at eventide.'"[111] Importantly, Rudrum concludes that biblical allusion "carries much of the 'encoding' of political comment in Vaughan's

poems and those of some of his contemporaries." Unlike other varia-
tions of the type scene, Vaughan's Isaac prays, and thereby affirms the
time of evening prayer. This affirmation combines biblical allusion with
the observance of evening prayer in the Book of Common Prayer in
a "message to that books adherents."[112] Philip West notes the importance of set hours for Vaughan. Emphasizing practical piety in both
texts, West observes that "Vaughan's holy liver" or devout reader "is
protected from distractions and disorder by the regularity of hourly
prayer" and the "careful use of man's internal clock."[113] The type scene
evokes the order and decency of Vaughan's lost church in typological
code. The antitype of Isaac's marriage in the marriage of Christ and his
Church preserves the integrity of the Church in the face of disunity and
impiety.

Mount of Olives and Silex Scintillans share Vaughan's distinctive diction. "Ray" is a key word in Silex Scintillans, occurring eighteen times as
verb or noun or adverb.[114] Mount of Olives begins with a meditation for
awakening: "Ray thy selfe into my soul that I may see what an Exceed-
ing weight of glory my Enemy would bereave me of for the mere shad-
owes and painting of this world."[115] The poem "Mount of Olives" also
echoes the preface to the prose Mount of Olives: "I am so warm'd now
by this glance on me, that midst all storm, I feel a ray of thee."[116] In
"Isaac's Marriage," Vaughan describes Isaac's prayerfulness" "Religion
was/Rayed into thee, like beams into a glass."[117] Pursuing the Christian
typology of the poem, the ray of light striking a mirror also signifies the
power of the Holy Spirit in the Annunciation. Mary's reception of the
Spirit comes from the tradition of the Specula sine macula or unspotted
mirror: "For she is the brightness of the everlasting light, the unspotted
mirror of the power of God, and the image of his goodness" (Wisdom
of Solomon 7:26).[118] Vaughan's image suggests not only Mary as ideal
reader, but also the source of Christ's Body.

How does Vaughan compare to the Catholic perspective? Vaughan's
dedicatory prayer in Silex Scintillans is addressed to God and the Virgin
Mary. As Dayton Haskin has shown, Mary could appeal to Protestants
as a model of an ideal reader.[119] Milton portrays her as such in Paradise Regained. Vaughan's dedicatory prayer is, however, focused by his
image of the ray of light that readers can receive. Vaughan suggests this
in "To the Holy Bible," where the speaker addresses his Bible:

> and thou cast by
> With meek, dumb looks didst woo mine eye,
> And oft left open wouldst convey

A sudden and most searching ray
Into my soul, with whose quick touch
Refining still, I struggled much.[120]

Vaughan depicts the relation of reader and text as a holy wooing. The eye, not ear, is wooed by the neglected Bible's "meek, dumb looks." Left open, the text sends a "searching ray" into the speaker's soul with an unexpected randomness. The result is spiritual struggle not unlike the unease that accompanies sexual attraction. The poem offers an unexpected and somewhat daring variation on the type scene of betrothal.

Vaughan also uses the textual ray to maintain the Anglican calendar. In "White Sunday," the Bible accommodates the greater light of God:

Yet while some rays of that great light
Shine here below within thy Book,
They never shall so blinde my sight
But I will know which way to look.

For though thou doest that great light lock,
And by this lesser commerce keep:
Yet by these glances of the flock
I can discern Wolves from the Sheep.[121]

White Sunday is Pentecost, when the fire of the Holy Spirit descends on the Apostles seven weeks after Easter Sunday. The title grounds the poem in the Book of Common Prayer while praising the Bible. The poem re-establishes the liturgical calendar while holding "Puritan pretensions up to the reasonable light of Anglican common sense."[122] Like Taylor, Vaughan asserts that the fiery inspiration of the Spirit remains in the lesser light of scripture. The accommodated light does not blind the speaker; rather, the light leads the speaker to discern truth and error amid the strife of wolves and sheep.

Meditations in the *Mount of Olives* complement the poems. These include preparations for journeys: "Meditate in the way upon the sojournings and travels of the Patriarchs and Prophets, the many weary journeys of Jesus Christ in the flesh, the travels of his Apostles by sea and land, with the pilgrimage and peregrinations of many other precious Saints that wandred in Deserts and Mountains, of whom the world was not worthy."[123] Possible collations of biblical texts, times, and themes for prayer also show Herbert's influence on *Silex Scintillans*. As Paul Dyck insightfully shows, Herbert's lyrics achieve a systematic intertextuality similar to a commonplace book.[124] Vaughan emulates this by copying Herbert.

Vaughan has few architectural reference points, in contrast to Herbert's lyrics on windows, monuments, and altars, marking an important contrast between the two poets. Instead, Vaughan depicts journeys through symbolic natural landscapes because the Church of Herbert is in exile.

Silex Scintillans, part one, for example, begins with "Regeneration" and "The Search." Both poems use the metaphor of pilgrimage to abridge the Gospel. "Regeneration" ends with the Spirit as Pentecostal wind; "The Search" echoes the *Mount of Olives* by dismissing the "skin, and shell of things" that do not inspire prayer. "Religion" takes stock of the state of religion in England in 1651. The poem emphasizes the interplay of voices, beginning with dialogue among angels and people:

> My God, when I walk in those groves,
> And leaves thy spirit doth still fan,
> I see in each shade that there grows
> An Angel talking with a man.[125]

Natural "groves" are settings for covert worship. The "leaves" are the pages of the Bible, as in "White Sunday," but also the pages of the Book of Common Prayer, since its prayers facilitate meditation.

The third stanza finds the biblical place where "Jacob dreames, and wrestles." Jacob dreams in Genesis 28:12, and wrestles with an angel in Genesis 32:24. As West observes, Jacob's dream is an important motif in Vaughan, notably in "Regeneration." Here, dreaming and wrestling depict different connections between heaven and earth in prayer. Dreaming is an angelic thoroughfare, while wrestling is intense struggle. Both are metaphors for prayer. The thoroughfare may represent collective worship, while struggle can depict the challenges of inward prayer. As Bishop Bryan Duppa wrote in 1675: "Prayer is in its own nature a kind of Wrestling and Striving for a Victory, which presupposeth an opposition; And rather than it shall be wanting, God himself will enter into the Lists as he did with Jacob in that famous Wrestling, when to shew the power of Prayer, he that was invincible, was content to be overcome by him, who had no other weapons but Tears and Prayer."[126] The metaphor adds to the trope of prayer as spiritual weapon.

The first seven stanzas treat the Old Testament connection between men and angels as "familiar," especially for patriarchs and prophets. The remaining five observe the decline of religion from its sources using the imagery of confused voices. Religion has become a din of "false Ecchoes, and Confused sounds." The well of betrothal is now a "tainted sink":

Just such a tainted sink we have
Like that Samaritans dead well,
Nor must we for the kernel crave
Because most voices like the shell.[127]

Again, we find Vaughan considering biblical symbols from different aspects. The "dead well" signifies the replacement of the church as bride of Christ with what Vaughan considers lifeless practices; dissonant voices register the loss of liturgical unity.

Silex Scintillans surveys conditions for prayer, meaning struggle, dryness, and uncertainty as well as confidence and assurance. In "The Call," Vaughan evokes Romans 8:26 in images of sighs and tears: "Who never wake to groan, nor weep,/Shall be sentenced for their sleep."[128] "The Storm" prays for prayer itself as sighs and tears, with an inner spiritual wind countering the storm outside: "Lord, then round me with weeping clouds,/And let my mind/In quick blasts sigh beneath those shrouds/A spirit-wind."[129]

"The Morning-watch" imitates Herbert's "Prayer I," but with a transformation of the elements that define prayer:

Prayer is
The world in tune,
A spirit-voice,
And vocal joys
Whose echo is heavens bliss.
O let me climb
When I lie down![130]

Climbing when lying down to sleep recalls Jacob's dream of the ladder to heaven. Sleep is a "Curtain'd grave" that makes awakening a type of resurrection. Vaughan longs for a union of voices. Prayer is an instrument of consummate harmony orchestrated by the Spirit.

Other poems elevate the liturgical decorum of prayer. "The Match" makes a solemn offering of prayer to God: "Accept, dread Lord, the poor Oblation,/It is but poor,/Yet through thy mercies may be more."[131] "Rules and Lessons" is a short devotional manual all its own. It offers spiritual rules for rising in the morning, the business and activity of morning and afternoon, and sleeping again at night. Morning prayer requires a functional inner clock and a mindfulness of the finite span of life:

Yet, never sleep the sun up; prayer should
Dawn with the day; There are set, awful hours
'Twixt heaven and us.[132]

Next, Vaughan asks the reader to enter the world in a spirit of devotion:

> Serve God before the world: let him not go
> Until thou hast a blessing, then resign
> The whole unto him; and remember who
> Prevailed by wrestling ere the Sun did shine.
> Pour oil upon the stones, weep for thy sin,
> Then journey on, and have an eye to heaven.[133]

The first four lines reiterate the typology of Jacob and Christ. Prayer is again Jacob wrestling. Effort in prayer brings submission to the will of God. Similarly, Christ wrestles in prayer in his agony in Gethsemane, but ultimately surrenders his will to God's. Christ's holy wrestling anticipates his resurrection after his suffering. The ending counsels reader and church to "journey on" in life's pilgrimage.

Vaughan's prose *Mount of Olives* is consolation for the loss of the Book of Common Prayer. Vaughan preserves order by making the biblical canon a template for prayerful occasions. Each prayer event is distilled from biblical narrative, character, or symbol. The dense typological networks that frame biblical episodes are like the network of believers who join in corporate prayer. The poetic and hermeneutic relationships possible among Vaughan's lyrics encourage readers in their spiritual journeys. These relationships invest in biblical typology, such as type scenes signifying the betrothal of Christ and his Church, in liturgical seasons and dates that impose order on the turbulence of current history, in literary influence seen in his reverent "copying" of Herbert, and, finally, in the central moments of the Gospel – the Incarnation, Passion, and the Last Judgment – which ground piety in times of crisis.

The Mount of Olives, which provides the title for Vaughan's prose devotions, the epigraph to his devotional poems, and the title of two different lyrics in the collection, orients us spatially in the textual complexity of Vaughan's collection. In "Mount of Olives (II)," the speaker recalls wandering "bleak and bare in body as in mind" before feeling "a Ray of thee."[134] The bare body suggests the lost Church. Like Andrewes in his Nativity sermon, Vaughan connects the kenotic moment to "the depth and dread of winter" when Christ relinquishes heavenly glory to appear in human form. The speaker experiences the divine ray in kenotic receptivity, and compares it to "a lively sense of spring," just as resurrection follows suffering and death. In "Mount of Olives (I)," the mount is similarly a place neglected by poets, but receptive to Christ:

> Their Lord with thee had most to do;
> He wept once, walked whole nights on thee,

And from thence (his sufferings ended,)
    Unto glory
    Was attended.[135]

Suffering and glory, darkness and light combine in Christ's exemplary meditations. Like Andrewes and Taylor, Vaughan maintains a deeply incarnational attitude to piety conditioned by exile and loss. His poems elaborate extensively on his central precept: watch and pray.

Chapter Three

John Milton (1634–1650): The Spirit of Utterance

They who use no set formes of prayer, have words from their affections; while others are to seek affections fit and proportionable to a certain doss of prepar'd words; which as they are not rigorously forbid to any mans privat infirmity, so to imprison and confine by force, into a Pinfold of sett words, those two most unimprisonable things, our Prayers and that Divine Spirit of utterance that moves them.

Milton, *Eikonoklastes*

Taylor elevates the term liturgy in the debate over prayer. He takes liturgy in its literal sense of public work or work for the people. Gregory Dix emphasizes the shape of liturgy: "Liturgy is the name given ever since the days of the apostles to the act of taking part in the solemn corporate worship of God."[1] As shape or form, it is a sequence comprising the single action towards which it leads. For example, if "the whole eucharist is essentially one action, the service must have a logical development as one whole, a thrust towards that particular action's fulfillment, and not merely a general purpose of edification."[2] Liturgies encompass both testaments and indeed most religions. As Taylor remarks, "Solemne Liturgies and Set formes of Prayer were made by the best and greatest Princes, by *Moses*, by *David*, and the Sonne of *David*." A liturgy is and contains within it set forms of prayer.

A liturgical drama draws from and responds to the relevant liturgical elements an occasion provides and considers, as Dix states, the dramatic "action's fulfillment, and not merely a general purpose of edification." I see three liturgical dramas in Milton's canon. The first is the masque called *Comus*. I call it a conformist liturgical drama because it draws from the prescribed readings from the Book of Common Prayer for the occasion of its performance on Michaelmas Eve 1634. The second occurs in Book 9 of *Paradise Lost*. I call this a liturgy of temptation since Satan tempts Eve by bearing false witness to the power of the forbidden fruit in a demonic Eucharist in which Eve consumes the element. As a rite of separation and alienation, its effect is anti-eucharistic. The third is *Samson Agonistes*. I call this a liturgy of dissent because it responds to forced conformity and the re-imposition of monarchy and the prayer book with a complex blend of mimetic form, scriptural allusion, prayerful contrition, and inner meditation.

This sequence marks out the trajectory for Milton's career from an early position of liturgical conservatism to his rejection of official liturgy as an instrument of state control. Milton sets his own markers to confirm this. These include the revision of *Comus* in 1637 and its inclusion in his 1645 *Poems of Mr. John Milton*, a text that deliberately synchronizes his early poems with his polemical prose. His response to the regicide of 1649 underscored his transition to radicalism. He saw the invasive power of the late king's voice-at-prayer in the *Eikon Basilike* as pernicious to religious and political liberty. Despite Milton's attacks on it in *Eikonoklastes*, the king's book aided the eventual restoration of the monarchy. These results deeply shaped themes of dissent and resistance in Milton's major poems.

i. Early Milton: *Comus* and the Trial of Liturgy

In 1634, Milton was not the radical figure he later became. His mature politics and ecclesiology emerged in the 1640s and 1650s, beginning with tracts on divorce, church government, and toleration. His polemic culminates in *A Treatise of Civil Power in Ecclesiastical Causes* (1659), written against state coercion of individual conscience in religion, and *The Ready and Easy Way to Establish a Free Commonwealth* (1660), a jeremiad against the restoration of monarchy. He became a republican committed to the politics of Christian liberty and an unorthodox and on some points heretical theologian. Whereas Milton saw prose as a cooler element than poetry, his poems recreate his polemics in verbal fireworks and tense debates. These verbal qualities are evident in a *Mask presented at Ludlow Castle*.

Who was the young poet whose masque entertained an aristocratic family in 1634? "On the Morning of Christ's Nativity," written in 1629, consecrates Milton's voice with the holy fire of Isaiah, but it is orthodox on the Trinity and celebrates a holy day in the calendar. "Sonnet 7" admits "no bud or blossom" has appeared in a poetic late spring, but recommends patience: "All is if I have grace to use it so / As ever in my great task-Master's eye." These themes owe less to radicalism than to biblicism, which informs every phase of Milton's career.

Masques were aristocratic entertainments for important occasions. Allegorical or mythological characters perform in speech, song, and dance to compliment an important figure. Court masques were spectacular and expensive compliments for Royal occasions. On this occasion, Milton collaborated with the musician Henry Lawes, brother of the composer William Lawes, to celebrate the installation of John Egerton, the Earl of Bridgewater, as Lord Lieutenant of Wales. Lady Alice Egerton, the Earl's daughter, played the Lady who prevails against Comus, a sorcerer and seducer. Milton produced a less visually lavish but more poetically and polemically discursive work conscious of literary tradition, political occasion, and religious polemic.

I examine *Comus* for three reasons. The first is Andrewes's influence on a compressed prayer the Lady speaks.[3] The second is Milton's use of prescribed scriptural readings. The third is the polemical discourse of the "trial of liturgy" that developed through the 1630s, which centred on the Book of Common Prayer. Milton affirms the prayer book, but not complacently. He tests it in the confrontation between the Lady and Comus, joining liturgical occasion with polemical debate.

Milton's religious position in *Comus* divides critics. Achsah Guibbory highlights Milton's "concern with the threat to true religion and the danger of carnal idolatry."[4] Cedric Brown sees an "ardent, idealistic reformist spirit"[5] in the poem. Gordon Campbell and Thomas Corns make a counter-argument: *Comus* "constitutes the most complex and thorough expression of Laudian Arminianism and Laudian style within the Milton oeuvre,"[6] evident in the ceremonialism of the genre. I argue that Andrewes rather than Laud is a main influence on *Comus*. The same distinction illustrated Herbert in chapter 1. To begin with, Milton's use of the prayer book readings for Michaelmas eve make *Comus* a liturgically oriented drama. Michaelmas celebrates the triumph of the angel Michael over Satan in the Book of Revelation.[7] 1 Corinthians 13 is a prescribed reading, and Milton adapts its themes of faith, hope, charity, and language. Paul contrasts the natural person who "knows not the things of God" with the spiritual person who discerns truth (I Cor. 2:14), a premise for the debate between Comus and the Lady. Paul also affirms the ceremony of the Eucharist as an expression of the unity of the early Church (1 Cor. 11). Importantly, Paul warns of the dangers of religious imaginings that elevate individual experience over collective unity (1 Cor. 1:12–13). This is Andrewes's concern in his sermons on prayer and in "Of Imaginings." Similarly,

Milton explores the relation between individual and collective spiritual experience.

Milton raises the problem of imaginings early in the poem when the Lady is alone in the forest:

> A thousand fantasies
> Begin to throng into my memory,
> Of calling shapes and beck'ning shadows dire,
> And airy tongues that syllable men's names. (205–8)

The memory comes from the "tumult of loud Mirth" Comus makes, but persists as potential fantasy. Comus later tempts her fancy: "here be all the pleasures/That fancy can beget on youthful thoughts" (669–70). This is more than carpe diem. The Lady is sufficient to stand but free to fall, so to speak: she can be vulnerable to imaginings, but capable of governing herself through virtue.

The Lady prays briefly when she follows Comus, disguised as a shepherd, to his "low/But loyal cottage": "Eye me blest Providence, and square my trial/To my proportion'd strength. Shepherd lead on (321–30)." Brief prayers like this were called "ejaculations." Brief as it is, the prayer has two petitions, the first for divine guidance, the second for inner strength. The second comes from Paul: "There hath no temptation taken you but such as is common to man: but God is faithful, who will not suffer you to be tempted above that ye are able" (1 Cor. 10:13). Where Paul says suffer, Milton says "square." "Square" can mean a rule or measure, evoking Tertullian's view of the Lord's Prayer as the sum of all prayers. The whole gospel is in it, including 1 Corinthians. For example, John Cosin, a member of the Durham House Group,[8] calls the Lord's Prayer: "the *Rule* or *Square* whereby all our Petitions are to bee formed."[9] Milton combines Paul's discursive, pastoral, at times polemical style with the poetic and parabolic brevity of Christ. The Lady's prayer converts the words of Paul and Christ into an epitome of the Gospel.

The Lady's "trial" evokes the trial of liturgy in treatises on prayer in the 1630s.[10] Cosin follows Andrewes, who called the Lord's Prayer "a platform of prayer" and "a pattern and complement of all their petitions." In Cosin's words, the Lord's Prayer was "used in all ages of the Church, not onely as a common part of her Praiers and Service, but as the chiefe & fundamentall part of them, the Ground whereupon she builds, the Patterne wherby shee frames, and the Complement wherewith she perfects all the rest of her heavenly Devotions, framing them all, as this is framed, with much efficacie, though not with any superfluitie of words."[11] By placing the prayer in a schedule of hours, however, Cosin sparked outrage. William Prynne, a lawyer sentenced to ear cropping in 1633 and 1637 for sedition by the court of Star Chamber, accused Cosin of using the "Horologe and Clocke of *Rome.*"[12] Prynne observes: "[T]he Creed, the Lords Prayer, and the eight Beatitudes are contained in the Scriptures, and in our Common Prayer Booke: but take both forme and matter together, and those other particulars which are here paraleld, and you shall never finde them but in Popish writers."[13] Prynne accuses Cosin of aligning the prayer book with Catholic devotions.[14]

Henry Burton, mutilated alongside Prynne and John Bastwick in 1637, attacked Cosin in a *Tryall of Public Devotions* (1628). Burton's trial is a dialogue between Lady Curia, a Catholic of the court, and Lady Charis, a Protestant of the country. Lady Curia's chaplain is Diotrephes ("nourished by Jupiter"), an enemy of the early Church (3 John 1:9). Lady Charis's chaplain is Iohannes, as in Epistles of John. Lady Charis receives Cosin's book from Lady Curia and is disturbed by its "Jesuiticall" frontispiece. She urges Lady Curia to meet Iohannes to hear his censures of Cosin's book. In his preface, Burton says Cosin is unexercised in the "Spirit of Christ, helping our infirmities in prayer, Rom. 8.26." He brings England "within the circle of his canonical houres."[15] Like Smart, Burton stirs up fears of Catholicism.

Ambrose Fisher's *A Defense of the Liturgie of the Church of England* (1630) is another dialogue. A blind scholar who dictated his work, Fisher speaks through Irenaeus, named for the early bishop who battled heresies. Irenaeus speaks with Novatus, named for a third-century schismatic condemned by Pope Cornelius as a seditious heretic for denying the power of the Church to give absolution to apostates. Fisher's Novatus voices the Puritan case: set forms prevent ministers from exercising the gift of prayer. Irenaeus replies that prayer can come by infusion, by the inspiration of the Spirit, by assistance, and by the reading of scripture. Fisher champions common prayer as an instrument of unity: "If every man at his own arbitrement composed liturgies, there would be as many liturgies as the Ethiopians had gods."[16] Multiplicity evokes chaos in church and state, whereas paganism equates extemporaneous prayer with vain imaginings.

Replies to Fisher include the anonymous *Triall of the English Liturgie* (1637), a fictional letter from a minister to a friend. Set forms force "matter & words, to be used without variation."[17] The question "is not of Prayer devised by a mans selfe, or of limiting the spirit in the people, but of Prayer devised by others and imposed, and of limiting the spirit of the minister."[18] The Lord's Prayer is the "rule and patterne according to which our Prayer should be framed,"[19] but it is not a set form. Christ, "knowing the minde of his Father, was able to frame a perfect and absolute Prayer for his Church, yet did not holde it meet to tye his people to those words always which himself devised, but left the Churches free therein."[20] Christ gives people "libertie to use that for a Prayer, being uttered with understanding, yet his purpose is thereby to direct us how to frame all our Prayers."[21] Freeing the minister to exercise the gift of prayer, moreover, will not cause "inconvenience" if ministers possess "fitnesse for the worke of the Ministrie."[22] Inconvenience was a synonym for disunity.

Last, John Ball's *A friendly triall of the grounds tending to separation in a plain and modest dispute touching the lawfulnesse of a stinted liturgie and set form of prayer* (1640) criticizes the *Triall of the English Liturgie*. Ball, an Anglican priest, stresses epitome: "Tertullian fitly calleth it, the law of prayer, and breviary of the Gospel: Calvine, The rule. That it may be used with right disposition and affection of soul, is confessed by them that dislike all stinted forms."[23] Ball seeks unity. He rebukes those who separate the godly from communion out of fear of defilement by the ungodly. His work appeared in the year of his death when the consequences of his dissent from Laud's reforms were affecting his health.[24]

Milton expanded the quarrel between the Lady and Comus in 1637, perhaps mindful of simmering polemics. Arguments between the Lady and Comus oppose Christian and "pagan" views of nature, virtue, and beauty. Responding to Andrewes's idea of "imaginings," the poem opposes her rational truths to his incantations. In particular, she mounts an iconoclastic attack on his seductive rhetoric, calling his arguments "magic structures."

Using the twofold purpose of polemic, the poem attacks error and builds community. Paul addresses divisions that occur when the "many gifts" of individual inspiration compete with the "one Spirit" that unites the Church (1 Cor. 12:4). He warns against false teachers with dazzling rhetorical powers. Revelation magnifies these tensions into types of true and false churches, envisioning the triumph of the true Church on a cosmic scale. Milton follows Paul by favouring collective edification over private gifts. The Lady destroys Comus's "magic structures high" in plain language.

1 Corinthians 13:13 states, "And now abideth faith, hope, charity." Milton converts this into faith, hope, and chastity throughout *Comus*. The shift from charity to chastity departs from Andrewes's view of charity as the virtue of public prayer for dramatic reasons. There is no scope for charity in the Lady's polemic against Comus, but the drama ends with her reunification with family and audience. Similarly, Jesus shows

no charity towards Satan in *Paradise Regained,* even as his polemic conveys Milton's idea of a church.

Comus uses art without grace. Accordingly, the Lady treats him as the "natural" man of Paul's letter.

> Thou hast nor Ear nor Soul to apprehend
> The sublime notion and high mystery
> That must be utter'd to unfold the sage
> And serious doctrine of Virginity. (784–7)

Her rejection of Comus could imply Calvinist reprobation. Andrewes, however, rejects this reading of 1 Corinthians, preferring Paul's concern for the Church. Similarly, the early Milton depicts a church edified by the Lady's resistance to Comus. Both follow Paul's exhortation to the Corinthians to value shared edification over private experience (1 Corinthians 14:14–17). Common prayer needs a common language, a value the masque maintains.

Reading *Comus* with the trial of liturgy discourse helps to measure the extent of its reformist leanings in 1637 and its role in the 1645 poems. From 1642 to 1645, Milton addressed prayer in debates over church reform. Milton supported "Smectymnuus," an acronym of five Puritan ministers who argued with Bishop Joseph Hall over church government.[25] Addressing Parliament, Hall was among those who argued the Lord's Prayer is a set form influenced by Jewish tradition. Christ taught "a direct forme of prayer; and such, as that part of the frame prescribed by our Saviour, was composed of the forms of devotion then formerly usuall."[26] In a second treatise answering Smectymnuus, he reinforced Jewish tradition: "Nothing can be more plain then that our Saviour prescribed to his Disciples (besides the rules) a direct form of Prayer, whiles he saith, *Pray thus:* Much of which form I find cited, as of ancient use, out of *Seder Tephilloth* of the Jews of Portugall."[27] Moreover, at the Last Supper, Jesus used "words which were usuall in the Jewish feasts" as "Cassander hath well shewed in his *Liturgica.*"[28] Hall does not discourage "conceived" prayers in private devotions: "[L]et the full soule freely poure it selfe in gracious expressions of its holy thoughts, into the bosome of the Almighty: Let both the sudden flashes of our quick ejaculations, and the constant flames of our more fixed conceptions mount up from the altar of a zealous heart, unto the Throne of Grace."[29] The flash of private devotion and the steady flame of common prayer are compatible. Hall shows the conformist position is accommodating.

Hall was right about Jewish precursors to the Lord's Prayer. Tertullian refused to contemplate this, and Smectymnuus simply rejects

Hall's appeal to Jewish tradition: "[W]e have read that the Rabbines since the daies of our Saviour have borrowed some expressions from that Prayer, and from other Evangelicall passages: But we never read till now, that the Lord Christ the wisdome of the Father borrowed from the wisdome of the Rabbines expressions to use in Prayer."[30] Smectymnuus channels Tertullian in breaking with Jewish tradition.

If Hall is accommodating, Milton's *Of Reformation* is apocalyptic. It ends with a fervent prayer for God's "almost spent, and expiring Church" (*CPW* 1: 614). God's enemies have been "consulting all the Sorceries of the great Whore," the demonized Church of Rome (615). The victory of truth brings celestial celebrations: "Then amidst the Hymns, and Hallelujahs of Saints some one may perhaps bee heard offering high strains in new and lofty Measures to sing and celebrate thy divine Mercies, and marvelous Judgements in this land throughout all Ages" (616). Milton celebrates spontaneity to galvanize the process of national reformation. The lofty strains of the saints must always be new.

Animadversions upon The Remonstrants Defence Against Smectymnuus (July 1641), satirizes Hall. Milton emulates earlier trial texts in a dialogue between a Remonstrant and an Answerer. Like Hall, the Remonstrant argues that Jesus used words at the Last Supper that "were usual in the Jewish Feasts" (*CPW* 1: 685). The Answerer, channelling Milton, distinguishes use from coercion, before arguing that an ancient text can become "superstitious, fruitlesse, or impious" (685). He does not argue that Christ's divinity makes all his words original, like Smectymnuus; instead, he warns that words can be habits. Prayer must be daily exercise, not rote repetition. He echoes the analogy of celestial music from *Of Reformation*, arguing that "variety (as both Musick and Rhethorick teacheth us) erects and rouses an Auditory, like the maisterfull running over many Cords and divisions; whereas if men should ever be thumming the drone of one plaine Song, it would be a dull Opiat to the most wakefull attention" (*CPW* 1: 691). The exasperated remonstrant asks plainly if the liturgy is good or evil. The answer: "It is evill" (691).

The relation of prayer and praise to music in both treatises anticipates angelic songs in *Paradise Lost* and *Paradise Regained*. The angels greet the revelation of the Son as redeemer in Book 3 of *Paradise Lost* and the first revelation of the Son in Book 5 with hymns and songs: "Thee Father first they sung Onmipotent,/Immutable, Immortal, Infinite" (3: 371–3). Milton states the subject of praise first before paraphrasing the words to avoid any sense of prescription. At the end of *Paradise Regained*, Angels also sing "Heavenly Anthems of his victory/Over temptation and the Tempter Proud" (4: 594–5), establishing the permanence of the topic and the potential variety of words. Since penitential prayers and lamentations are not needed in heaven, hymns of praise are the prayer life of good angels. These spontaneous productions illustrate Milton's idea of the fit minister who creates new words and new prayers for every topic at every turn.

Eikonoklastes attacks the conflation of king and God, state and church. In the 1650s, Milton's *De Doctrina Christiana* and *A Treatise of Civil Power* (1659) uphold the authority of individual conscience in religion. On the brink of the restoration, *The Ready and Easy Way* confronts the spectre of civil idolatry in the fantastic pageantry of a restored court. This is the worst kind of collective religious "imagining" in Milton's view. These prose works shape prayer in *Paradise Lost* in two ways. First, in key episodes Milton makes free prayer typical of a free conscience. Second, he represents external temptation as a threat to the inner voice of conscience. Prayer requires one's true voice. The early rejection of liturgy as rote repetition in *Of Reformation* and *Animadversions*, and the exposure of the king's voice as invasive and idolatrous in *Eikonoklastes*, shaped his later sympathy for religious dissent.

ii. Milton versus Taylor: *Eikon Basilike* and *Eikonoklastes*

On 30 January 1649, King Charles I stepped onto the scaffold from the window of the Banqueting Hall in Whitehall. Once a site of masques and entertainments devised by Ben Jonson and Inigo Jones, it was now a theatre of judicial punishment and suffering. His attendants included Bishop Juxon, who mentored Jeremy Taylor in the 1630s, a time when this event was unthinkable. The king had a speech impediment but spoke briefly, though his words were muffled by drums and the crowds were kept at a distance by mounted horsemen. Witnesses reported that a terrible groan rose from the assembled crowd when the axe fell. Peter Rudnytsky remarks that England experienced regicide as trauma: it was a "reenactment of the Fall, as well as a sacrilegious act of parricide or deicide."[31] When Charles was buried at Windsor Castle on 8 February 1649, the government forbade mourners to use the Book of Common Prayer.

The King's chaplains and bishops, including Taylor, had been editing his writings to preserve his memory. The result was the *Eikon Basilike: The Portraiture of his Sacred Majesty in his Solitudes and Sufferings*. John Gauden, the main editor of the book, wanted to name it *Suspiria Regalia* or sighs of the king. Jeremy Taylor coined the final title, which prevailed over Gauden's second choice, *The Royal Plea*, a title certain to provoke anti-Royalists.[32] The *Eikon Basilike* appeared in the streets soon after his death. It made Charles a royal martyr, helping to ensure the restoration of monarchy in 1660.

Its chapters present Charles in his own voice. He reflects on pivotal events of his reign and defends his decisions. As Daems and Nelson remark, Charles emerges as "the defender of both Church and State," while his enemies appear as "fanatical zealots intent on subduing the conscience of the king and obliterating the biblically based ecclesiastical body."[33] The book begins with a frontispiece, produced by William Marshall, showing the King kneeling in prayer, exchanging an earthly crown for a martyr's crown[34] (see Figure 6).

Its chapters end with the king in prayer, beseeching God for vindication, or interceding for his country and at times even for his enemies. Prayer deepens the sense of intimacy the book creates between reader and king.

Intimacy implies privacy. In fact, the king's "solitudes" integrate private and public prayer. Laura Lunger Knoppers argues that differences between private and public prayer do not apply to the *Eikon Basililke*. Throughout, "Charles meditates on public matters."[35] His meditations are private, but they "form a mirror or pattern for his son, not as a private person, but as future head of church and state."[36] The book evokes the *Basilikon Doron*, the "gift of the king," written by King James for his eldest son Henry, whose death made Charles the heir. Similarly, the *Eikon Basilike* prays for Charles II as if foreseeing his restoration.[37] The prayers assert hereditary continuity from James to Charles II. The Psalms are the main model for the king's prayers. Psalm references identify King Charles with King David, recreating the Davidic typology in Taylor's 1644 *Psalter*. The king also prays for his people, making him a public intercessor.

Intimacy requires a sense of presence. Elizabeth Skerpan-Wheeler makes this observation: "[T]he *Eikon Basilike* literally took the place of the king. In the absence of direct royal control or effective government censorship, this image took on an autonomous life, appropriated by readers and the book trade to create a publishing phenomenon."[38] Its "autonomous life" offers an ironic illustration of Milton's thesis in *Areopagitica*: a book contains "the pretious life-blood of a master spirit, embalm'd and treasur'd up on purpose to a life beyond life" (*CPW* 2: 493). This analogy validates the view of Daems and Nelson: "[W]ith kingly absence, *Eikon Basilike* served as an incarnational text, for it provided a revered, material, textual body for Charles I. Many early-modern readers experienced the volume as the sacred, authoritative Word."[39] One half of this experience comes from belief in *sacred* majesty. The other comes from the prayers, psalm paraphrases, and meditations the king speaks from its pages.

Figure 6. Frontispiece: *Eikon Basilike,* engraved by William Marshall (1649).
Courtesy of the Huntington Library.

In Chapter 1, *On his Majesty's Calling this last Parliament*, the English people are knit closely to the heart of the king: "No man was better pleased with the convening of this Parliament, than My self; who knowing best the largeness of My own Heart toward My People's good and just contentment, pleased My self most in that good and firm understanding, which would hence grow between me and My People."[40] The idea of incarnation expands here, since the nation is the king's second body. The king uses plural pronouns in citing Psalm 23: "O Lord, thou hast deprived us of many former comforts; yet grant me and My People the benefit of our afflictions, and thy chastisements; that thy rod as well as thy staff may comfort us."[41] Psalm 23 prefigures Christ as the good shepherd of the flock. It speaks of a table prepared in the "presence of mine enemies," prefiguring the Eucharistic meal. It concludes with the "house of the Lord" as an eternal dwelling place, signifying the Church.

A second biblical reference identifies the king with Christ. "Chastisements" echoes Isaiah 53:5: "But he was wounded for our transgressions, he was bruised for our iniquities: the chastisement of our peace *was* upon him; and with his stripes we are healed." Christians read this as a prophecy of Christ's crucifixion. The theme of blood sacrifice continues: "If nothing but my blood will satisfy My Enemies, or quench the flames of My Kingdoms, or thy temporal Justice, I am content, if it be thy will, that it be shed by Mine own Subjects' hands. But O let the blood of Me, though their King, yet a sinner, be washed with the blood of my Innocent and peace-making Redeemer."[42] Charles emulates Christ's passion by becoming a sacrifice for his kingdom in accordance with God's will while also expressing his need for redemption through Christ's sacrifice.

Chapter 16 addresses the Book of Common Prayer. King Charles commends recent defenders of the prayer book: "As for the matter contained in the Book, sober and learned men have sufficiently vindicated it against the cavils and exceptions of those, who thought it a part of piety to make what profane objections they could against it."[43] These "sober and learned" vindicators included Jeremy Taylor. Charles commended Taylor's *Discourse concerning prayer ex tempore*, encouraging its expansion into the *Apology for authorized and set forms of liturgie* in 1649. In his prefatory letter to the king in the *Apology*, Taylor observes that, in the two years "since your Most Sacred Majesty was pleased graciously to looke upon" the *Discourse*, its leaves "are growne into a Tract, and have an ambition (like the Gourd of *Jonas*) to dwell in the eye of the Sunne from whence they received life and increment" (*Apology*, A3r). While Taylor's total contribution to the *Eikon Basilike* is hard to quantify, his defences of liturgy impressed the king, and no doubt influenced the ways in which the *Eikon Basilike* promotes set forms of prayer.

Taylor's *Apology* is a subtext for Chapter 16 of the *Eikon Basilike*, and so we can read the attack on Chapter 16 in Milton's *Eikonoklastes* as an implicit attack on the *Apology*. Milton attacked set forms of prayer as early as 1641 in *Animadversions*: "[T]here is a large difference in the repetition of some patheticall ejaculation rays'd out of the suddain earnestnesse and vigour of the inflam'd soul, (such as was that of Christ in the Garden) from the continual rehearsal of our dayly orisons" (*CPW* 1: 682).[44] In 1649, the image of the King as Christ in Gethsemane drove Milton to attack his sincerity as a false image. As Achinstein remarks, prayer "held a special meaning for a Protestant: it was the direct and above all *sincere* communication between humans and God, and it represented the voice of conscience."[45] Milton needed to strengthen the voice of conscience. His strategy was to divide king and people. Where the king speaks constantly of "My People" throughout the *Eikon Basilike*, Milton speaks of "the people." Where the king gathers his people like children into the metaphor of a nurturing parent, Milton exhorts the people to understand Christian liberty as outgrowing monarchy in a revolutionary moment. Where the king subdues his people in self-vindication, Milton involves them in his new national vision.[46]

Milton's iconoclasm is therefore both destructive and constructive. Iconoclasm shows readers how to "resist propaganda by relying upon inner judgment," as Achinstein suggests.[47] David Ainsworth sees Milton's spiritual reader as one who questions images "instead of uncritically accepting them."[48] *Eikonoklastes* asks readers to break the *Eikon Basilike* "apart, as Milton does," and separate "the divine wheat from the worldly chaff."[49] If idolatry is a disease that can "contaminate the inner man" and "grip the body politic," Ernest Gilman argues, then "iconoclasm becomes the necessary instrument of public health."[50] Erin Henriksen observes a paradoxical tension of "corrective breaking" in *Eikonoklastes*: Milton "shatters the image set up by the king's book, breaking it precisely in those places that threaten to ensnare its audience in idolatry. It goes further as well, to make from the broken pieces a new work, an image that corrects the mistaken beliefs of the original."[51] Andrewes saw "imaginings" as leading to idolatries; however, both he and Taylor traced this tendency to the spiritual presumption of some Puritans. For Milton, the equation of the king with Christ in propaganda suborns the national religious imagination.

Emphasizing Charles's theatrical self-fashioning of in the *Eikon Basilike*, David Loewenstein argues that iconoclasm creates "a new orientation towards the past."[52] Charles's "Penitential Meditations" strengthen his connection to "the biblical line of kingship represented by David and Christ."[53] Loewenstein cites Charles's inclination to "hold to primitive and uniform antiquity" rather than "comply with divided novelty."[54] Continuity echoes Taylor on set forms of liturgy: the "primitive and ancient formes of Church service" are "composed according to those so excellent Patterns," and "publick Forme of Lyturgie was the great instrument of Communion in the Primitive Church" (*Apology* 54, 69). Loewenstein recognizes a larger tension between the prayerful Charles who transcends suffering and the polemical Milton who addresses his adversary in the revolutionary sphere of history.

Milton fought this textual battle, but he could not win unless England established a functional republic. A public weary of civil war responded to the piety in the king's voice. The monarch is the head of the Church, and this tradition remained alive in the king's "solitudes" and "sufferings" after his death. Milton applied the free and open encounter of truth and error modelled in *Areopagitica* to his reading of the *Eikon Basilike*, but knew the king's voice could impress the reader's mind. This theme shaped his major poems profoundly. Satan's temptation, for example, wins too "easy entrance" into the ear of Eve.

What does this receptivity to outside voices mean for the individual experience of prayer and, by extension, the religious imagination? For Andrewes and Taylor, the Book of Common Prayer fills the reader with inspired and artful prayers. For Milton, and for Bunyan, true prayer means making room inwardly for the mind and Spirit to work. Making room evokes the Christian doctrine of "kenosis," a self-emptying that precedes the incarnation of Christ, who "being in the form of God, thought it not robbery to be equal with God: But made himself of no reputation, and took upon him the form of a servant, and was made in the likeness of men" (Phil. 2:6–7). The original Greek for "no reputation" is "kenosis," or "to become empty."

James Mensch offers a phenomenological model of prayer as a dialectic between kenosis and incarnation. If kenosis is a mode of receptivity that makes room for the Holy Spirit in the individual, incarnation is a mode of empathy, which is "a feeling (a suffering or undergoing) of the world in and through another person."[55] Prayer involves receptivity to the Spirit and empathy for others. The model illuminates Andrewes, who favoured a movement from the "I" of individual zeal (as receptivity to the Spirit) to the "we" of collective charity (or membership in the incarnate church). Receptivity for Puritans requires the interior space of conscience they protected from the intrusion of "other men's words." For Anglicans, it requires internalizing the forms of common prayer. Incarnation for Puritans requires the gathered community. For

Anglicans, it requires the mystical Body of Christ. The *Eikon Basilike* activates this model of prayer in an apprehension of sacred majesty. In Marshall's frontispiece, the king, who is also the head of the Church, appears as a sacred image who also apprehends the sacred by receiving holy light in prayerful suffering. Milton considered this image of the sacred as a dangerously "phantastick" imagining. It is within these competing claims to sanctity that Milton's *Eikonoklastes*, Taylor's *Apology*, and the *Eikon Basilike* collide.

Chapter 16, "Upon the Ordinance against the Common-Prayer Book," treats the *Directory of Public Worship* as a usurping text. Proponents of the prayer book equate it with a constant God. Opponents preferred variety. King Charles speaks for the prayer book: "Nor is God more a God of variety, than of constancy; Nor are Constant Forms of Prayers more likely to flat, and hinder the Spirit of prayer, and devotion, than unpremeditated and confused variety to distract, and lose it."[56] This passage is close to Taylor's *Apology*, perhaps revealing his special involvement with Chapter 16. Extemporaneous prayer depends "upon irregular variety for which no antecedent rule can make particular provision" (*Apology* 36). Constancy is not stasis. The prayer book provides various encounters with the Spirit within the constancy of its forms. The "irregular variety" of extemporaneous prayer exposes worshippers to randomness.

Taylor dedicates the *Apology* to the sacred image in a prefatory letter to the king that reinforces the "portraiture" of Charles I as a Christ-like martyr: "I present your MAJESTY with a humble persecuted truth, of the same constitution with that condition whereby you are become most Deare to God, as having upon you the characterisme of the Sonnes of God, bearing in your Sacred Person *the markes of the Lord Jesus*, who is your Elder Brother, the King of Sufferings, and the Prince of the Catholique Church." Taylor connects devotion to monarchy, a connection that would prove potent in the *Eikon Basilike*. He emphasizes the authority of "princes" who "have a speciall obligation for the defence of Liturgies, because they having the greatest Offices" (*Apology* A3v–A4r). The similitude of Christ and King Charles in his sufferings becomes a metaphor for the Book of Common Prayer, the "humble persecuted truth" that is the subject of Taylor's *Apology*.

The trope of the book as suffering martyr in Chapter 16 may also reveal Taylor's hand. The prayer book was "crucified by an Ordinance" in 1645.[57] Like that book, King Charles bears the stigmata of Christ. In 1644, Milton compared censorship to homicide and martyrdom, "and if it extend to the whole impression, a kinde of massacre" (*CPW* 2: 493). As "good almost kill a Man as kill a good Book" is a central premise in *Areopagitica* (*CPW* 2: 492). But the *Eikon Basilike* is a bad book, and so Milton exposes it as a travesty of sanctity. He deflates the king as martyr by shifting his image to secular entertainments, court masques, in fact: "[Q]uaint Emblems and devices begg'd from the old Pageantry of some Twelf-nights entertainment at *Whitehall*, will doe but ill to make him Saint or martyr" (*CPW* 3: 343). He accuses Charles of stealing prayers from "heathen" sources like Sidney's *Arcadia*: "[T]his King, not content with that which, although in a thing holy, is no holy theft, to attribute to his own making other men's whole Prayers, hath, as it were unhallow'd, and unchrist'nd the very duty of prayer it self, by borrowing to a Christian use Prayers offer'd to a heathen God. Who would have imagin'd so little feare in him of the true all-seeing Deitie, so little reverence of the Holy Ghost, whose office is to dictate and present our Christian Prayers" (*CPW* 3: 362). Accusations of plagiarizing empty the king's image of legitimacy.[58] Andrewes, we recall, distinguished Christians from "heathens" in his reading of 1 Corinthians, and Matthew rebuked the "vain repetitions" of heathens in framing the Lord's Prayer. Milton places the prayer from *Arcadia* on the "heathen" side.

Milton believed the Spirit of prayer to be a spirit of discernment. God allows our emotions "to be guided by his sanctifying spirit, so did he likewise our words to be put into us without our premeditation; not onely those cautious words to be us'd before Gentiles and Tyrants, but much more those filial words, of which we have so frequent use in our access with freedom of speech to the Throne of Grace" (*CPW* 3: 506). The Spirit itself is the greatest gift: "to lay aside for other outward dictates of men, were to injure him and his perfect Gift, who is the spirit, and the giver of our abilitie to pray" (*CPW* 3: 506). Evoking Romans 8:26, Milton describes the Spirit dwelling in each conscience in the formation of a minimal religious community:

> Though we know not what to pray as we ought, yet he with sighs unutterable by any words, much less by a stinted Liturgie, dwelling in us makes intercession for us, according to the mind and will of God, both in privat, and in the performance of all Ecclesiastical duties. For it is his promise also, that where two or three gather'd in his name shall agree to ask him any thing, it shall be granted; for he is there in the midst of them. (*CPW* 3: 507)

As we will see, Milton adheres to the precept of "where two or more are gathered" in the bonds between Adam and Eve at the end of *Paradise Lost*, and Jesus and Mary at the end of *Paradise Regained*.

In three images, Milton portrays Charles's prayers as confining. First, stinted prayer is a confining pinfold:

> They who use no set formes of prayer, have words from their affections; while others are to seek affections fit and proportionable to a certain doss of prepar'd words; which as they are not rigorously forbid to any mans privat infirmity, so to imprison and confine by force, into a Pinfold of sett words, those two most unimprisonable things, our Prayers and that Divine Spirit of utterance that moves them. (*CPW* 3: 505)

"Pinfold" means a "pen our pound for cattle." As Merritt Hughes suggests, this word echoes the Attendant Spirit in *Comus,* who sees men "with low-thoughted care/Confin'd and pester'd in this pinfold here" (6–7). The Lady in *Comus* voices a higher, inexpressible language of the spirit beyond physical confinement.

Second, stinted prayer "is a tyranny that would have longer hands then those Giants who threatn'd bondage to Heav'n" (*CPW* 3: 505). The image returns in *Paradise Lost* to compare the rebel angels to the "Earth-born" Titans who "warr'd on Jove" (1.198).[59] Such giants are the enemies of heaven. Third, stinted prayer is corrupt rather than wholesome food. If set forms are "savory words and unmix'd, suppose them *Manna* it self, yet if they shall be hoarded up and enjoynd us, while God every morning raines down new expressions into our hearts, instead of being fit to use, they will be found like reserv'd *Manna*, rather *to breed wormes and stink*" (*CPW* 3: 505). Taylor, in contrast, counters Manna as a metaphor for extemporaneous prayer:

> When the formes are dayly changed, it is more probable that every Man shall find something proportionable to his fancy, which is the great instrument of Devotion, then to suppose that any one forme, should be like Manna fitted to every tast; and therefore in prayers, as the affections must be naturall, sweet, and proper, so also should the words expressing the affections, issue forth by way of naturall emanation. (*Apology* 34)

Manna is monotonous to the restive Israelites; likewise, Puritan reformers compare manna to forced uniformity: [T]hey "long for variety, and then they cry out that *Manna* will not nourish them, but prefer the *onions of Egypt* before *the food of Angels*" (*Apology* 41). Milton responds with imagery: he describes the bread as corrupt rather than spiritual, and he combines private and public devotion in plural forms – God inspires "our hearts."[60] The distinction between idolatry and devotion is paramount. Milton's motivation is to attack what Lana Cable calls the "idolatry of words" in the *Eikon Basilike*.[61]

Taylor and Milton present radically different views of the sacred image. Taylor venerates the image in the preface to his *Apology* as a necessary to the Church. Milton blasts the image as an idol that subdues reason and discernment. On the eve of the Restoration, Milton contrasted a republic led by ordinary citizens with a monarch demanding adoration. His major poems respond to the restoration as a failure of the national imagination, both religious and political.

Chapter Four

John Milton (1650–1674): The Spirit of Prayer

Thus they in lowliest plight repentant stood
Praying, for from the Mercy-seat above
Prevenient Grace descending had remov'd
The stony from thir hearts, and made new flesh
Regenerate grow instead, that sighs now breath'd
Unutterable, which the Spirit of prayer
Inspir'd, and wing'd for Heav'n with speedier flight
Than loudest Oratorie

(*Paradise Lost* 11: 1–8)

The invocation to Book 1 of *Paradise Lost* performs the progression from poetry to prayer Milton describes in *The Reason of Church Government*: inspiration is not "obtain'd by the invocation of Dame Memory and her Siren daughters, but by devout prayer to that eternall Spirit who can enrich with all utterance and knowledge" (*CPW* 1: 820–1). The poem begins with a recognizable epic convention, and ends by praying to the Spirit that moved over the face of the deep in Genesis 1:

And chiefly Thou O Spirit, that dost prefer
Before all Temples th' upright heart and pure,
Instruct me, for Thou know'st; Thou from the first
Wast present, and with mighty wings outspread
Dove-like satst brooding on the vast Abyss
And mad'st it pregnant, What in me is dark
Illumine, what is low raise and support;
That to the highth of this great Argument
I may assert Eternal Providence,
And justify the ways of God to men. (1: 17–26)

The poet is unformed material petitioning for the separation of darkness and light, order and chaos in his creative consciousness. He dictates the poem in blindness to an amanuensis, having lost his sight at age forty-three. To be sure, he revised and edited orally as well, but speaking a poem never before heard out of darkness is a powerful affirmation of extemporaneous prayer.

Milton's experience of the royal voice of the *Eikon Basilike* may have influenced this prayerful invocation. He advocated resistance to an invasive voice seeking to pray in and through subjects. Creation in Hebrew is *bara* – the separation of entities.[1] Light and darkness, Heaven and Earth are distinguished in the invocation. So are Jesus and Charles II in the phrase "till one greater Man/Restore us" (4–5). As Keeble observes, the word "restore" had "an inescapable topicality" in 1660. Restoration rather than revolution "instantly became the usual word to denote what had occurred."[2] Milton forgoes options like "redeem." "Restore" places the early modern reader in the midst of seventeenth-century things while distinguishing divine restoration from its political parody. Jesus, not Charles II, is the "greater man." Distinctions are central to reading and writing in Dissenting culture. Milton supported Restoration Dissenters and Nonconformists in protecting the voice of individual conscience amid the din of slander and invective hurled at them in print polemic or public trials. Discerning, distinguishing, and differentiating can raise readers above the din.

Milton's Satan prefers confusion. Many readers still find Satan the most attractive character, and even the hero of the poem. I subscribe to another key distinction made by Keeble: yes, Satan is *a* hero, but he is not *the* hero of the poem.[3] He is a hero because he carries the cultural baggage of classical martial heroism that defined Western civilization by suborning Christianity to its code of war. Satan is a charismatic warrior who puts his mark on history. The Son, in contrast, expresses the "better fortitude of patience and heroic martyrdom," and suffers the marks of history on himself. Milton would understand but not endorse a reader's view of Satan as *the* hero.

i. "under saintly show": Satan and the Art of Prayer in *Paradise Lost*

Epic similes in Books 1 and 2 present a visually magnificent Satan. Even more compelling is his voice. He speaks some of the most memorable lines in the poem, whether in public speeches or private soliloquies. A gap between the public and private self is not viable in honest contrition or in prayer. Suffering impels prayer. Dissembling does not. Satan, to be sure, does not pray for forgiveness, but it does occur to him. What if he could repent? Of all the great "what if" questions posed in the poem, only Satan's has no future. Suffering and self-examination, memory and deliberation, all hardened by sin, lead Satan to think about God. If his speeches sought reconciliation rather than revenge, they would be prayers.

A main example is in Book 4. Satan pauses before entering Eden, and speaks to the Sun:

> O thou that with surpassing Glory crown'd,
> Look'st from thy sole Dominion like the God
> Of this new World; at whose sight all the Stars
> Hide thir diminisht heads; to thee I call,
> But with no friendly voice, and add thy name
> O Sun, to tell thee how I hate thy beams. (4: 32–7)

The first sixteen lines of this speech are the oldest part of the poem, dating from the early 1650s. According to Edward Phillips, Milton's nephew and early biographer: "This subject was first designed as a tragedy, and in the fourth book of the poem there are six verses, which, several years before the poem was begun, were shown to me, and some others, as designed for the very beginning of the said tragedy."[4] Phillips told John Aubrey, another biographer, that he heard Milton recite the lines in the early 1650s.[5] This implies a tragic source for the speech.[6] Francis Blessington sees the soliloquy as a failed classical supplication: "From Satan's soliloquy, we know that the Father keeps open the possibility for Satan's plea." In this "the Father excels the more arbitrary classical deities – but Satan still refuses to sue for grace."[7] He finds models in Virgil and Homer, and argues that Milton assimilates these to Christian supplications "to fuse the classical and Christian worlds." Satan's classical heroism is not the Christian heroism Milton promotes in the Son, whose name plays on "Sun." This is the first of three word-plays Milton applies to prayer. This pun develops Milton's emphasis on the Son of God as redeemer, intercessor, and mediator, and the main heroic figure in the poem.

A dramatic soliloquy is perceived as extemporaneous. Its private nature also implies candour and authenticity. The same can be said of the king's solitary meditations in the *Eikon Basilike*, yet Milton saw them as neither extemporaneous nor authentic. Phillips's recollection places Satan's speech close in time to *Eikonoklastes*. Milton questions the authorship of "these Soliloquies" at one point in the treatise, encouraging the reader's sense of a dissembling monarch. Satan's speech is solitary but he still dissembles as a religious figure "under saintly shew."

The Lord's Prayer is a subtext for Satan's speech. He begins with wordless "sighs' (4: 29), an allusion to Romans 8:26. What follows parodies elements of the prayer. Satan hates rather than hallows the divine name. He separates his will from God's will, deviating from "Thy will be done": "Nay curs'd be thou; since against his thy will/Chose freely what it now so justly rues." He complicates the petition, "Forgive us our debts," by lamenting his "debt immense of endless gratitude" to God. He claims he was not delivered from temptation: "lifted up so high/I sdein'd subjection, and thought one step higher/Would set me highest." Finally, he inverts the first petition, "Thy Kingdom come on earth," and the doxology, "For thine is the kingdom," by seeking a "divided kingdom" with God on earth. As a parody of the Lord's Prayer, this speech amplifies the contrast between the Son and Satan that defines the epic.

Angels are formed for prayer, praise, and service. Fallen angels retain this formation. Satan's intellectual, volitional, and emotional faculties remain powerful, adding to his pain. Meditation exercises the faculties God endows. Prayer and meditation are linked in early modern devotional guides. Thomas Rogers, in his *Pretious Booke of Heavenlie Meditations* (1597), says that "Prayer bringeth us unto the ende of our journey," and "Meditation sheweth the way." Joseph Hall, in his *Meditations and Vowes, Divine and Morall* (1606), sees prayer and meditation "as two loving turtles, whereof separate one, the other languisheth."[8] Prayer and meditation make our "inventions quickened, our wills rectified, our affections whetted to heavenly things, our hearts enlarged to God-ward, our devotion enkindled; so that we may find our corruptions abated, our graces thriven, our souls and lives way bettered by this exercise."[9] Satan meditates with memory, will, understanding, and emotion.

Mary Fenton aptly calls the speech an "anti-prayer." Satan "addresses the 'Thou' who is external to himself, and mimics the behaviour of one in a reverent, prayerful state."[10] Satan cannot pray because he "simultaneously rejects and desires fusion with divinity."[11] His speech uses methods of prayerful meditation, particularly the Augustinian method of self-analysis, scriptural contemplation, psychic quest, and inward illumination. This method developed as a Protestant response to Catholic methods. Accordingly, the soliloquy reflects a deeper tension in early modern religious culture.

Louis Martz shows the influence of meditative techniques on seventeenth-century poetry, including the Catholic spiritual exercises of St Ignatius Loyola. Jean Baptiste de Medina, illustrator of the 1688 edition of the poem, explicated the "Sun" as "Son" in an elaborate baroque image of Christ exalted above Satan (see Figure 7).

Figure 7. Illustration by Jean-Baptiste de Medina. *Paradise Lost; A Poem in Twelve Books* (1688). © British Library Board 643.m.10.(1) p. 60.

Perhaps Medina considered the Ignatian meditative method of composing a place in the mind, this one being the place that first provoked Satan to rebel. Several of Donne's *Holy Sonnets* use this three-stage sequence of imagined place, meditative apostrophe, and prayerful colloquy. These stages stimulate the faculties of memory, understanding, and will, which correspond to the three persons of the Trinity. These faculties all function in Satan's speech, but not in the formal Ignatian order; instead, I argue that Satan uses an Augustinian method favoured by Protestants. This method explores the inwardly divided self through autobiography interwoven with biblical references, as Augustine does in his *Confessions*. Martz remarks: "[I]n Augustinian meditation there is no such precise method; there is, rather, an intuitive groping back into the regions of the soul that lie beyond sensory memories. The three powers of the soul are all used, but with an effect of simultaneous action, for with Augustine the aroused will is using the understanding to explore the memory, with the aim of apprehending more clearly and loving more fervently the ultimate source of the will's arousal."[12] The Augustinian model informs Satan's speech.[13]

Illumination is a part of Augustinian meditation. This makes Satan's address to the Sun, which is the light of nature, more ironic. Illumination is the incomprehensible light of God the meditator contemplates with human intellectual light. "Discovery of truth," Martz argues, "consists in the operations of man's intellect, working within the 'illumination' granted by divine power. To define the manner of this interior working, Augustine says, 'We must find, in the rational or intellectual soul of man, an image of its Creator planted immortally in its immortal nature.'" The image remains, "'whether it be obscured and defaced, or fair and clear.'"[14] The invocations to Books 1 and 3 of *Paradise Lost* illustrate this process. The invocation to Book 1 is a prayer for light: "what is dark in me illumine." The invocation to Book 3 is a meditation on "holy light." In contrast, natural light stirs Satan's memory of Heaven and the divine light of the Son. Satan will not repent, but meditation is the vestige of the divine image that remains in him.

As Frank Huntley shows, the militant Protestant mode of meditation came into "being at the beginning of the seventeenth century in direct conflict with the *Spiritual Exercises of St. Ignatius*."[15] Thomas Rogers's *A Pretious Book of Heavenly Meditation*, a collection of passages translated from Augustine and other sources, rejects Ignatian meditation as "pernicious."[16] He offers meditation in three volumes: Augustine's meditations; Augustine's prayers; and Augustine's manual, and calls meditation a "private talk of the soul with God." Augustine's style is comparable to Satan's. Augustine uses the pronoun "I" and interweaves scriptural quotations into his thoughts. Satan's style is self-centred, emphasizing I, me, and my, and he echoes familiar scriptural places: the Lord's Prayer; the Parable of the Talents, a deeply personal parable for Milton; and the Parable of the Prodigal Son, a key motif in Augustine's *Confessions*.

Milton evokes the Parable of the Talents when Satan meditates on grace and debt. He remembers God as an easy taskmaster:

> he deserv'd no such return
> From me, whom he created what I was
> In that bright eminence, and with his good
> Upbraided none; nor was his service hard. (4: 42–5)

He understands that grace was not onerous: "What could be less than to afford him praise,/The easiest recompence, and pay him thanks,/How due!" (4: 46–8). He was "Forgetful what from him I still receiv'd,/And understood not that a grateful mind/By owing owes not, but still pays, at once/Indebted and dischargd; what burden then?" (4: 54–7). His memory and understanding failed in the past but function in the present. Ron Corthell calls meditation "a distinctive form of rhetoric: it is an art of persuasion designed for a particularly fit audience, one 'prevented' by the grace of Christ."[17] In Milton's sonnet on the Parable of the Talents, "When I consider how my light is spent," the first eight lines meditate on labour and payment; prevenient grace then marks the *volta* as Patience prevents "That murmur" and explains the paradoxical economy of what the angel Raphael in *Paradise Lost* calls "voluntary service" (5: 529). Satan's meditation has no *volta* apart from the shifts and turns of his own intellect.

As Thomas Merrill suggests, the purpose of a parable is "not to present information but to change people's lives."[18] Satan contemplates the parable without changing. He insists that he cannot repent, but insists with language resembling Christ's Passion, another subject for meditation:

> For never can true reconcilement grow
> Where wounds of deadly hate have pierc'd so deep:
> Which would but lead me to a worse relapse
> And heavier fall: so should I purchase dear
> Short intermission bought with double smart. (4: 98–102)

Piercing wounds and "purchase dear" evoke Christ's suffering. Meditation on the Passion should lead to repentance. But this is an anti-prayer and anti-meditation. It replaces love with "deadly hate," redemption with a "heavier fall," and eternal life with "short intermission." Satan's meditation starts with an improbable repentance and ends with an ineffectual Passion. A true meditation would begin with Christ's Passion and end with repentance, as in Donne's "Good Friday 1613, Riding Westward."

After the exercise, the epic narrator describes its effects on Satan.

> Thus while he spake, each passion dimm'd his face,
> Thrice chang'd with pale, ire, envy and despair,
> Which marr'd his borrow'd visage, and betray'd
> Him counterfeit, if any eye beheld.
> For heav'nly minds from such distempers foul
> Are ever clear. Whereof hee soon aware,
> Each perturbation smooth'd with outward calm,
> Artificer of fraud; and was the first
> That practis'd falshood under saintly show. (4: 114–22)

Milton exposed a "saintly show" in the *Eikon Basilike*. He expects readers to do the same here. Satan speaks to himself and affects himself but cannot resolve or compose himself. Perturbation and distemper are signs of bad art.

In Book 4, Satan uses "his Devilish art" to produce "Phantasms and Dreams" in a slumbering Eve (4: 801–3). Satan's art enters Eve's mind in words spoken into her ear. The design of the dream exploits the poetic sensibility Satan saw in Eve while spying on her and Adam earlier, and shows Milton's concern with the invasion of the ear by coercive voices. For this reason, Books 4 and 5 contrast right prayer and dissembling prayer as good and bad art.

When Eve awakes, Adam clears her of blame for the dream by emphasizing the role of conscious will in sin. Since Satan is unknown to them, Adam sees the origins of the dream in fancy ungoverned by waking reason. Good poetry allays "the perturbations of the mind, and set the affections in right tune" (*CPW* 1: 817). So can good prayer:

> Lowly they bow'd adoring, and began
> Thir Orisons, each Morning duly paid
> In various style, for neither various style
> Nor holy rapture wanted they to praise
> Thir Maker, in fit strains pronounct or sung
> Unmeditated, such prompt eloquence
> Flow'd from thir lips, in Prose or numerous Verse,
> More tuneable than needed Lute or Harp
> To add more sweetness. (5: 144–52)

Set hours for prayer were controversial, but creation is the template for ceremony in Eden, not the clock. These prayers are also unscripted ("unmeditated") and extemporaneous ("prompt eloquence"). "Prose or numerous Verse" is a matter of choice, not compulsion. They do not need "holy rapture" to harmonize their voices as the first instruments of music.

Like Satan, Adam and Eve speak to the Sun:

> Thou Sun, of this great World both Eye and Soul,
> Acknowledge him thy Greater, sound his praise
> In thy eternal course, both when thou climb'st,
> And when high noon hast gain'd, and when thou fall'st. (5: 171–4)

All of nature is vocal in Eden. The sun's course brings additional hours for praise: morning, noon, and evening. The word "fall'st" is perhaps portentous, but Milton invites us to imagine innocent praise from our place in fallen time. The beauty of these prayers illustrates elevated and uncorrupted artistic power.

The prayer ends with a petition: "If the night/Have gather'd aught of evil or conceal'd,/Disperse it, as now light dispels the dark" (5: 206–9). The alignment of light and dark with good and evil prefigures God's work of bringing good out of evil in the fallen world. This contrasts with Satan's final resolution: "Evil be thou my Good" (4: 110). Confusion is Satan's work; separation is God's work. Milton expects readers to resist confusion through discernment and discretion.

ii. Prayer and Intercession in *Paradise Lost*

Raphael is God's answer to the morning prayers of Adam and Eve. He is a poet-teacher who accommodates divine realities to human understanding by choosing genres for ethical as well as literary reasons.[19] His choices exercise discernment and teach obedience. His theme in Books 5 and 6 is spiritual combat in the War in Heaven, with zeal being the virtue suited to his theme. Zeal opposes its Satanic opposite, blasphemy. Milton places zeal and blasphemy together in *De Doctrina Christiana*: an "eager desire to sanctify the divine name, together with a feeling of indignation against things which tend to the violation or contempt of religion, is called Zeal" while the "opposite of this is to talk about God's name in an impious and shameful way, which is commonly called blasphemy" (*CPW* 6: 697–8). Zeal characterizes "true" religion. "Sonnet 9," for example, compliments a young lady whose zeal is an "odorous Lamp"; *Of True Religion* (1673) describes "zealous labourers" who resist false religion. Andrewes and Herbert elevate charity over zeal as a corporate virtue, and so does Milton in the closing moments of *Paradise Lost* when the angel Michael advises Adam, "add Love/By name to come call'd charity" (12: 583–4). He does, however, explain the virtue of zeal as the individual's strength of conscience that is indispensable to a true church.

The paragon of zeal is Abdiel, the "servant of God" who confronts Satan in Book 5.

> Abdiel, than whom none with more zeal ador'd
> The Deity, and divine commands obey'd,
> Stood up, and in a flame of zeal severe
> The current of his fury thus oppos'd.
> O argument blasphemous, false and proud!
> Words which no ear ever to hear in Heav'n
> Expected, least of all from thee, ingrate,
> In place thyself so high above thy Peers. (5: 805–12)

Abdiel is the archetype of the conscientious Dissenter. He is like those who endured disparaging invective in Restoration England. Raphael chooses him out of millions of stories to help Adam distinguish zeal from blasphemy. Abdiel is also a prophet as he calls to Satan to repent. Repentance requires prayer: "hast'n to appease/Th'incensed Father, and th'incensed Son,/While Pardon may be found in time besought" (5: 846–8). This is a second wordplay on prayer after the Sun/Son pun in Book 4. Incensed means righteous anger, but it resonates with the penitent prayers of Adam and Eve that later ascend to the Father "clad/With Incense" (11: 18). If Satan were to "appease" the Father, he would, like Adam and Eve, have to "incense" him with prayer instead of blasphemy. Combining prayer and prophecy, Abdiel's speech offers a typically two-fold polemic of rebuke and reformation, confrontation and meditation.

Satan's rebellion parodies taking Heaven by spiritual violence, a traditional metaphor for prayer. Abdiel, he retorts, will see "Whether by supplication we intend/Address, and to begirt th'Almighty Throne/Beseeching or besieging" (5: 867–9). This is a third wordplay on prayer. "Beseeching" and "besieging" have a minimal difference in pronunciation. As a spiritual weapon, genuine prayer is beseeching *and* besieging, but Satan divides them with "or." This disjunction isolates blasphemy as profane violence. In Book 3, the Son asks the Father if blasphemy rather than prayer will assault heaven when the Fall is foreseen: "So should thy goodness and thy greatness both/Be question'd and blasphem'd without defence" (3: 165–6). The Father reveals his redemptive plan, and prayer is integral to his purpose: "To Prayer, repentance, and obedience due,/Though but endeavor'd with sincere intent,/Mine ear shall not be slow, mine eye not shut" (3: 191–3). Human prayers, mediated by the Son, will reach the throne of grace. Blasphemies will not.

The temptation of Eve in Book 9 also parodies prayer, but as fraud rather than force. Just as Satan's soliloquy in Book 4 is an anti-meditation, so too is his temptation of Eve in Book 9 an anti-liturgy. The Serpent testifies of his conversion to human sapience. He then makes the source of sapience, the forbidden fruit, a eucharistic element to tempt Eve. Satan gives thanks to the "sacred, wise and wisdom-giving plant" for the gifts of speech and reason. When Eve falls, she deliberates on whether to keep her experience private or to go public by converting Adam. Her deliberation replicates Satan's logic, and becomes the first fallen human soliloquy. Still, it is not original. It illustrates Milton's concern for invasive voices: "his words replete with guile/Into her heart too easy entrance won" (9: 732–3). The melding of Eve's voice with Satan's initiates idolatry as replication and conformity. Dissent from temptation would need a spontaneous prayer of the kind spoken by the Lady in *Comus*.

Adam suppresses the option of praying when he falls. As Dennis Danielson has shown, his fall encourages us to consider what Adam might have done.[20] His willingness to die with Eve evokes the redeeming death of the Son, and so excites our sympathies, but where the Son's death is effectual, Adam's is not. Danielson argues for intercessory prayer as Adam's best option to emulate the second Adam. To wait on God in prayer, moreover, is to grasp Milton's idea of heroism as patience. His fall initiates false heroism by elevating outward action over the "better fortitude."

Eve becomes more Christ-like than Adam when they consider options in the fallen state. In Book 10, she suggests prayer as a way forward:

> both have sinn'd, but thou
> Against God only, I against God and thee,
> And to the place of judgment will return,
> There with my cries importune Heaven, that all
> The sentence from thy head remov'd may light
> On me, sole cause to thee of all this woe,
> Mee mee only just object of his ire. (10: 930–6)

Her contrition moves Adam:

> If Prayers
> Could alter high Decrees, I to that place

> Would speed before thee, and be louder heard,
> That on my head all might be visited,
> Thy frailty and infirmer Sex forgiv'n,
> To me committed and by me expos'd. (10: 952–7)

Adam appropriates intercession to restore the hierarchy he abandoned in his fall: "Hee for God only, shee for God in him" (4: 299). His offer develops the redemptive counter-movement that Eve conceives. Needing grace to remove the "stony from thir hearts" (11: 4), they pray with the Spirit: "sighs now breath'd/Unutterable, which the Spirit of prayer/Inspir'd, and wing'd for Heav'n with speedier flight/Than loudest Oratory" (11: 5–8). "Oratory" rebukes both verbal art and Adam's claim to be "louder heard." "They" is the equal of "Our" in "Our Father." The plural pronoun pushes the redemptive counter-movement further along, as "they in lowliest plight repentant stood" (11: 1).

The Father sends Michael to comfort Adam and Eve in their expulsion. Eve's immediate dream of a redeemer complements Adam's mediated vision of biblical history. At the close, Michael counsels Adam on the virtues he most needs:

> only add
> Deeds to thy knowledge answerable, add Faith,
> Add Virtue, Patience, Temperance, add Love,
> By name to come call'd Charity, the soul
> Of all the rest: then wilt thou not be loath
> To leave this Paradise, but shalt possess
> A Paradise within thee, happier far. (12: 581–7)

This passage echoes 1 Corinthians 13:13, "[N]ow abideth faith, hope, charity, these three; but the greatest of these is charity." Charity and zeal are often contrasting virtues in the polemics of prayer, with zeal attributed most to radical sects. Raphael chose Abdiel for his individual "flame of zeal," whereas Michael calls charity the soul of the first church where two or more are gathered. Milton balances the two virtues to project a future church out of a paradise where prayers were not confined or compelled.

iii. Prayer and Temptation in *Paradise Regained*

Andrewes's *Seven Sermons on, the wonderfull combate (for Gods glorie and mans salvation) betweene Christ and Sathan* appeared in 1627, one year after his death. They appeared again in 1642 in a single volume and in an anthology.[21] *Seven Sermons* defines a "good" temptation as a test of virtue. Good temptation is a premise of the Book of Job, a model for *Paradise Regained*.[22] Good temptation is beneficial, but the Lord's Prayer says, "lead us not into temptation." How can the two be consistent? Andrewes explores this question in the first sermon. His text is Matthew 4:1: "Then was Jesus led aside of the Spirit into the wildernesse, to be tempted of the devil." Andrewes reads the event as a second kenosis:

> Our Saviour Christ by his Nativity, tooke upon him the shape of man; by his Circumcision, he tooke upon him, and submitted himselfe to the degree of a servant. By the first, he made himselfe in case and able to performe the worke of our redemption: By the second, he entred bound for the performing of it. All was to this end, that he might restore the worke of God to his original perfection.[23]

He "submitted himself" is a translation of "kenosis" in Philippians 2:7. Jesus is receptive to the Holy Spirit that leads him into temptation. Setting divinity aside, Jesus empathizes fully with human suffering.

The temptation is the third descent of the Spirit in the life of Jesus. The first is the Annunciation, as Mary conceives Jesus by the power of the Holy Spirit (Matt. 1:20). The second is the Baptism, when the Spirit descends from Heaven as a dove (Matt. 3:16–17). Andrewes emphasizes the leading of the Spirit: "We must not be ledde by the Spirit whence the Revelation came, *Math.* 16, 22. from whence revelations of flesh and blood do arise; but by the Spirit from whence the voice came, *This is my beloved sonne, in whom I am wel pleased.* It came not by the spirit that ministreth wise counsel, but by that which came downe upon them."[24] The descent of the Spirit signals a good temptation:

> Good temptations may as matters serving for our experience, not onely for our selves, that we may know our own strength, *Rom.* 5, 3. and to worke patience in us: but to the divell also, that so his mouth may be stopped, as in *Job 2, 3. Hast thou marked my servant Job, how upright he is, and that in all the world there is not such an one?* Howsoever they be, the devill hath not the rod or chaine in his hands, but the holy Ghost to order them, as they may best serve for his glory and our good: and as for the devill, he bindeth him fast, *Revel.* 20, 2.[25]

Milton paraphrases the ideas in this passage in Book 1 of *Paradise Regained* where Job is mentioned three times. Job, a figure of "constant perseverance" (1: 148) engages in spiritual combat, the primary metaphor for temptation in *Paradise Regained*.

Andrewes uses the Lord's Prayer to define "good" temptation. He contrasts "lead us not into temptation" from Hebrews 13:20: "Now the God of peace, that brought again from the dead our Lord Jesus, that great shepherd of the sheep, through the blood of the everlasting covenant." The difference lies in the Greek originals:

> by the Greeke word here used, is set forth the difference between the temptations of the Saints, and Reprobates. In the Lords Prayer one petition is, *Lead us not into temptation:* but there, the word importeth another manner of leading, than is heere meant. We do not there pray against this manner of leading here, which is so to leade us, as to be with us, and to bring us backe againe, *Heb.* 13, 20. but we pray there, that hee would not cast or drive us into temptations; and when we are there, leave us, by withdrawing his grace and holy Spirit, as hee doth from the reprobate and forsaken.[26]

"Lead us not" uses the Greek "eisenenke." Bringing Christ back from the dead (Hebrews 13:20) uses the Greek "anagagon," a leading upwards. Thus, leading in the Lord's Prayer can mean exposure to bad temptation, whereas leading in Hebrews 13:20 is fulfilled in the Resurrection. In the context Andrewes provides, we see that Jesus's good temptation will be an anagogic journey. Hebrews 4:15 is a second source for the doctrine of kenosis: Jesus "was in all points tempted as we are, yet without sin." Claiming authority as a strong Protestant reader in the preface to *De Doctrina Christiana*, Milton divested orthodox Christology in his theology. The hero of *Paradise Regained* is Jesus, the deliverer, the messiah, the anointed, but never "Christ." Divesting titles is a kenosis of doctrine. Milton emphasizes temptation in Jesus's human nature to affirm the power of reason and choice in the human Jesus and his human reader.

The third temptation completes the anagogic journey. Satan bears Jesus to the pinnacle of the temple. He tempts Jesus to hurl himself down, but unwittingly assists the leading upwards of anagogy when Jesus prevails. Satan's defeat prefigures his resurrection and glorification:

> True Image of the Father, whether thron'd
> In the bosom of bliss, and light of light
> Conceiving, or remote from Heaven, ensrhin'd
> In fleshly Tabernacle, and human form,
> Wand'ring in the Wilderness, whatever place,
> Habit, or state, or motion, still expressible
> The Son of God, with Godlike force endu'd
> Against th' Attempter of thy Father's Throne (4: 596–603)

This anagogic outcome makes the Lord's Prayer a subtext in *Paradise Regained*. Milton shares Andrewes's idea of good temptation, though he denies the Lord's Prayer is a set form; nevertheless, the taxonomy of prayer Ken Simpson identifies in *De Doctrina Christiana* includes elements of the Lord's Prayer: "There are two kinds of prayer prescribed in Scripture – invocations and the sanctification of God's name – and four kinds of invocations: petitions, thanksgivings, oaths, and casting lots."[27] Petitions "take two forms – the petition for good and the petition to take away evil." The sanctification of God's name "is often associated with zeal in defending and promoting God and professing the faith, even in the face of death."[28] "Give us this day our daily bread" is integral to the first temptation. Satan appears as an old and therefore mortal man who suffers hunger and thirst. Jesus may be the answer to his prayers, but Jesus sees through Satan and refuses to turn stones into bread. Instead, he continues to fast, and speaks of hunger as matter for the "petition for good":

> But now I feel I hunger, which declares,
> Nature hath need of what she asks; yet God
> Can satisfy that need some other way,
> Though hunger still remain: so it remain
> Without this body's wasting I content me,
> And from the sting of Famine fear no harm,
> Nor mind it, fed with better thoughts that feed
> Mee hung'ring more to do my Father's will. (2: 252–9)

Natural hunger would make bread the first petition, not "thy kingdom come, thy will be done," a point Andrewes stresses. The Lord's Prayer places "Thy will be done" before "daily bread" to elevate God's will above natural hunger.

Similarly, the second temptation – the kingdoms of the world – gives God's kingdom ("thy kingdom come") precedence, while the third temptation – to fall from the pinnacle of the temple – is a deliverance from evil. Jesus stands, prefiguring the triumph of the Resurrection. A frustrated Satan "departed from him for a season" (Luke 4:13). Satan will return to tempt Jesus in Gethsemane, an episode that stirred debate on set forms of prayer because Jesus repeats "let this cup pass from me" three times (Matt. 26:39, 42, 44). Matthew, Andrewes's preferred source, writes that Jesus "prayed the third time, saying the same words" (26:44). Luke, Milton's source for *Paradise Regained*, makes no reference to repetition, stating simply that Jesus "prayed more earnestly" (22:44).

Milton preferred Luke's order of temptations to Matthew's. As the first book of the New Testament, however, Matthew assumed precedence.[29] This may be why Andrewes used Matthew. Luke reverses Matthew's second and third temptations, placing kingdoms second and the Temple third. This order permits a long analysis of the world before a dramatic climax, which would appeal to Milton's interest in polemical debate between Jesus and Satan. If we consider Luke's order with prayer in mind, however, we find a second reason. An epic, even a brief one, is a national poem. The restored Stuart regime used the prayer book to force religious uniformity. Nation and religion intersect throughout Milton's career, but with new urgency after the Restoration. Luke's order gave Milton another opportunity to juxtapose kingdom and temple, state and church, in a poem of national significance.

What difference does this make? The three kingdoms of the world – Parthia, Rome, and Athens – explore the roots of Western nationhood: militarism, imperialism, and classicism. Jesus rejects all three, but Satan still controls these kingdoms in the final temptation. He cannot offer Jesus the Temple because it is God's house, but he can control it if Jesus will serve him. The result would be a union of church and state which Milton spurned. Luke's order separates the temple-church from imperial state power at the moment Satan exhausts the earthly kingdoms. Jesus revolts against Satan's rhetoric of conformity in exemplary resistance to state control. He stands in perfect discipline above the temple, accommodating a priesthood of believers without state coercion.

Liah Greenfeld sees a shift in Milton's treatment of religion and nationalism. As his thesis of liberty evolved, the religious content of his argument declined: "His pronouncements, full of religious fervor and still employing the authority of religious texts, became devoid of any religious content."[30] Liberty, she concludes, became the "distinguishing characteristic of Englishness."[31] In fact, the decline Greenfeld perceives is also a separation of church and state consistent with Milton's mature republicanism and religious toleration. If Greenfeld is correct, Milton would have preferred Matthew's order of temptations to Luke; instead, he prefers the Jewish temple, not the Roman imperial throne. For Milton, subduing monarchy is a necessary development in national and religious maturation.

Athens, the third kingdom, is also significant for prayer. Prayer polemics emphasize the relationship between the gifts and graces of the Spirit and human art. In Athens, Satan tempts Jesus with the arts of language. Jesus judges classical literature to be "ill-imitated." The Bible is original poetry:

Or if I would delight my private hours
With Music or with Poem, where so soon
As in our native Language can I find
That solace? All our Law and Story strew'd
With Hymns, our Psalms with artful terms inscrib'd. (4: 331–5)

This passage echoes the exaltation of biblical literature in *The Reason of Church Government*: "[T]hose frequent songs throughout the law and prophets beyond all these, not in their divine argument alone, but in the very critical art of composition may be easily made appear over all the kinds of Lyrick poesy, to be incomparable" (*CPW* 1: 816). Moreover, biblical prophets surpass Greek and Roman "statists" as political teachers:

In them is plainest taught, and easiest learnt,
What makes a Nation happy, and keeps it so,
What ruins Kingdoms, and lays Cities flat;
These only with our Law best form a King. (4:361–4)

The Athenian temptation places the Bible at the centre of English national consciousness *and* literary culture.[32] The prophet's voice, not the king's, is the standard by which nations rise or fall. For this reason, the Bible should not serve literary instruments of nationhood such as the Book of Common Prayer. The Psalms, as Patrick Miller observes, range "through the gamut of experiences (disaster, war, sickness, exile celebration, marriage, birth, death) and emotions (joy, terror, reflections, gratitude, hate, contentment, depression)."[33] "Sion's Songs" are sufficient to connect Jesus to his nation in prayer.

This may be why Satan's final temptation of Jesus is a Psalm:

Cast thyself down; safely if Son of God
For it is written, He will give command
Concerning thee to his Angels, in thir hands
They shall up lift thee, lest at any time
Thou chance to dash thy foot against a stone. (4: 555–9)

Satan quotes Psalm 91:11–12: "For he shall give his angels charge over thee, to keep thee in all thy ways. They shall bear thee up in their hands, lest thou dash thy foot against a stone." Satan tries to invert the upward anagogic direction of good temptation by asking Jesus to cast himself down. Jesus responds by embodying the Word in Deuteronomy 6:16: "Also it is written,/Tempt not the Lord thy God; he said, and stood." To speak and then stand is to become the Word incarnate.

The third temptation foreshadows the Passion where bystanders mock Christ on the cross: "And they that passed by railed on him, wagging their heads, and saying, Ah, thou that destroyest the temple, and buildest it in three days, Save thyself, and come down from the cross" (Mark 15:29–30). As Russell Hillier and Erin Henrikson point out, *Paradise Regained* foreshadows the Passion not least in its use of the Psalms.[34] The Passion sparked debate over set forms. Psalm 31:5 – 'into thine hand I commit my spirit" – offers Christ's last words in Luke. "My God, my God, why hast thou forsaken me?" is Psalm 22:1. Milton abandoned a short poem on the Passion in his youth, but approached the subject typologically in his later poems. *Samson Agonistes,* the companion poem to *Paradise Regained,* is a major example.

iv. Prayer and Uncertainty in *Samson Agonistes*

In 1662, a revised Book of Common Prayer appeared with the Acts of Uniformity as its preface. The Act required conformity to the prayer book. A mass ejection of ministers who would not conform occurred on 14 August of that year, known as Black Bartholomew's Day. Moreover, by 1662 the newly restored regime and Church used liturgies to narrate the Restoration as a providential event, vindicating the discourse started with the *Eikon Basilike* in 1649. *Samson Agonistes* is both prayerful and meditative. Milton again draws on Augustinian meditation to probe Samson's obsessive and depressive state of mind. His memory is a dialectic of the failed leader (memory) and the promised deliverer (expectation). If Satan presents an anti-meditation of non-repentance in Book 4 of *Paradise Lost,* Samson, I argue, presents a meditation at first hopeless and then hopeful, and a counter-liturgy that critiques the divine fiction of celebratory Restoration liturgies reflected in the poem's internal occasion: a Philistine holiday of deliverance.

Samson Agonistes is prayerful from its first line: "A little onward lend thy guiding hand." The hand may be human or divine, a duality the poem never relinquishes. Samson appears to pray before he pulls down the Temple of Dagon. Judges 16:28 records this prayer for revenge: "And Samson called unto the Lord, and said, O Lord God, remember me, I pray thee, and strengthen me, I pray thee, only this once, O God, that I may be at once avenged of the Philistines for my two eyes." Milton conceals this prayer. The Messenger sees it from a distance: "he stood, as one who pray'd/Or some great matter in his mind revolv'd" (1637–38). Between these moments is a rich network of psalm-like prayers and allusions: "God of our Fathers, what is man!" (l. 667); "My trust is in the living God" (l. 1140); God's "ear is ever open; and his eye/

Gracious to re-admit the suppliant" (1172–3); "Go, and the Holy One/ Of Israel be thy guide" 1427–8); "With God not parted from him, as was fear'd,/But favoring and assisting to the end" (1719–20). In particular, the poem evokes psalms of lamentation, which give form and voice to individual suffering and collective history. Importantly, as Hugh Mac-Callum observes, the Bible in this poem is the Torah and some oral fragments of still-to-be-written scripture.[35] The dramatic genre imagines prayer and poetry in oral form.

The Samson story comes from the book of Judges, a text that reflects turbulence and instability between the Exodus from Egypt and the founding of monarchy in ancient Israel. If, as Robert Alter argues, biblical narrative is a dialectic of design and disorder, then Judges is at the extreme end of disorder. Humans follow their own impulses and suffer for it. *Samson* is full of local wars and violence against women, such as the burning of Samson's first wife, the superstitious sacrifice of Jephthah's daughter, and the rape, murder, and dismemberment of a nameless concubine in the last chapter. The entire book shadows Milton's treatment of Samson. Biblical authors rarely editorialize, but they do not condone these actions; in fact, Judges supports feminist counter-readings, as Mieke Bal shows, and Milton agreed.[36] Narrative is not simply a basis for critical thinking in the Hebrew Bible; narrative *is* critical thinking, so Judges is very ambivalent towards charismatic leadership.[37] Milton understood the Bible, including its more violent texts, as sites for deep critical thinking, not moral complacency, and he tried to make his poems do likewise.

How could Milton make prayer and meditation out of these materials? The one ordering principle in Judges is its narrative frame: the recurring cycle of apostasy. People turn from God, suffer, then turn back to God by praying for a deliverer. God raises often flawed judges who partially deliver them. We have seen how this cycle reminded other writers of the turbulence of their times, notably Jeremy Taylor in his 1644 *Psalter*. In *Samson Agonistes*, Milton aligns this cycle with the lament psalm structure to express bitter memories and broken expectations in a short time frame. Although apostasy is a tragically repetitive cycle, the lament psalms provide a U-shaped structure open to hopeful, prayerful transformation. Walter Brueggemann describes this structure: address (or introductory petition); lament; a turning towards God (confession of trust); petition; vow of praise.[38] Milton uses the patterns of exile and return, suffering and redemption of the Psalms as a foundation for his *mimesis* of the Samson *mythos*. The outcome is a liturgical poem of dissent.

Liturgically, *Samson Agonistes* explores the shape of time. It begins on a day of Philistine celebration for deliverance from Samson, and ends as a day remembered for Samson's destruction of the Philistine temple. This conflict over the meaning of a single day evokes interpretations of history in solemn days of prayer and thanksgiving in Restoration England. Special liturgies devised for the restored king's birthday articulated restoration as providential. Milton regarded the Restoration as a loss of liberty, not a moment of deliverance. He resists these state-prescribed prayers as narratives of history at the most enigmatic moment in the drama: the moment in the Temple of Dagon when Samson stands "as one who pray'd" (1637). The poem confronts the state's use of public prayer to prescribe its interpretation of recent history. This is why interpretive conflict is at the core of Milton's meaning.

Milton's attitude to the destruction of the temple is much debated. A consensus among many twentieth-century critics affirms Samson's inward regeneration as divine grace prepares him to act as a hero of faith. Inward regeneration answers Samuel Johnson's view of the poem's supposed missing middle: it "has a beginning and an end which Aristotle himself could not have disapproved; but it must be allowed to want a middle, since nothing passes between the first act and the last, that either hastens or delays the death of Samson."[39] Anthony Low applies Milton's understanding of repentance to the regenerationist solution: "Samson makes use of the basic five-act Greek structure, and also of the traditional five stages of Christian regeneration conviction of sin, contrition, confession, departure from evil, conversion to good."[40] Low's articulation seeks a stable reconciliation of Hebrew, Greek, and Christian poetics. Samson's visitors – the Chorus, Manoa, Dalila, and Harapha – exercise his spirit as he passes through confession, contrition, confidence, and illumination.[41] This sequence organizes the discordant and concordant aspects of time in relations of probability and necessity, and even suggests a valid liturgical design. The questions *Samson Agonistes* raises, however, unsettle our stable answers, much like the questions in the Book of Job, a biblical model for this poem.

This consensus has, however, proved untenable in twenty-first-century criticism, and has given way to a more productive uncertainty. Revisionist critics see tragic repetition rather than meaningful emancipation in the story.[42] Some argue that Samson is an ironic contrast to Jesus, who rejects violence in *Paradise Regained*. These debates create what John Shawcross calls the "uncertain world" of *Samson Agonistes*, a world where unresolved ambiguities are part of the meaning of the poem.[43] In addition, terrorism has figured in critical discourse since the attacks of 11 September 2001, prompting debates on the figure of the terrorist and religious violence and challenging each critic's need for a cleansed and concordant reading. Uncertainty is like the dissonance that affected Dissenters after 1660. Dissonance comes from suffering, persecution, and defeat. Dissonance requires patience, discretion, and discernment in the exercise of faith. It also, I suggest, requires an understanding of uncertainty itself as a quality of Dissenting writing: covert, ambiguous signifiers energize literary representation in the culture of Dissent, and Samson is now an ambiguous and unstable figure for twenty-first-century readers.

Theoretical models can illustrate conflicting temporalities in *Samson Agonistes*. Paul Ricoeur, for example, constructs a dialectic of experiential time, based on Augustine's *Confessions,* and mimetic time, based on Aristotle's *Poetics*.[44] Augustine portrays the restless patterns of mind and memory in self-examination. Aristotle affirms the power of plot to give form to tragic suffering. *Samson Agonistes* is such an amalgam of memory and mimesis. Discord is found in Samson's obsessive remembering of his transgressions. Concord is implied in Milton's "disposition of the fable," but concord in this poem is unstable.

Can different temporalities co-exist without reconciliation, and can that co-existence be part of the poem's meaning? The poem provokes our need for what Frank Kermode calls fictions of concord: "We achieve our secular concords of past and present and future, modifying the past and allowing for the future without falsifying our own moment of crisis. We need, and provide, fictions of concord."[45] Characters also need concord. Manoa and the Chorus express certainty in the final scene of the drama as they interpret the unexpected but perhaps vindicating end of Samson's life. Temporal compression adds intensity to their questions and answers. The unity of time is a Greek convention, as Milton notes in the preface: "The circumscription of time wherein the whole Drama begins and ends, is according to ancient rule, and best example, within the space of twenty-four hours." Aristotle cites the "unity of time" to compare tragedy and epic.[46] Milton's use of time, however, is not simply conventional. It magnifies uncertainties in preparation for the catharsis Manoa describes in the final lines:

> His servants he with new acquist
> Of true experience from this great event
> With peace and consolation hath dismist,
> And calm of mind, all passion spent. (1755–8)

Peace, consolation, and dismissal add to our sense of the poem as liturgy.

Aristotle also discouraged staged violence. Gratuitous spectacles do not enhance thought and feeling in tragedy. The Messenger narrates the violent catastrophe in the Temple of Dagon. He testifies that Samson "stood, as one who pray'd/Or some great matter in his mind revolv'd" (1637–8). While this either/or construction heightens the poem's tensions, it also raises the subject of prayer. As Achinstein states, prayer for Dissenters "represented a creative type of speech that was unaccountable in the worldly sense of human institutions and governance. It could thus be a space for the expression of emancipatory hopes, and was politically dangerous."[47] In addition, as Targoff notes, Milton's idea of prayer emphasizes "the unpremeditated devotional voice, the 'freedom of speech' that each individual ought by right to possess."[48] *Samson Agonistes* explores the politics of prayer. In particular, prayer calls attention to the inspiration of the Spirit, a focal point for prayer in dissenting polemic. Samson's claim to freedom in the Temple of Dagon entails both speaking and praying, and devolves controversially on that enigmatic moment of the Spirit's action or, for some critics, absence, in the "rouzing motions" that change the course of events.

Samson's prayer is a pivotal moment. We can ask why Milton does not record Samson's prayer in Judges 16:28–30. Hideyuki Shitaka sees this omission as transformative: "Milton stresses that God approved Samson's prayer or perhaps his sincere efforts to pray."[49] Derek Wood observes that the prayer of Judges 16:28–30 "associates his lost eyes with his imminent revenge," unsettling Samson's relation to Milton's ethic of patient heroism.[50] Achinstein views Samson's prayer as resistance to fixed words. The prayer in Judges 16:28–30 might "have been too dangerous to write in 1670." As she argues, the "only way to represent the Spirit's instantiation is in an efflux of metaphor: crashing together are a blinding pastiche of biblical images for Spirit: Dragon, Eagle, Phoenix," a triptych the Chorus creates to avow that Samson was inspired.[51] The redemptive vision of *Paradise Regained* and violence of *Samson Agonistes* are neither ironically opposed nor mutually subsumed. Instead, they construct an "uncertain temporality after the promise and before the fulfillment – very much like the time of Milton's dissent."[52] Milton's poetic challenge was to represent prayer without recording it. Transcription would be a compromise with the Book of Common Prayer. Milton does not transcribe any prayers in his poems after the innocent morning orisons in Book 5 of *Paradise Lost*.

The prayer in Judges 16:28–30 is private, whether it is internal revival, vindictive desire, or verbal circumspection. The omission actually enhances the public context of Samson's prayer. Public prayer in Restoration England narrated history to harmonize collective memory with the return of monarchy. It was, in other words, a fiction of concord. Milton's poem rejects this facile harmony. Samson's moment of prayer is uncertain but for his reader's knowledge of Judges. This knowledge arguably folds readers into a covert moment of dissent, but the Messenger depicts a lone individual claiming a space of speech in a hostile assembly. Still more was at stake for Milton. While he would find the imposition of the prayer book objectionable, he would also find public prayer as a narrative of restored monarchy pernicious. Ambiguity in Samson's prayer challenges the state's use of public prayer to expel ambiguity from history.

Authorized narratives of history occur in scripted worship services composed for public celebrations after 1660. Likewise, the Philistine holiday in *Samson Agonistes* is a special day proclaimed to celebrate deliverance. In the early 1660s, the Restoration government proclaimed a special holiday to highlight the coincidence of the king's birthday, his coronation, and the Restoration itself. Samson obsesses over his "nativity" and his commission as a judge. The Chorus wonders if God "restored" Samson's sight (1503, 1528). These ruminations connect the poem to official liturgies of restoration.

The ecclesiastical calendar of early modern England was a site of conflict. Horton Davies coins the phrase "calendary conflict" to characterize tensions between Anglicans and Puritan reformers over issues such as Sabbath recreation or Christmas. Royal "state services" comprised one component of the Anglican calendar. These services inculcated "veneration for the King and thus social stability."[53] A prayer commemorating James I's deliverance from the Gowry plot implores God to leave the "slaughtered carckises" of conspirators as "a worthy spectacle of thy dreadfull judgements." This prayer may be "political propaganda under the guise of theological diction."[54] Nevertheless, it uncannily anticipates Samson's recollection of desecrated "carcases" exposed "to dogs and fowls a prey" (694) displayed "under change of times" (695), which recalls the punishment of the regicides in 1660.

The national day of deliverance was the fifth of November, the date of the Gunpowder Plot. A service for 5 November entered the Book of Common Prayer in 1605, and remained until 1859.[55] A second date was 30 January 1649, the date of the execution of Charles I. This event was a national sin demanding annual repentance after the Restoration. Preaching on 28 June 1660, a national feast day celebrating the Restoration, John Spencer equates the two dates: "[T]he Papists seem to have now a 30th of January to return us for 5th of November."[56] Spencer's juxtaposition of dates, however, creates an alternating pattern of national light and darkness: "As for the Nation, never was that more eclipsed and fuller of darkness, then, when (like the Moon) in most direct opposition against our Sun (our lawful Sovereign.)."[57] There is more cause for shame on 30 January than for pride on 5 November. Restoration propaganda illuminates the regicide, resolving the impasse of pride and shame in sermons.

As Achsah Guibbory observes, sermons show the "early modern English habit of drawing Israelite analogies, for this habit was deeply bound up with the conceptualizing of the English nation."[58] Some returned to the theme of temple building Guibbory identifies in the sermons of the English revolution. Edward Reynolds, for example, begins, "It is now at last, by Gods assistance, come forth, and sheweth how easily the Spirit and providence of God; can erect his Temple, and provide for the Interests of his Truth and Worship, though the instruments of it be utterly destitute of humane power."[59] Others made Charles II a type of King David, as in *Davids deliverance and thanksgiving* by Gilbert Sheldon, who preached this sermon before the king at Whitehall, and went on to direct the Savoy Conference.[60] These writers identify England and Israel by linking the rebuilt temple of the state Church to King David and Charles II.

A permanent date for celebration was needed. Charles II did not celebrate the anniversary of his accession because he marked the date on 30 January, the date of his father's death. In 1661 Parliament decreed 29 May, the king's birthday, to be the anniversary of the Restoration. Hence, on Sunday, 20 May of that year, ministers read out a Royal proclamation declaring the new holiday. The proclamation is not just a date in the calendar; it is an extended narrative of England's deliverance:

> that being the day which the Lord had made, and crowned with so many publick blessings, and signal deliverances, both of us and Our People, from all our late most deplorable Confusions, Divisions, Wars, Devestations and Oppressions: to the end it might be kept in perpetual remembrance in all ages to come, and that We would with all Our Subjects of this Our Realm, and the Dominions thereof, and Our Posterities after Us, might annually celebrate the perpetual memory thereof, by sacrificing their unfeigned hearty publick thanks thereon to Almighty God, with one heart and one voice in a most devout and Christian maner.[61]

The proclamation ordered a day of rest:

> And we strictly command all persons whatsoever, for the better observation of the said day, to abstain from all servile works and business on that day, and cheerfully and orderly to repair to the publick place of Gods Divine Worship, for the due performance of the Duties of that day, according to the good intentions of the said Act.[62]

Samson remarks that his rest is forced upon him:

> This day a solemn Feast the people hold
> To Dagon thir Sea-Idol, and forbid
> Laborious works, unwillingly this rest
> Thir Superstition yields me. (12–15)

Echoing proclamation rhetoric, Samson says "this day" rather than today. Taking leave of the Hebrew Chorus, he issues a counter-proclamation: "This day will be remarkable in my life/By some great act, or of my days the last" (1388–9). Likewise, his last words to the audience defy their proclamation: "Hitherto, Lords, what your commands impos'd/I have perform'd, as reason was, obeying" (1640–1).

Those who ignore the day are blind to the work of providence:

> And we declare, That such persons as shall be faulty herein, shall be esteemed by Us, contemners and infringers of Our Laws and Commands, and as prophane persons, shutting their eyes against such evident manifestations of mercy and goodness vouchsafed by Almighty God to us and Our People.

As Isaiah says, the profane "shut their eyes, lest they see with their eyes, and hear with their ears, and understand with their heart, and convert, and be healed" (6:10). Matthew applies this to those who do not perceive the messiah:

> And in them is fulfilled the prophecy of Esaias, which saith, By hearing ye shall hear, and shall not understand; and seeing ye shall see, and shall not perceive: For this people's heart is waxed gross, and their ears are dull of hearing, and their eyes they have closed; lest at any time they should see with their eyes, and hear with their ears, and should understand with their heart, and should be converted, and I should heal them. (13:14–15)

Milton reverses this attribution of blindness, as the Chorus portrays a revelling Philistine crowd "with blindness internal struck" (1686).

A formal liturgy for 29 May accompanied the proclamation. Bishop Matthew Wren, its likely author, based it on the form used for the Gunpowder anniversary.[63] Psalm 95, the "Venite," is a regular feature of services of sung morning prayer: "O come, let us sing unto the Lord; let us heartily rejoice in the strength of our salvation. Let us come before his presence with thanksgiving, and show ourselves glad in him with psalms. For the Lord is a great God, and a great King above all gods."

Psalm 95 has no images of retribution. It sees God as a "King above all gods" without reference to David. The special liturgy incorporates texts that vindicate the King through the destruction of his enemies into the text:

> For he hath found David his servant: with his holy oyl hath he anointed him. (Psal. 89.21) His hand hath held him fast: and his arm hath strengthened him. The enemy hath not been able to do him violence: the son of wickedness hath not hurt him. (Psal. 89.22) He hath smitten down his foes before his face: and plagued them that hated him.[64]

Anointing, strength, and violence are prominent in the Samson narrative. The theme of retributive justice continues in a sequence of Psalm texts: Psalm 20:8: "They are brought down and fallen; but we are risen and stand upright"; Psalm 21:8: "All thine enemies shall feel thy hand"; Psalm 118:7: "I shall see my desire upon my enemies." The selection also includes Psalm 85, which announces a golden age through the reunion of righteousness, peace, mercy, and truth, the four daughters of God.

The Old Testament lesson is 2 Samuel 19, David's return to Jerusalem after Absalom's rebellion. In this chapter, David pardons Shimei, viewed as a type of blasphemer, for cursing him. The story parallels Charles's pardoning of enemies on his return. The Epistle includes Romans 13:1 – "Let every soul be subject unto the higher powers" – and the Gospel includes Matthew 22:21, with its distinction between God and Caesar. The texts inculcate subjection.

Set prayers intersperse the texts, emphasizing the harmonized temporality of Charles's nativity and his return:

> And we are now here gathered together before heaven, and before thee, to make a thankful commemoration of the time and of the day, wherein this thy unspeakable goodness was poured out upon us.[65]
>
> O God, who didst this day first bring into the World, and since that didst this Day also restore to us, and to his own just and undoubted Rights, our most gracious Soveraign Lord thy Servant King CHARLES.[66]

The gathering of the community parodies the Eucharist, a memorial of Christ's sacrifice. Despite this hyperbole, a liturgy proclaiming the king's birthday as a "day the Lord hast made" was predictable to Londoners who recalled coronation or birthday liturgies long past. Official narratives could induce familiarity as well as awe.

Given Milton's attitude to such proclamations, it is significant that Samson's death does not produce a new holiday. After Samson's death,

Manoa does not proclaim a new anniversary; instead, he predicts that "Virgins also shall on feastful days/Visit his Tomb with flowers" (1741–2). Thus, an existing calendar of "feastful days" takes precedence, though celebrants may remember Samson's actions in "copious Legend, or sweet Lyric Song" (1737). Samson, in contrast, is obsessed with his nativity:

> O wherefore was my birth from Heaven foretold
> Twice by an Angel, who at last in sight
> Of both my Parents all in flames ascended
> From off the Altar, where an Off'ring burn'd,
> As in a fiery column charioting
> His Godlike presence, and from some great act
> Or benefit reveal'd to Abraham's race?
> Why was my breeding order'd and prescrib'd
> As of a person separate to God,
> Design'd for great exploits; if I must die
> Betray'd Captiv'd, and both my Eyes put out,
> Made of my enemies the scorn and gaze. (23–34)

Samson's naive notion of a scripted life stirred his hubris, leading to his downfall. *Samson Agonistes* begins as a fiction of discord expressed as alienation and exile. The Coronation liturgy offers a "fiction of concord." Where the liturgy prints apt lessons and psalms, *Samson Agonistes* imagines the Bible as oral and fragmented. This shows Milton's solidarity with Dissenters who resisted the Book of Common Prayer after 1660. When the new regime established 29 May as a permanent holiday, John Bunyan was beginning his long imprisonment and preparing to write *I Will Pray With the Spirit,* his attack on the Book of Common Prayer, and *Grace Abounding to the Chief of Sinners,* his spiritual autobiography. *Samson Agonistes* is about a prisoner who works through his own autobiography obsessively. That solidarity tends to focus synchronically on the emblematic image of Samson standing "as one who pray'd." This prayer is internal, momentary, and wordless to the public, even if it points to Samson's explicit prayer for revenge in Judges. Milton was not solving history so much as challenging its reduction.

The "circumscription of time" invests the whole of the past in a single day. Synchronic time is the epitome of diachronic time. Similarly, liturgy can express the whole of redemptive history in an hour. For Anglicans and Royalists, that pattern passes through the trauma of the regicide and the abolition of the prayer book to the Restoration, framed in the Davidic narrative of monarchy. For Dissenters, the pattern repeats the cycle of apostasy in the Judges narrative, with the hope that the creating light of Genesis will reappear as the light of Christ, illuminating his saints and his biblical precursors. The temporality of Judges corresponds to the structure of the psalms of lamentation. The narrative frame of Judges repeats a cycle in which the children of Israel fall into apostasy, remember God and cry out to him, and are delivered until the cycle begins again with a new generation. The psalms of lamentation distill this broader temporality into the voice of a suffering individual whose time is too short to bear much repetition. These psalms do not end where they begin. They typically present a turn or transformation from lamentation to praise analogous to the turn from apostasy to deliverance in history. As Brueggemann remarks, this "turn is a move beyond remembering. But it could not be done without the painful part of remembering."[67] Milton wrote *Samson Agonistes* to undertake the painful part of remembering both for himself and his nation. The poem is not simply a partisan rejection of the narrative of the royal liturgy; instead, the turning structure of the lament psalm revalues tragic mimesis biblically and is crucial to seeing this liturgical poem as an extended exercise in religious meditation and prayer.

Chapter Five

John Bunyan: The Nameless Terrible Instrument

There was also an instrument invented by *Emanuel*, that was to throw stones from the Castle of *Mansoul*, out at *Mouth-gate*; an instrument that could not be resisted, nor that would miss of execution; wherefore for the wonderful exploits that it did when used, it went without a name.

John Bunyan, *The Holy War* (1682)

From his early anti-Quaker writings in the 1650s to *Grace Abounding*, his spiritual autobiography, Bunyan defined the Dissenting experience as resistance to error and blasphemy filtered through a cultural din of invective and hostility towards Dissenters. His writings model and teach the discernment of right prayers and true voices. He sustained his polemic against the prayer book in his allegorical fictions through a poetics of discretion and circumspection addressed primarily to Dissenters. The "nameless terrible instrument" illustrates the role of uncertainty and enigma in his poetics. Just as Milton's Samson is both riddler and warrior, this instrument is both visible spiritual weapon and hidden hermeneutic crux. In my closing analysis of *The Holy War*, I will argue that it is an emblem of the Lord's Prayer; this solution should not, however, diminish part of the emblem's meaning, which is uncertainty itself.

i. Bunyan's Restoration Context

John Bunyan (1628–88) was born in the town of Elstow near Bedford. When Milton published *Areopagitica* in 1644, Bunyan was sixteen years old and serving in a garrison of the Parliamentary Army at Newport Pagnell ten miles west of Bedford. In 1649 he married his first wife. Her name is unknown: "[T]his woman and I, though we came together as poor as poor might be, (not having so much as a Dish or Spoon betwixt us both) yet this she had for her part, *The Plain Mans Path-way to Heaven,* and *The Practice of Piety*, which her Father had left her when he died" (*GA* 9). His father was a brazier; he became a tinker. The family grew to include four children, including Mary, who was blind. They moved to Bedford and joined an independent congregation through the mentorship of its pastor, John Gifford. Bunyan became pastor in 1672 on his release from prison. The appointment reflects Bunyan's godly character and gift for preaching.

His life changed dramatically in 1660 when the Restoration regime banned religious meetings outside of the Church of England. Bunyan would not voluntarily abandon his pastoral responsibilities as the government required, and suffered trial and imprisonment. At his trial, Justice Kelynge took aim at tinkering, Bunyan's humble trade, to dismiss his claim to be a minister: "[A]s every man hath received a trade, so let him follow it, as thou hast done, let him follow his tinkering. And so other men their trades. And the divine his calling" (*GA* 109). Tinkers should not meddle in things divine, yet Bunyan had far more knowledge of the Bible than his judges imagined. He and Kelynge debated 1 Peter 4:10: "As every man hath received the gift, even so minister the same one to another, as good stewards of the manifold grace of God." Bunyan rejected Kelynge's restriction of "calling" to tinkering: "[T]he Holy Ghost doth not so much in this place exhort to civil callings, as to the exercising of those gifts that we have received from God. I would have gone on, but he would not give me leave" (*GA* 110). Bunyan was anxious for the needs of his family as he went to prison, but also confident in his vocation.

The Book of Common Prayer was a main issue at his trial. Consequently, his treatise on prayer written from prison, *I Will Pray with the Spirit*, evolved from the exchanges. Bunyan attacks "stinted prayers" or set forms and makes the Lord's Prayer a flashpoint for religious hypocrisy in one of the most blistering polemical works of the time. His title quotes 1 Corinthians 14:15, pitting Paul's familiar precept against the Book of Common Prayer. To appreciate the uncompromising nature of this polemical treatise, we can examine the political manoeuvring around the return of the prayer book in 1660.

The return of monarchy in 1660 meant the return of the Church of England and the Book of Common Prayer. These events did not bring the immediate expulsion of ministers who could not conform to the state church. There was time for compromise. Charles II issued the Declaration of Breda before returning from the continent to Dover. He offered toleration: "And because the passion and uncharitableness of the times have produced several opinions in religion, by which men are engaged in parties and animosities against each other, which, when they shall hereafter unite in a freedom of conversation, will be composed and better understood, we do declare a liberty to tender consciences."[1] A bill of toleration was one option; however, as J.P. Kenyon remarks, "Charles II's final undertaking in the Declaration of Breda, that he would give his assent to any legislation that offered a measure of religious toleration, was never implemented, because no such legislation was ever presented."[2] Instead, the Convention Parliament that negotiated the king's return called a national conference to settle religious differences. The Savoy Conference, named for its location in London, met from 15 April to 24 July 1661 under the direction of Gilbert Sheldon, bishop of London.

Prior events had hardened attitudes. In January 1661, Thomas Venner led a violent uprising of Fifth Monarchists in London. Fifth Monarchists expected Christ's kingdom to appear based on their reading of the four kingdoms portrayed in Daniel 2. The uprising failed and Venner was executed on 19 January. Knoppers shows that the "uprising provided the government with an opportunity to link political subversion with religious enthusiasm."[3] Compromise vanished. As Kenyon remarks, the "elections of March and April 1661 returned a parliament opposed to any compromise. One of their first Acts sent the bishops back to the House of Lords, and they then busied themselves with a stringent Uniformity bill."[4] Events were moving towards the suppression of dissent and the production of a revised prayer book. The Act of Uniformity, passed on 19 May 1662, required all ministers to perform the prayers, rites, and sacraments prescribed in the Book of Common Prayer. Parliament set a deadline of 24 August 1662 for ministers to swear to use the prayer book.[5] This date, called "Black Bartholomew's Day," saw the ejection of 936 nonconforming ministers who refused.[6]

The possibility of compromise at the Savoy Conference was never great, but one leading Puritan tried. Richard Baxter (1615–91) was a Presbyterian minister opposed to separation from the national church. He supported the return of monarchy, and accepted an appointment as a chaplain to the king on 25 June 1660.[7] Kathleen Lynch observes, "Baxter's life mission was to reconstitute the established church on more inclusive (the contemporary code was comprehensive) grounds."[8] Nuttall describes Baxter's frustration with the Savoy Conference: three months of "hopefulness and sudden prominence were to be followed by two years of increasing frustration, and then by nearly thirty more of inactivity and disgrace. He never preached again before the King."[9] He left the re-established church in 1662 before Black Bartholomew's Day.

Baxter produced his *Reformed Liturgy* to overcome the differences. Biblicism is a main feature of his liturgy: "The safest way of composing a stinted Liturgie, is to take it all, or as much as may be, for words as well as matter out of the Holy Scriptures."[10] Importantly, he thought of the Lord's Prayer as a set form, while professing that he never used any form of prayer "since I was 17 or 18 years of age; except the Lord's Prayer, which I use most Lord's Days once."[11] A liturgy comprised of scriptural texts could, Baxter hoped, unite all parties. He wrote his liturgy in two weeks, but shaped its principles before the Restoration. It was published as *A Petition for Peace with the Reformation of the Liturgy* (1661). As Keeble notes, Baxter faced instant adversity: "During the period of reaction that followed the Restoration, 'party' was to dominate men's thinking in England to a cruel degree. All opinions were in danger of being simplified that they might be categorized and judged. Sympathy and charity barely survived in an intellectual climate which knew no mean between vituperation and adulation."[12] The *Petition for Peace* laments these hostilities: "one party calling the other Factious, Schismaticall, Singular, and Disobedient, the other calling them Antichristian, Proud, Tyrannical, Superstitious, Persecutors and Formalists."[13] He asks ministers to "forbear one another in love, instead of hating, reviling and persecuting one another."[14] Behind this appeal we hear the din of invective against and also among sects.

Anglican leaders who suffered during the Interregnum were ready to push back. John Gauden published *Considerations Touching the Liturgy of the Church of England, In Reference to His Majesties late Gracious Declaration, and in order to an Happy Union in Church and State* (1661). Gauden dilutes the toleration offered in the *Declaration of Breda*, calling it a "temporary condescension."[15] He mentions it to highlight other options: punishment and persecution. He speaks of the "Majesty" of God to link monarchy with divinity. He uses disease and deformity to portray prayer book and king as good medicines. Decent liturgy preserves "the sanctity and solemnity of holy Duties from the contagion and deformity of private Ministers frequent infirmities."[16] Disorder in worship has, "like a scab or leprosie, prevailed over the common sort of people in England."[17] He stirs doubt in Nonconformists about inspiration, a common tactic. Extemporaneous prayer is utter nonsense: "[T]hey are so dubious between wind and water, Sense and Non-sense, Faction and Sedition, Boldness and Blasphemy, that it makes sober Christians, who have a due reverence of the Divine Majesty, dread to hear them."[18] Bunyan would learn to see through this confusion.

To summarize, we see three reasons for Bunyan's uncompromising attitude to set forms. First, unlike Baxter, Bunyan was in no position to influence national debate. Second, he experienced arrest, trial, and prison very soon after the Restoration, refusing compromise as conformity. Third, he felt some of Gauden's disparaging views through the judges at his trial. This stiffened his resolve to defend the godly from slander and invective and strengthen them in their faith.

ii. Attacking the Prayer Book: *I Will Pray with the Spirit*

Bunyan's Baptist congregation met freely in Bedford for most of 1660. As Richard Greaves records, by November 1660, "Bunyan and his pastoral colleagues had no compelling reason to anticipate severe punishment if they continued to preach. Moreover, the Bedford congregation finally accepted the Restoration," as shown in their willingness to mark 12 November as a day of prayer for the government.[19] Bunyan agreed to preach at a prayer meeting at Lower Samsell knowing that Francis Wingate, a local Justice of the Peace, would issue a warrant for his arrest if he appeared. Bunyan kept his commitment. Constables arrested him and took him to Harlington Manor, twenty-two miles south of Bedford, where he faced questioning by a rather close-knit group: Wingate himself, William Lindale, Wingate's wife's stepfather and vicar of Harlington, and William Foster, Wingate's brother-in-law and a Bedford attorney.[20] All three saw Bunyan as seditious. Remanded in custody in Bedford, Bunyan later faced five judges at the quarter sessions in January 1661.

The Act of Uniformity appeared in May 1662. In 1660 the government used old laws to stifle preachers. An act passed in 1593 under Elizabeth I and renewed under Charles I gave grounds for Bunyan's arrest. *An Act to retain the Queen's subjects in obedience* was passed for "the preventing and avoiding of such great inconveniences and perils as might happen and grow by the wicked and dangerous practices of seditious sectaries and disloyal persons."[21] Bunyan could have avoided prison since law prescribed imprisonment of offenders "until they shall conform and yield themselves to come to some church, chapel or usual place of common prayer and hear divine service."[22] Michael Mullett remarks that Wingate "left the outcome of the situation entirely within [Bunyan's] hands: by refusing the conditions for bail, he *chose* to go to prison."[23] Impatient with Bunyan's resolve, Wingate advised Bunyan to look to his family, but the choice was not simple. As a congregational leader, he had to be an example to his followers, including new converts.

Bunyan's next interview with Dr William Lindale was more heated. As Greaves relates, Bunyan and Lindale "traded biblical verses as if they were weapons." Bunyan's scriptural texts asserted his vocation while suggesting that Lindale typified "the priests and Pharisees whose hands were stained with Christ's blood." This exchange marks "a transition from the relatively limited question of Bunyan's right to preach" to the "much broader insistence of each disputant that the other's church was false."[24] The transition from narrow legal manoeuvring to broad Reformation polemic shows Bunyan's determination to lead from prison:

> I was not at all daunted, but rather glad, and saw evidently that the Lord had heard me, for before I went down to the justice, I begged of God, that if I might do more good by being at liberty than in prison, that then I might be set at liberty: But if not, his will be done; for I was not altogether without hopes, but that my imprisonment might be an awakening to the Saints in the country, therefore I could not tell well which to chuse. Only I in that manner did commit the thing to God. And verily at my return, I did meet my God sweetly in the prison again, comforting of me and satisfying of me that it was his will and mind that I should be there.[25]

The subject of prayer was a focal point. Lindale calls extemporaneous prayer a "pretence" for extortion and fraud.

> LIND. Aye, saith he, and you are one of those scribes and pharisees: for you, with a pretence, make long prayers to devour widows' houses.
> BUN. I answered, that if he had got no more by preaching and praying than I had done, he would not be so rich as now he was. But that scripture coming into my mind, Answer not a fool according to his folly, I was as sparing of my speech as I could, without prejudice to truth. (*GA* 101)

The Holy Spirit brought a text to his remembrance at his trial. Bunyan had an answer but restrained himself. He discloses his reasons to his reader. When brought before "magistrates, and powers" the "Holy Ghost shall teach you in the same hour what ye ought to say" (Luke 12:11–12). Bunyan chose not to bring wisdom to fools. His intended audience is his community, not the court. This bi-level exposure of natural response and prevenient grace would shape the complex narrative frames in his later allegories.

Inevitably, Bunyan's trial at the quarter sessions of January 1661 became a debate over conformity. The indictment states that he "devilishly and perniciously abstained from coming to church to hear divine service, and is a common upholder of several unlawful meetings and conventicles." Bunyan answered that he was, in fact, a "common frequenter of the church of God" (*GA* 106). "Church of God" meant Bunyan's congregation, not the state church. Bunyan's main adversary was Kelynge, who later helped to frame the Act of Uniformity. When another judge asked him if he wrote down prayers and read them to his congregation, Bunyan insisted it is "none of our practice." The judge was hoping to uncover hypocrisy. Kelynge pushed the point, arguing that it is "lawful to use the Common Prayer" because Christ taught his disciples to pray the Lord's Prayer, "and therefore prayers made by men, and read over, are good to teach, and help men to pray." Again, Bunyan confides only in his readers:

> While he was speaking these words, God brought that word into my mind, in the eighth of the Romans, at the 26th verse. I say, God brought it, for I thought not on it before: but as he was speaking, it came so fresh into my mind, and was set so evidently before me, as if the Scripture had said, Take me, take me. (*GA* 107)

Bunyan hears scripture inwardly during the question. He tells Kelynge that the Spirit, not the book, "helpeth our infirmities." He reports his trial as Spirit-filled and Spirit-led, inspiring speech that validates his theory of prayer.

Prayer was central to Bunyan's polemical mission. *I Will Pray with the Spirit, or A Discourse Touching Prayer* appeared in 1662 and with some revisions in 1663. Keeble calls the treatise "an openly oppositional text" that "contrasts the sincerity of true spirituality with the hollow formalism of liturgies and prescribed rites."[26] This contrast typifies Bunyan's determination to "dissent from, and stand against, prevailing ideology."[27]

I Will Pray with the Spirit has the shape of a sermon. Part I – "What Prayer Is" – defines prayer in seven elements. Bunyan calls prayer an "Ordinance of God," adopting the legal diction of state control. It is the "means by which the soul, though empty, is filled" (*MW* 2: 235). It is also the "affectionate pouring out of the heart or soul to God" (*MW* 2: 235) with prayers bubbling "out of the heart when it is over-pressed with grief and bitterness, as blood is forced out of the flesh"; the soul in prayer "will spend itself to nothing, as it were, rather than go without that good desired, even communion with Christ" (*MW* 2: 239). Lori Branch analyzes the diction of commerce in the treatise. Emotion becomes a "currency in which all true prayer traded"; it merges with the mercantile discourses of value that Bunyan uses for spirituality.[28] A "feeling of misery" which forces words is true substance in prayer."[29] Fervency certifies the value of words expressed from within rather than prescribed from without.

The prayerful soul finds the world vain: "[T]he Soul that thus prayeth indeed, sees an emptiness in all things *under heaven*; That in *God* alone there is rest and satisfaction for the Soul" (*MW* 2: 240). "Right *Prayer* sees nothing substantial, or worth the looking after, but *God*" (*MW* 2: 241). It carries a "mighty vehemency in it," unlike the prayer book: many "are very great strangers to a sincere, sensible, and affectionate pouring out their hearts or souls to God; but even content themselves with a little lip-labour, & bodily exercise, mumbling over a few imaginary Prayers" (*MW* 2: 239). Bunyan rejects the charge of "imaginings" brought against Puritans by Andrewes and Taylor.

The individual comes to God as a member of Christ "so that God looks on that man as part of Christ, part of his Body, flesh and bones, united to him by election, conversion, illumination"; moreover, "by vertue of this union, also, is the holy Spirit, conveyed in to him" (*MW* 2: 242). This body implies the Church: "For God, and Christ, and his People, are so linked together, that if the Good of one be prayed for, to wit, the Church, the glory of God, and advancement of Christ must needs be included" (*MW* 2: 244). Bunyan's church is not the state church. There is no prior "we" as there is for Andrewes and Taylor. Bunyan highlights the singular individual in his title: *I Will Pray with the Spirit*. His church is a godly community of selves gathered within a "crooked and perverse Nation."

Part II of the treatise – What it is to pray with the Spirit – attacks the Book of Common Prayer. Without the Spirit, Bunyan argues, "though we had a thousand Common-Prayer-Books, yet we know not what we should pray for as we ought" (248). Common Prayer is "none of God's Ordinances; but a thing since the Scriptures were written, patched together, one piece at a time, and another at another; a meer human invention and institution" which God forbids (*MW* 2: 249). The prayer book is an instrument of hypocrisy because it both compels and allows the ungodly to pray through it. In reality, when "the Spirit gets into the heart then there is Prayer indeed, and not till then" (*MW* 2: 257). Paradoxically, the ungodly "are counted the only honest men, and all because, with their blasphemous throats and hypocritical hearts, they will come to Church and say, *Our Father*" while conscientious Dissenters "must be looked upon to be the only Enemies of God and the Nation" (*MW* 2: 253).

Parts II and III treat conformity as a temptation. Paul, Bunyan argues, produced no prayer book because we "know not what we should pray for as we ought; but the Spirit it self maketh intercession for us, with groaning which cannot be uttered. And he that searcheth the heart, knoweth the meaning of the Spirit, because he maketh intercession for the Saints according to the will of God" (*MW* 2: 246). Bunyan underscores not knowing throughout Part II: "Consider the person speaking even Paul, and in his person all the Apostles. We Apostles, we extraordinary Officers, the wise Master-Builders, that have some of us been caught up into *Paradise,* I Cor. 3. 10. 2 Cor. 12. 4 We know not what we should pray for" (*MW* 2: 246). He notes Paul's account of "a man who was caught up into Paradise, and hears unspeakable words which it is not lawful for a man to utter. Of such a one will I glory, yet of myself I will not glory, but in mine infirmities" (2 Cor. 12:2–5). The word "infirmities" echoes Romans 8:26, "the Spirit helpeth our infirmities" (Romans 8:26). Through Paul, Bunyan distinguishes true prayer from private ecstasies on the one hand and set forms on the other. Hence, in Part III, Bunyan emphasizes collective edification through the use of the "Mother tongue," protecting himself from the imputation of ecstatic enthusiasm.

Bunyan admits his own struggles in prayer: "For, as for my heart, when I go to pray, I find it so loth to go to God, and when it is with him, so loth to stay with him, that many times I am forced in my Prayers; first, to beg of God that he would take mine heart, and set it on himself in Christ, and when it is there, that he would keep it there" (*MW* 2: 256–7). He adds: "[M]any times I know not what to pray for, I am so blind, nor how to pray, I am so ignorant; onely (blessed be Grace) the Spirit helps our infirmities" (*MW* 2: 257). Conti sees this as an illustration of how autobiographical reflection emerges from polemic in a writer's confession of faith.[30] In this instance, the confession reveals dry moments in Bunyan's prayer life, while professing trust in God, Christ, and the Holy Spirit. I suggest that the passage links pastoral care to personal confession. He addresses his followers, assuring them that they are not alone in their struggles. The confession is part of the dual purpose of polemic: it undertakes to strengthen Bunyan's community through empathy, lest he seem a spiritual superman.

Loss of language places the soul in God's sight: "Ah sweet soul! It is not thy word, that God so much regards, as that he will not mind thee, except thou comest before him with some eloquent Oration. His eye is on the broken-ness of thine heart" (*MW* 2: 267). Eloquence makes the Book of Common Prayer "Antichristian": it "hath nothing but Tradition of men, and the strength of Persecution to uphold, or plead for it" (*MW* 2: 285). He situates his reader in the field of vision of a dominant, persecuting culture. The godly individual is "looked upon as factious, seditious, erroneous, heretical; a disparagement to the Church, as seducer of people" (284). Concurrently, the godly soul is in the sight of God who affirms authentic prayer. As with Milton's Abdiel, this dual perspective typifies dissenting polemic, which serves to oppose the persecutor and commend the godly.

iii. Prayer, Blasphemy, and Discretion in *Grace Abounding* and *Pilgrim's Progress*, Part One

Blasphemy is a potent attack word in *I Will Pray with the Spirit*. In *Grace Abounding* Bunyan turns the word inward. In *I Will Pray with the Spirit*, the rebuke of false prayer as blasphemy is categorical. In *Grace Abounding*, Bunyan fears that he might commit blasphemy. On one occasion, Bunyan meditates on Luke 21:32, when Christ says to Peter, "Simon, Simon, behold, Satan hath desired to have you." Bunyan hears the texts "sounding and ratling in mine ears." Next, a "very great storm" came "down upon me." Eventually, "all my comfort was taken from me, then darkness seized upon me; after which whole flouds of Blasphemies, both against God, Christ, and the Scriptures, was poured out upon my spirit, to my confusion and astonishment" (*GA* 29). The power of blasphemy raises doubts about "whether there were in truth a God or Christ, or no? and whether the holy Scriptures were not rather a Fable and cunning Story, then the holy and pure Word of God?" (*GA* 29). These questions, along with others he would "dare not utter, neither by word nor pen," carry him away "as with a mighty whirlwind" (*GA* 30). On one level, natural tempests convey the chaotic power of blasphemy. On another, blasphemy mimics extemporaneous prayer. In prayer, the Spirit inspires the godly person. In blasphemy, a more demonic spirit supplants the Spirit with a "mighty whirlwind." Bunyan did not write down the prayers he spoke in religious meetings. Blasphemy also produces thoughts he dared not record by "word nor pen." Blasphemy can be a demonic parody of prayer in its rush of words and sounds.

Bunyan sees blasphemy as "a sin of the flesh, waged against the spirit," as Vera Camden suggests.[31] It is also a problem of language, since "it was through language that men and women knew their consciences, and their God."[32] *Grace Abounding* reflects a nation of blasphemers and prophets. The *Blasphemy Act* of 1650, for example, targeted the supposed excesses of Ranters. The Rump Parliament claimed a certain power to discern blasphemy, but was really grasping for respectability after the regicide. As Camden notes, "Bunyan found himself in the middle of the conflict of state and sect, given his imprisonment for sedition on the one hand, and his distrust of Ranters and Quakers on the other."[33] Bunyan works through this conflict by differentiating himself from radical groups he opposed while maintaining his integrity as a Dissenter.

Like Milton, Bunyan juxtaposes zeal and blasphemy. Religious dissemblers are "hot" for the form but not for its power. "Hot" suggests false zeal. In *Grace Abounding*, however, he questions his own zeal. He imagines God mocking his efforts to pray, or that Satan is tempting him: "Then hath the Tempter come unto me also with such discouragements as these: You are very hot for mercy, but I will cool you; this frame shall not last always; many have been hot as you for a spirit, but I have quenched their Zeal" (*GA* 32). If the two voices in this passage are imaginary, they are also distinct. Allegory would become Bunyan's tool for distinguishing true and false voices. Discretion is the first allegorical figure Christian meets at the Palace Beautiful in *Pilgrim's Progress*, part one. She questions him before he meets her family: Prudence, Piety, and Charity. The episode shows the discretion needed to safeguard an illegal meeting.

Christian has not yet learned discretion. When he passes through the Valley of the Shadow of Death, one "of the wicked ones got behind him and stept up softly to him, and whisperingly suggested many grievous blasphemies to him, which he verily thought had proceeded from his own mind." He "had not the *discretion* neither to stop his ears, nor to know from whence those blasphemies came" (*PP 1*, 65, emphasis mine). The episode allegorizes the uncertainty Bunyan confessed in *Grace Abounding* when his mind seemed to generate blasphemies. The reader sees this event through the narrator who discerns the difference.

If zeal is a sacred flame and blasphemy a vicious flood, then discretion is the faculty that distinguishes them. If prayer is harmonic, volitional, and sincere, blasphemy is dissonant, volatile, and irrepressible; in fact, blasphemy imitates the "inexpressible groanings" of prayer in the spirit. Blasphemies were "poured out upon my spirit" (*GA* 29). Recalling Fenton's term, we can think of blasphemy as an extreme case of anti-prayer. "Poured out" clearly echoes the story of Pentecost, when the Spirit is poured out on the early church in the Book of Acts. Bunyan surely grasped the symmetry of prayer and blasphemy he was constructing when he wrote that sentence. Discretion is modelled in allegory. In *The Holy War*, for example, when the Diabolonians lay siege to Mansoul, "there was nothing heard in the camp of Diabolus but horrible rage and blasphemy; but in the town good words, prayer, and singing of psalms." This contrast is an allegory of discretion. While Diabolonians and Mansoulians mingle in earlier parts of *The Holy War*, and prayer and blasphemy interpenetrate in *Grace Abounding*, Bunyan's allegories instill discretion in readers.

In *Grace Abounding* Bunyan is obsessed with the unpardonable sin: "But he that shall blaspheme against the Holy Ghost hath never forgiveness, but is in danger of eternal damnation" (Mark 3:29). This spontaneous – indeed extemporaneous – torrent of words was terrifying because Bunyan did not really know where it came from or if he had crossed a line. He fears this verbal torrent "might be that sin unpardonable."[34] Many Puritans feared this was the otherwise unnamed and unknowable and possibly unforgiveable sin against the Holy Spirit. As Baird Tipson remarks, the early Christian Church identified the sin against the Holy Spirit "as an extreme form of blasphemy, the ultimately sacrilegious act." In early modern Protestantism, however, "discussions of the sin ranged beyond such literal explanations. In a development that would eventually affect Protestant England, the scope of the sin against the Holy Spirit expanded enormously."[35] This expansion made the sin uncertain and indefinite. As Stachniewksi observes, this sin's "vagueness made it a vortex of terror to those whose minds had been drawn to the question of whether they were elect or reprobate" (*GA*, n. 31, 238). Vagueness produces crisis. Crisis demands resolution.

Fear of blasphemy drives Bunyan's prayers: "I thought I was as with a Tempest driven away from God, for always when I cried to God for mercy, this would come in, 'tis too late" (*GA* 45). Despair gives way to another elemental image when a sudden rushing wind, another metaphor for the Spirit, pours through a window and assures him of his justification:

> Once as I was walking to and fro in a good mans Shop, bemoaning to my self in my sad and doleful state, afflicting my self with self abhorrence for this wicked and ungodly thought; lamenting also this hard hap of mine, for that I should commit so great a sin, greatly fearing I should not be pardoned; praying also in my heart, That if this sin of mine did differ from that against the Holy Ghost, the Lord would shew it me: and being nor ready to sink with fear, suddenly there was as if there had rushed in at the Window, the noise of Wind upon me, but very pleasant as if I had heard a voice speaking, *Didst ever refuse to be justified by the Blood of Christ?* And withal, my whole life of profession past, was in a moment opened to me, wherein I was made to see, that designedly I had not; so my heart answered groaningly No. (*GA* 48)

Despair may be the underlying unpardonable sin and blasphemy merely a symptom. Camden suggests, "Bunyan's greatest blasphemy and the blasphemy which Luther most roundly condemns is the desperation of one who clings to his despair despite all assurances to the contrary of grace and forgiveness."[36] Bunyan's "No" in this passage means he has not refused grace. Importantly, the anecdote simulates prayer: it begins as the inward bemoaning of his condition, and ends "groaningly" before the power of the Word overcomes him. Throughout Bunyan is "praying also in my heart" to understand the unpardonable sin.

The idea of this sin led some strict Calvinists to distinguish the godly from reprobates: "[T]he sin against the Holy Ghost became a means whereby those people who had appeared to be elect were revealed as reprobate," Tipson observes. If "their faith were false they would eventually slip into final apostasy and maliciously blaspheme the Spirit."[37] Bunyan accepted election and reprobation as realities that put a sharp edge on human existence. The elect, however, can suffer the confusion of prayer and blasphemy only to find that prayer prevails. He testifies candidly to this process to reassure his community of readers.

iv. Bunyan and the Quakers

John Coffey records that "more than 4000 Quakers and Baptists were arrested and imprisoned in the space of a few weeks"[38] in 1660. Eventually, 400 Quakers died in prison and 15,000 endured arrest and prosecution.[39] Bunyan was hostile to the Quakers before the Restoration. His first polemical writings in the 1650s attacked the Quaker writer Edward Burrough. Tensions between sects brings our story full circle. Andrewes, we recall, disliked Calvinism, seeing predestination as presumption; conversely, Bunyan disliked Quakers, seeing their anti-Calvinism as presumptuous. The inner light is the main Quaker doctrine. As Hilary Hinds describes it, this light "unsettles the Calvinist binary of elect and reprobate and identifies a third class – those who can or will turn to the light."[40] All people could come to the light, which Quakers identified as Christ within. The Bible is a fountain of light, but is subordinate to the light within. Bunyan was appalled. Christ as inner light in the present could devalue Christ as redeemer in historical time, discounting atonement and a final judgment at the end of time.[41]

Quakers endured attacks on many fronts. Baxter was a harsh critic. Quakers were known to disrupt services in churches, which they called "steeple houses." Some invaded Baxter's church while he was away sick and tried to suborn the service into a disputation with the curate who refused. In *The Quaker's Catechism* (1657), Baxter charges Quakers with "horrible pride" in their claim to immediate revelation; moreover, they are guilty of presumption: "If you presume that you are so much more beloved of God than he, that God will reveal that to you without seeking and study which upon the greatest diligence he will not reveal to him, what can this conceit proceed from but pride?"[42] Baxter's attack, like Bunyan's, reflects the threatening success of Quakerism. As T.L. Underwood notes, the movement began in 1652 and by 1660 had gained some 40,000 members, in a nation of five million people (*MW* 1: xvii). Moreover, by 1660 "anti-Quaker tracts averaged about twenty per year and nearly all of their authors received replies from Quakers" (xxi). These polemical responses also indicate alarm at Quaker success.

A challenge in studying Quaker prayers is the absence of printed records. Thomas Corns notes that only one printed sermon survives from 1652–70: "[C]ommitment to impromptu composition and hostility to the printed sermon militated strongly against the survival of all such speech acts."[43] Hugh Barbour and Arthur O. Roberts observe that Quakers "preached as they felt they were led by the Spirit." Hence, Quaker writings such as proclamations or warnings may reveal qualities of their sermons, but not their prayers.[44] As Richard Bauman states, we lack "the *texts* of prayers, sermons, and other religious utterances. Quaker religious speaking was all spontaneous," and there were "principled reasons for not taking down those utterances in writing."[45] In keeping with the Quaker belief "concerning inward worship through attendance on the Light within, the prayerful expressions of individual Quakers were inward and silent."[46] An exception, Bauman notes, is the prayer of "spiritual struggle," uttered in sighs and groans. A Quaker worship meeting could consist of long silences interspersed with words or expressive sounds. Silence is not the absence of sound; it is a means to the "direct personal experience of God within oneself"[47]

Biased evidence comes from their adversaries. In *A Brief Relation of the Irreligion of Northern Quakers* (1653), Francis Higginson, a minister in Westmoreland, refers to prayer while disparaging Quaker meetings: "In these their assemblies, for the most part they use no prayer, not in one meeting often. When they do, their praying devotion is so quickly cooled that when they have begun, a man can scarce tell to twenty before they have done."[48] He reports no singing of "psalms, hymns or spiritual songs," and no "exposition of scripture." They wait "which of them the Spirit shall come down upon in inspiration and give utterance to." Higginson measures Quaker prayers against the norms of conventional churches, sites of "carnal" speech in "steeple houses." Sensing scandal, Higginson reports meetings of "both sexes lately, and not infrequently continued all night long."[49] The hint of scandal shows the aspersions hurled at Quakers and also Ranters, a name that could mean radical antinomians more than an organized group. Despite his bias, Higginson correctly identifies the equal role of women in Quaker worship. As for Quaker silence, he assumes any speech is better than no speech, a premise Quakers rejected.

Quakers do write *about* praying, as their founder George Fox (1624–91) often does in his *Journal*. He also shared Bunyan's hostility to the Book of Common Prayer because of its set times and liturgical seasons, and wrote against it in 1656 and 1660. I argue that we can glean much about

Quaker prayer from their polemical writings on prayer. A style of praying is evident in the style and subliminal sound patterns evident in these texts.

Fox uses a fiery style to attack common prayer.[50] In *A word from the Lord unto all the faithlesse generation of the world*, Fox writes: "[W]o to you that paint your selves with other mens words, that appear beautifull to men outwardly, but within are full of poyson, whited Walls, painted Sepulchres, full of Deceit and Hypocrisie, outside-Churches, outside-Forms, outside-Teachers, Formal-Pray-ers." The light shines inward; hence, externals or outward things constitute apostasy, and require a prophetic, confrontational style that repeats "outside" to great effect. Here at least Fox is not that far from Bunyan, who called set prayers "a false voice; they in person appear as Hypocrites, and their Prayers are an Abomination." The rejection of "other men's words" was a common rallying point for all opponents of the prayer book.[51]

This kind of polemic tells us little about Quakers prayers. Fox's *A Declaration concerning fasting and prayer* (1656), in contrast, is more revealing:

> Now that all may *come to know* the true praying, which is with the Spirit, & with the understanding, and here you *come to know* the praying with *sighs and groans* which cannot utter words with a *sigh and a groan*, & so as this spirit *comes to guide* & lead, yee come to the Father of Spirits, whom he hears, & he is *nigh unto all* that *call upon him* in truth, who *call upon him* with their hearts, whose hearts are *nigh unto* him; these *come to know* the praying, every where lifting up holy hands without wrath & doubting.[52] (emphasis mine)

This passage cites the texts from Paul shared by all supporters of extemporaneous prayer, specifically 1 Corinthians 2 and Romans 8:26. But Fox's style is different. He blends the texts seamlessly. His paratactic style linked by successive "ands," approximates inspired speech. It is a run-on sentence that repeats words and phrases:

> *come to know ... come to know ... sighs and groans ... sigh and a groan, comes to guide... nigh unto all ... call upon* him ... *nigh unto* him ... call upon him

The treatise is polemical, but it *prays* for the implied reader of the text as a potential convert who experiences these sonic waves, and who is urged to come, know, call. It is a prayer that "all may come to know" the Quaker experience of illumination and understanding. We can see some of the shape and substance of Quaker prayers in this passage.

Fox then turns to the Lord's Prayer. Bunyan keeps his distance from the prayer, calling it the "so-called" Lord's Prayer and preferring Paul's "Abba, father" to "Our Father." Fox, in contrast, paraphrases the Lord's Prayer by subsuming its petitions into his Spirit-led voice:

> And such as pray not with the Spirit wait not for the *Kingdome of God to be done in earth as it is in heaven,* nor *know not the daily bread,* nor the day, *neither do they forgive* men their trespasses that trespass against them; so when you pray forgive men that trespass against you, then your heavenly Father will *forgive* you your trespasses that you have transgressed contrary to the Spirit; and here you shall pray without wrath or doubting; for it teacheth to pray *which doth forgive,* and that is *forgiven* which inherits the Kingdome, and *eats the daily bread,* which witnesseth the Will of God *to be done in earth as it is in heaven,* and he calls him father which is in heaven.[53] (emphasis mine)

The phrases in italics reveal the Lord's Prayer as a subliminal text that unfolds in sonic waves. Fox constructs triads of "kingdom," "earth" and "heaven" with repetitions of "trespass." Pray and forgive are the most frequent words. The first half is negative, stating prayer is not possible without forgiveness; the latter half is positive, as the Spirit "teacheth to pray which doth forgive." It is a chiastic structure, with the words "Kingdome," "daily bread," and "in earth as it is in heaven" mirroring each other on either side. The constant echo is "forgive," which occurs five times. Recombining key words "enhances fluency in oral spontaneous composition."[54] so there is an art to this performance of inspiration: where Bunyan simply opposes the Lord's Prayer as a set form, Fox unsettles the text, creating what Hinds calls "paratactic accumulation" and "incantatory effect."[55] This effect conveys spontaneity, encouraging a sense of immediacy in readers. The purpose, described in Fox's *Journal,* is conversion, meaning "to bring people off from all their own ways, to Christ, the new and living way" and "to know the Spirit of Truth in the inward parts, and to be led thereby" and "to bring them off from all the world's fellowships, and prayings, and singings, which stood in forms without power; that their fellowship might be in the Holy Ghost."[56]

Fox takes the whole of the Lord's Prayer as his matter, but there are risks in his manner. By saying "it teacheth to pray," Fox answers the question posed to Jesus by his disciples: "teach us to pray." By answering with, "when you pray," Fox merges his voice with Christ's. While the merger may seem innocuous to us, it was potentially dangerous to identify with Christ too literally. To do so could be blasphemy.

The most memorable and misunderstood blasphemy case of the seventeenth century began on 24 October 1656. During a heavy downpour, the Quaker leader James Nayler and his followers performed Christ's entry into Jerusalem on Palm Sunday at the gates of the city of Bristol. Nayler rode a horse and played the role of Christ. His followers walked beside him shouting Hosannas like the crowds in the Gospel narratives. The *Blasphemy Act* of 1650 defines blasphemy as speaking evil of God and also any act or speech by a person claiming or affecting equality with God. Nayler's offence was affecting equality with God, meaning staging or performing blasphemy. The case should have been heard in Bristol, but Parliament ordered Nayler to London and convicted him of "horrid" blasphemy. He suffered flogging in the streets, public branding on the forehead with the letter B, and tongue boring, meaning a hole bored through his tongue with a red-hot iron, and finally imprisonment. Staging a biblical story peacefully was criminal; ramming molten steel into a man's mouth was not. Nayler was released in broken health in 1659 and died while trying to make his way home to Yorkshire.

Parliament wanted to make an example of Nayler. Some sought to curb the whole Quaker movement by punishing one of its leaders. To others he was an enigma. As Leo Damrosch notes, "all parties agreed upon the folly of Nayler's ill-judged sign," but not all agreed that Nayler blasphemed.[57] His testimony persuaded several that he was not insane since he distinguished sign, his own body, from signified, the body of Christ. Blasphemy requires some confusion of the two bodies. The episode deeply disturbed Fox, who had quarrelled with Nayler some months earlier. Fox describes it in his *Journal*: "[A] little before this time we were set at liberty, James Nayler run out and a company with him into imaginations. And they raised up a great darkness in the nation."[58] Running into imaginations – Andrewes's complaint against Puritans sixty years earlier – shows Fox's concern for Quaker dignity. Though angry, Fox visited Nayler in prison: "I saw he and his company were wrong but I did not admonish them: but James Nayler and some of them could not stay the meeting but kept on their hats when I prayed and they was the first that gave that bad example among friends."[59] The wearing of hats during prayer came as a shock to Fox in his recollection, but this moment came after the events at Bristol, where Nayler and his followers were hatless.

Quakers refused to doff their hats to social superiors and even to judges, who often hardened their punishments for it. Yet when they entered Bristol on that fateful day, and despite a thundering downpour, "Nayler's followers went bareheaded" according to the interrogation transcript in *The Grand Imposter: Or, The Life, Tryal, and Examination of James Nayler, the Seduced and Seducing Quaker With the Manner of his Riding into Bristol*, published in 1657. This fact emerged in an interrogation where one of Nayler's followers, Timothy Wedlock, was asked this question: "You will not put off your hat to a magistrate, yet you came bare in a hard rain through the town before him." To this, Wedlock replied, "I did as I was moved by the Spirit."[60] This admission is significant. To be moved by the Spirit is to pray, even in silence or in bodily movement; and prayer is not blasphemy.

As Hinds observes, the Friends did not "look to the historical Christ as a sign of a remote divinity."[61] Possessed of the inner light, their own bodies served as signs, and the state inflicted horrific violence on Nayler's body. Clearly Nayler's performance was as much of an enigma to his more thoughtful contemporaries as Bunyan's nameless terrible instrument is to us. I once thought Nayler was suffering from literal imaginings, but now I think that he and his rain-soaked followers were doing what Quakers did when their hats were off: they were praying. When asked if his name was James Nayler at his interrogation, he answered, "the men of this world call me James Nayler."[62] When asked later if his name was Jesus, he kept silent. Broken by a system of violent religious justice, Nayler was quite the opposite of a blasphemer, or one who assumes divinity. He rendered himself nameless while claiming he was an instrument of God: in short, as Damrosch argues. he was not delusional since he understood himself as a signifier understandable to enlightened Quakers. His entry into Bristol was, at least on one level, an embodied prayer, perhaps even the specific petition in the Lord's Prayer: "thy kingdom come." Enigma and circumspection are qualities of Dissenting writing, and moreso after the Restoration. Though not written, Nayler's performance might be meant for discerning Quakers or a broader fit audience.

The episode shadows the writings of Bunyan and Milton. Bunyan conflates Quakers with Ranters, the apparent target of the Blasphemy Act. As Underwood states, Bunyan "and many like him felt conflicting pressures to communicate their particular Christian identity and yet publicly distance themselves as far as possible from radicalism in order to gain respect and acceptance within society – all this in the midst of political turmoil and uncertainty as well as religious persecution."[63] Milton did not comment on Nayler by name, but he admired the Quakers, and he argued that the state should have no power to coerce individual conscience in his *Treatise of Civil Power* (1659). He considers words like blasphemy and heresy to be scare tactics. Milton inverts the Nayler case when the angel Abdiel charges Satan with blasphemy because he affects equality with God in a show of force.

Bunyan is just as confrontational in *I Will Pray With the Spirit* when he seems to interrogate his readers:

> Therefore give me leave a little to reason with thee, thou poor, blind, igno-
> rant Sot; It may be thy great prayer is to say, *Our Father which art in Heaven,*
> *&c. Dost thou know* the meaning of the very first words of this Prayer?
> *Canst thou* indeed, with the rest of the Saints, *cry, our Father? Art thou* truly
> born again? *Hast thou* received the Spirit of Adoption *Dost thou see* thyself
> in Christ? And *canst thou come* to God as a member of him? Or, *art thou*
> *ignorant* of these things, and yet darest say, *Our Father?* Is not the Devil
> *thy Father* (John 8.44), and dost thou not do the deeds of the flesh? And yet
> *darest thou* say to God, *Our Father?* Nay, *art thou not* a desperate Persecutor
> of the Children of God? And *hast thou not* cursed them in thy heart many a
> time? And yet, thou dost out of thy blasphemous throat suffer these words
> to come, even, *Our Father?* (254 emphasis mine)

Who is this "blind, ignorant sot"? The language is too strong to mean his followers. Clearly, he intends his persecutors, though without naming any. He spoke carefully at his trial; here he gives his judges a potent if veiled rebuke. Presuming Bunyan to be ignorant, Justice John Kelynge baited Bunyan on prayer, even saying, in Bunyan's recollection, that the prayer book "hath been since the apostle's time." Art "thou not a desperate Persecutor" is the angry retort Bunyan could think but not utter in court.

Bunyan refuses to quote the prayer because of its place in the Book of Common Prayer. He does not venture beyond the first six words. Fox, in contrast, sees scripture as a source of illumination, but not the light itself. Hence, paraphrasing scriptural prayers is not problematic. Where Fox emphasizes calling and forgiving, Bunyan highlights the word "Father." For Bunyan, the father is the ultimate judge of heaven and earth, and thus a scourge not only for the magistrates who sent him to prison, but also potentially for the Quakers, who angered him with their claim that the Last Judgment has already passed. Where Quaker religion is familial, Bunyan's is paternal.

Quakers could impress their judges. Stories circulated of judges converting to Quakerism during their hearings. For example, during an earlier trial for blasphemy in Appleby, Westmoreland in 1653, Nayler "exonerated himself so convincingly that the judge, Anthony Pearson, joined the Quaker movement."[64] As Douglas Gwyn notes, he did this

by "expounding Quaker theology while answering the various petitions against him."[65] This outcome suggests that prayers for conversion
within Quaker polemic sometimes worked.

In 1660, Fox resumed his defence of Quakers in *Something in answer
to that book called The church-faith* (1660). He attacks Independents and
Presbyterians for preaching national edification while calling for the
imprisonment of Quakers. Their debates on prayer are carnal, not spiritual combat:

> But the Independent will stand up for his Church-Faith, and stir up the
> Powers of the Earth to hold it up, & the Presbyterian he will cry out to the
> Magistrate to hold up his Directory, and take the Common-Prayer-man by
> the throat, and pluck him out of his Authority; and the Common-Prayer-
> man, he will cry out for the Authority to hold it up, and he will take the
> Papist by the Throat to pluck him out of his Authority; and the Papist, he will
> cry out to uphold his Mass, and take the Common-Prayer-man by the Throat.
> Away for shame, hold your hands still, and come to spiritual Weapons.[66]

Fox observes divisions among Presbyterians, Anglicans, and Catholics in the polemics of prayer. All "Directories and Faiths which men
invent" have no spirit, and require the "Powers of the earth" to maintain them.[67] Thus, the violence he represents is actually a common feature of all non-Quakers: dependence on earthly power. Fox proclaims
that the "Spirit of Truth which gave forth Scriptures is our Directory."
He advocates prayer as spiritual weapon in the tradition of Tertullian.

Fox comes closer to Bunyan's polemical style in *Something in answer
to the old Common-prayer-book*, published in 1660. He again paraphrases
the Lord's Prayer, while asking how people can pray "Thy Kingdom
come; That be so cross one against another," and can "you say, your
daily bread, who are persecuting about Religion?"[68] "And where did
the Apostles say, that they should say the Lords Prayer with a loud
voice, and different from which they said other Prayers?"[69] In a post-
script entitled, "Testimony concerning the Book of Common-Prayer
(so-called)," Fox calls the prayer book an "Invention and Tradition, tra-
duced into the world long since the Apostles dayes."[70] "Apostles days"
here contradicts Justice Kelynge's remark to Bunyan: the Book of Common Prayer "hath been ever since the Apostles' time." Kelynge may
have meant that the book is based on scripture. Fox knew that the book
appeared centuries later. His raising of the question could mean that
the apostolic authority of the prayer book arose at other trials, perhaps
as a disingenuous method of tricking Dissenters. Fox adds that the
book foments persecution: "[W]hen it was formed, it being imposed on

this Nation, by force and penalty; and set up by compelling all people into the practice of it, by violent Laws upon Bodyes and Consciences of men, this was great abomination in the sight of God, and made the practice of it detestable unto him."[71] This combative remark shows that differing sects shared common pressures.

A plainer style emerges in the 1670s. William Loddington defends the movement from charges of presumption and indiscretion in *Quakerism no Paganism* (1674). "The first Charge against the Quakers is, That the light in every Man is God" and "that when they pray, they only pray to a God within them and that they make as many Gods as there are men in the world."[72] Loddington responds: "Far be it from us to assert, every such illumination to be the only Lord and Saviour and very God."[73] Quakers distinguished general from particular inspiration, mental from vocal prayer, and inner light from the "very God." Loddington may have been haunted by the Nayler case. "Far be it from us" concedes the dangers of religious "imaginations" that led Nayler to identify with Christ too literally. Ironically, Nayler authored one explicit prayer in print, addressed to Cromwell and appended to a tract by Fox, a year before this episode: "[M]y prayer to God for you is that you may lay down all your Crowns at his feet who hath Crowned you with victory, that so the Lord being set up as King in every conscience, all may be subject to your Government for conscience sake."[74] There is no confusion between Christ and Cromwell in this prayer.

Robert Barclay's *Catechism and Confession of Faith* (1673) presents Quaker beliefs plainly:

> Q. Must we then pray always in the spirit? A. Praying always, with all prayer, and supplication in the spirit, and watching thereunto with all perseverance, and supplication for all saints. (Eph. 6:18)[75]

The catechism is a conventional tool, and therefore a respectable one. It protects Quaker prayers from scrutiny, while emphasizing the shared scriptural sources of prayer. The questioner turns his attention to the outsider: "This is strange; it seems the Spirit is much more necessary than many called Christians suppose it to be, some of which can scarce give a good account whether they have it or want it." The movement of the Spirit means that prayer "is not limited to a certain place, neither to any certain time."[76] The catechism assures readers that Quakers discern inspiration with great care. Fox's probing questions in *Something in answer to the old Common-prayer-book* are moderated in Barclay's catechism. The pronouns shift from the "you" of persecuting groups to the "we" of the Quaker movement.

In *Quakerism Confirmed* (1676), Barclay and George Keith explain dis-
cretionary responsibilities further: "If men may have an influence or
inspiration of the Spirit, to wait, fear and love God, and yet want an
influence or inspiration to preach, and pray vocally, then the influence
and inspiration to preach, and pray vocally, is a distinct superadded
influence."[77] Here, the movement from silence to speech is a "a distinct
superadded influence." If it is vocal, it "requireth an influence of life
to flow forth into the words, that it may in a living and powerfull way
reach the hearers." They conclude:

> As for us, it doth suffice unto us, that God heareth us in secret, although
> men do not frequently hear us; yet we owne with all oure hearts publick
> expressive prayer, as it is performed in Spirit and in truth, and all of us
> have our share and testimony therein, as God moves thereunto, even those
> who are outwardly silent, as these who speak, when as both agree toge-
> ther in one spirit, and with one heart and soul joyne together in the same.[78]

Quakers use silence to discern the "reall life and living virtue" in
words. Silence is a more radical rejection of human invention in prayer
than we find in Bunyan. The emphasis here is on reasonable testimony,
social compatibility, and spiritual unity, not extraordinary experience.
The simulacrum of inspired prayer in early Quaker polemic becomes
discrete prayer for toleration and respect.

Bunyan engaged the Quakers in the 1650s. His first work, *Some
Gospel Truths Opened* (1656) responded to Edward Burrough. Bunyan
rejected Quaker teachings concerning Christ's role as redeemer. His
Calvinism requires the "external" Christ as redeemer through a sacrifice in historical time, and the reading of scripture for signs of election.
Burrough, Greaves observes, believed that "the Spirit's inner testimony
was a more reliable witness to both justification and condemnation
than external words."[79] To be sure, Quakers accepted the inspiration
of scripture and the historical existence of Jesus. The barrier, however,
is "the second coming, Christ's presence in the saints, and resurrection
of Jesus" in his physical body.[80] Bunyan wrote *The Resurrection of the
Dead* from prison to place the general resurrection and last judgment in
future time against the Quaker claim that the resurrection has passed
for those in the Spirit. As Underwood notes, Quakers saw the resurrection "as a soteriological event occurring within men in the present"
(*MW* 3: xx). Bunyan feared Quaker beliefs would "open a Flood-gate
to all manner of impiety." To say that the Resurrection has occurred,
meaning it "is past either with him or any Christian," leads "directly
to the destruction and overthrow of the faith of them that hear him"

(*MW* 3: 214). Bunyan's fear of the "Floud-gate" recalls his depiction of blasphemy in *Grace Abounding*.

Burrough's "efforts in Bedfordshire in the middle of the 1650s threatened the stability of the Bedford congregation."[81] In *Some Gospel Truths Opened*, Bunyan calls the light of conscience the true inner light. This light is "falsely called Christ" by Quakers, who multiply errors in their misunderstanding of conscience. Bunyan added a list of Quaker errors to the 1680 edition of *Grace Abounding*. The central error, Camden remarks, is "one of emphasis: while the Friends may not deny the soteriological structure that is set in place by Christ's work for humanity, they remain silent about the objective work of Christ, preferring to emphasize that work as it is experienced in the communion of Christ within his worshippers."[82] Bunyan insists on the historical fact of Christ's sacrifice and the imperative of self-examination. As Hinds observes, the Friends did not "look to the historical Christ as a sign of a remote divinity."[83] Possessed of the inner light, their own bodies served as signs. Again, the Nayler case unfortunately illustrates this conviction. Bunyan considered this blasphemous.

A Case of Conscience Resolved, published in 1683, responds to a request from women in his community to hold separate prayer meetings. Bunyan rejected the request: "I do not believe they should Minister to God in Prayer before the whole Church, for then I should be a Ranter or a Quaker; Nor *do* I believe they should do it in their own Womanish Assembly" (*MW* 4: 305). His conflation of Ranters and Quakers tars them with the licentiousness attributed to Ranters in anti-sectarian propaganda. As Underwood states, Bunyan "and many like him felt conflicting pressures to communicate their particular Christian identity and yet publicly distance themselves as far as possible from radicalism in order to gain respect and acceptance within society – all this in the midst of political turmoil and uncertainty as well as religious persecution."[84] Earning respect was a shared goal for Bunyan and Fox.

Bunyan may not have read Margaret Fell's *Women's Speaking Justified*, published in 1667. Fell, who married George Fox in 1669, empowers women to speak in church, claiming the authority of the "everlasting gospel" to make her case. Her analysis of biblical texts is impressive by any standard. She presents a compelling typological analysis of biblical women from Genesis to Revelation. She cites women disciples and prophets to counter the rigid applications of 1 Corinthians 14:34: "Let your women keep silent in churches." Women prayed in public: "And why did the Apostles join together in Prayer and Supplication with the Women, and *Mary* the Mother of Jesus, and with his Brethren, *Acts* 1:14. if they had not allowed, and had Union and Fellowship with the Spirit of God, where-ever it was revealed, in Women as well as others?" The prophetess Anna is at the Temple where she "served God with Fastings and Prayers night and day."[85] The *Magnificat* is important to Fell: "Are you not here beholding to the Woman for her Sermon, to use her Words, to put into your Common Prayer? and yet you forbid Womens Speaking."[86] The inclusion of the *Magnificat* in the Book of Common Prayer makes the suppression of women's voices hypocritical.

Likewise, the women who asked Bunyan for separate prayer meetings may not have read Fell. They had the support of a "Mr K.," and asked Bunyan to reply to him in writing, "for Mr. K. Expects it" (*MW* 4: 296). Mr K. may be the Baptist minister William Kiffin, who quarrelled with Bunyan over baptism in the 1670s. Kiffin's meddling may have sharpened Bunyan's refusal. He threatened to divide the community. As Ross observes, the women asked simply to spend time together in prayer. They did not seek public leadership in prayer or preaching, making Bunyan's invocation of Quakers excessive.[87] His answer emphasizes scripture where he finds no warrant for women's prayers: "But in all the Scripture, I find not that the Women of the Churches of Christ, did use to separate themselves from their Brethren, and as so separate, performe Worship together among themselves, or in that their Congregation: or that they made, by allowance of the Word, appointment so to do" (*MW* 4: 301). He dismisses Mr K. as a promoter of human invention.

Bunyan classified the women's request under public worship. Calling people to worship is "an Act of Power: which Power, resideth in the Elders in particular, or in the Church in General. But never in the Women as considered by themselves" (*MW* 4: 303). He denies that scripture gives such power to women. Unlike Quakers, Bunyan forbids women to lead prayers: "The Holy Ghost doth particularly insist upon the inability of Women, as to their well managing of the Worship now under Consideration, and therefore it ought not to be presumed upon by them. They are forbidden to teach, yea to speak in the Church of God. And why forbidden, but because of their inability" (*MW* 4: 306). Like Eve, the women risk usurping "Authority, and of their own Head and will" (*MW* 4: 307). Prayer is a daunting enough task for men:

> Men though strong and though Acting by Lawfull Authority in this, are not able but with unutterable grones to do it. How then shall all those that attempt it without that Authority, perform it, as acceptable Worship to God? This work therefore, is as much too heavy for our Women, now, as that about which Eve ingaged in at first, was too heavy for her. (MW 4: 308)

Bunyan seeks decorum in his own community, knowing the state saw Dissenters as seditious. The request for separate meetings makes women agents of misrule. Order requires the government of men: "Wherefore in this, Laws and Statutes; and Government, is to be looked after, and given heed unto, for the Edification of that which is to arrive at last to a perfect Man: To the measure and the Stature of the Fulness of Christ" (*MW* 4: 323). Order and government require distinctions of "Sex, Degrees, and Age" (*MW* 4: 323). Bunyan considers it lawful for women to pray, but not to separate from men or to be the voice of the church: "They should also not be the mouth of the Assembly, but in heart, desires, grones, and Tears, they should go along with the Men" (*MW* 4: 324). Only in the private "closet" are they permitted to pray at liberty.

In his conclusion, Bunyan assures the women they are "an Ornament in the Church of God on Earth, as the Angels are in the Church in Heaven" (*MW* 4: 325). Women should cover their faces in worship, while men, who can worship God "with open face before him," serve "as the mouth in Prayer for the rest" (*MW* 4: 325). He reveals his life-long anxiety over his relationships with women. Scandal stirred when he conveyed Agnes Beaumont to a meeting, as she recounted in 1674.[88] Importantly, *Pilgrim's Progress*, part two follows *A Case of Conscience Resolved* in Bunyan's writings. It tells of the pilgrimage of Christian's wife and family who follow his lead in seeking salvation. Throughout her journey, Christiana defers to men, particularly Mr. Great-heart who guides her. Great-heart's battle with the Giant Maul reflects *A Case of Conscience Resolved* in the representation of prayer. Pausing during the battle, "they sat down to rest them, but Mr. Great-heart betook him to prayer; also the women and children did nothing but sigh and cry all the time that the battle did last" (*PP* 2, 229). Great-heart then slays the giant "in the full heat of his Spirit" (*PP* 2, 230). Here, the man is the main voice of prayer, although Bunyan strictly avoids inventing any set prayer. The women support Great-heart with sighs and cries which, though consistent with the "groanings past utterance" of Romans 8:26, are inarticulate and immature. The role of the "Spirit" makes the combat an allegory of prayer. While *Pilgrim's Progress*, part two met the demand for more of a popular story, it maintains the gender order found in *A Case of Conscience Resolved*, which came from a simple request for prayer meetings by the women of Bunyan's church.

v. The Name of the Prayer in *The Holy War*

In 1682, Bunyan published *The Holy War Made by King Shaddai Upon Diabolus, to Regain the Metropolis of the World, Or, The Losing and Taking*

Again of the Town of Mansoul. The title summarizes the allegory. The human soul is a "fair and delicate Town" found in the "Continent of Universe" (*HW* 7). The frontispiece to the first edition presents Mansoul as an emblem. (See Figure 8.)

It is a walled town with five main gates: Ear-gate, Eye-gate, Mouth-gate, Nose-gate, and Feel-gate. The gates are the five senses, and their order is important. Faith "cometh by hearing" (Rom. 10:17), so Ear-gate takes precedence. The eye is vital to discernment. The mouth can speak and pray. Smell and touch can convey the effects of faith or sin. The town walls are "Impregnable, and such as could never be opened or forced, but by the leave and will of those within (*HW* 9). Sin is willful capitulation to Satan, who cannot otherwise enter the town.

A castle in the middle of town signifies the human heart. Bunyan is the central figure standing before the town. "Heart Castle" is visible through the slight transparency of Bunyan's heart, superimposing the human heart on the heart of the town. Jesus, called "Emanuel" in the allegory, stands to our right. Satan or "Diabolus" in a form suggesting Apollyon in Revelation stands to the left. Diabolus, or the Devil and his legions, lays siege to the town. Weapons signifying spiritual combat appear on the landscape and also fortify the town from within. Mansoul means the individual soul under siege from temptation and evil.

The allegory works on three levels: "those of Christian or world history, of the life of the individual soul, and of recent and contemporary English history" (*HW* xxvi). The first conquest of Mansoul by Diabolus (Satan) signifies the Fall in Genesis, while its deliverance by Emanuel, the Son of Shaddai, signifies the redemptive work of Christ. Town officials represent faculties such as memory, will, understanding, and conscience. These faculties are strong when connected to the Lord Chief Secretary or Holy Spirit but weak under the influence of sin. The allegory of local history reflects "the intense divisiveness of the time, and the treatment of religion as an instrument of state policy" (*HW* xxii). It was now twenty years after Bunyan's trial in 1660. In 1678, anti-Catholic feeling fuelled by the "Popish Plot," a fraudulent claim that Jesuits were plotting against the life of the king, intensified religious polarization. In 1681, the government intensified the repression of conventicles and imposed new controls on local governments. Richard Greaves observes *The Holy War* is in part Bunyan's response to "the government's new interest in enforcing the Corporation Act of 1661, which required all municipal officials to swear the oaths of allegiance, supremacy, and non-resistance" and "take the sacrament of the Lord's Supper in the Church of England."[89] The political allegory supports Bunyan's primary concern with the the invasion of conscience by external powers.

Figure 8. Frontispiece: *The Holy War* by John Bunyan (1682). Courtesy of the Huntington Library.

After retaking Mansoul from Diabolus, Emanuel fortifies the town. He orders "great slings" to be mounted on the battlements. He installs a "nameless terrible instrument" at Mouth-gate:

> There was also an instrument invented by *Emanuel*, that was to throw stones from the Castle of *Mansoul*, out at *Mouth-gate*; an instrument that could not be resisted, nor that would miss of execution; wherefore for the wonderful exploits that it did when used, it went without a name, and it was committed to the care of, and to be managed by the brave Captain, the Captain *Credence*, in case of war. (*HW* 117)

Bunyan's marginal glosses often cite biblical sources, but not here; in this case, the gloss simply reinforces the enigma, calling it a "nameless terrible instrument in Mansoul" (*HW* 117). The gloss favours inwardness, since the instrument is *in* Mansoul. It is hard to visualize this instrument. It is external as symbol and internal as some conscious activity. Spiritual weapons in *The Holy War* range from slings to swords, but this enigmatic weapon has no name. If the instrument is prayer, why not say so in the gloss? Once again, uncertainty is part of the question and the answer.

James Forrest and Roger Sharrock, Oxford editors of *The Holy War*, observe that earlier editors, notably Mason in 1782, took Mouthgate's "nameless terrible instrument" as the "prayer of faith" described in Matthew 21:22: "whatsoever ye shall ask in prayer, believing, ye shall receive." In support of faith, they note that Emanuel assigns the instrument to Captain Credence, or faith. Prayer as weapon recalls Herbert's "Engine 'gainst the Almighty" in "Prayer 1." Bunyan, however, aims the weapon at persecutors. So too does Benjamin Keach, a Baptist minister pilloried for sedition in 1664. Keach calls prayer an engine "that makes the Persecutors tremble; and wo to them that are the Buts and Marks that it is levell'd at, when it is fired with the Fire of the Spirit, and discharged in the Strength of Faith."[90] Defending the dissenting conscience is a main purpose of prayer.[91]

Daniel Runyon challenges this critical consensus in *John Bunyan's Master Story: The Holy War as Battle Allegory in Religious and Biblical Context*, and his annotated edition of *The Holy War*. Runyon argues that prayer is "pervasively present in *The Holy War*. There is no call for making it nameless now." Moreover, Bunyan "places allegorical labels on everything within reach, yet he will only label this machine 'nameless.' It therefore seems obvious that 'nameless' is nothing more than yet another allegorical label of something he has seen in scripture and wishes to include in his narrative."[92] Runyon's challenge demands a new interpretation.

Runyon offers no single solution. He points to Revelation 19:12, 2:17, and 3:12 for motifs of naming and namelessness within a narrative of cosmic battle.[93] The enigma persists and new questions arise.[94] Why do Forrest and Sharrock rely on the figure of Captain Credence for interpretive certainty when Emanuel is the inventor of the instrument?[95] Could the inconsistency of the nameless instrument with other representations of prayer in *The Holy War,* such as letters or petitions, direct us, not away from prayer but towards a specific prayer? Finally, if the emblem represents prayer artistically, is it consistent with Bunyan's critique of human invention in *I Will Pray with the Spirit*?

The nameless instrument is indeed a specific prayer, and one that has been a touchstone throughout this study. *I Will Pray with the Spirit* emphasizes the inspiration of the Holy Spirit in prayer. The key to the nameless instrument, in contrast, is not the role of the Holy Spirit. We must shift our focus from Captain Credence, who works the instrument, to Emanuel, the inventor of the instrument. If Emanuel is the inventor, and if the instrument is prayer, then it is the prayer invented by Jesus. It is the Lord's Prayer.

This reading works with the general treatment of prayer in *The Holy War.* The Lord's Prayer is a spiritual weapon in tradition. Bunyan elsewhere represents prayers as diplomatic letters and petitions in the allegory. As a scriptural text, the Lord's Prayer merits inclusion in an epic that treats Emanuel as a hero and the Bible as its template. As an invention, it concedes that Jesus composed an order of words even if he did not, as Bunyan insists, intend a set form. A question persists: why must it be nameless? It is because "The Lord's Prayer" is a name that Bunyan could not accept. For Bunyan, "The Lord's Prayer" evokes, not the Bible, but the Book of Common Prayer. The prayer is real but its name is a human invention. The name "Lord's Prayer" does not occur in scripture; it is a gloss attached by later translators of the Bible. To name the instrument would concede validity to the Book of Common Prayer. The placement of the instrument at "mouthgate" signifies words spoken from the heart rather than read from a book. Namelessness, moreover, is covert representation: the ministers of Charles II named the Lord's Prayer within the Book of Common Prayer; they would therefore have difficulty interpreting Bunyan's nameless emblem. Covert representation empowers dissenting readers as a select audience. The emblem includes discerning readers and excludes those who persecute or conform. This division of audience typifies the writing and reading strategies of dissenting literary culture.[96]

It is tantalizing to imagine that Bunyan read Tertullian, who compares the prayer to a weapon capable of many exploits. Bunyan's nameless instrument produces "wonderful exploits":

> Prayer alone it is that conquers God. But it was Christ's wish for it to work no evil: he has conferred upon it all power concerning good. And so its only knowledge is how to call back the souls of the deceased from the very highway of death, to straighten the feeble, to heal the sick, to cleanse the devil-possessed, to open the bars of the prison, to loose the bands of the innocent. It also absolves sins, drives back temptations, quenches persecutions, strengthens the weak-hearted, delights the high minded, brings home wayfarers, soothes the waves, astounds robbers, feeds the poor, rules the rich, lifts up the fallen, supports the unstable, upholds them that stand. Prayer is the bulwark of faith, our defensive and offensive armour against the enemy who is watching us from every side.[97]

These exploits help to explain namelessness since they exceed any one name.[98] Liturgical titles are confining while emblems are copious, as with Herbert's "Prayer I."[99]

In comparing prayer in *The Holy War* with *I Will Pray with the Spirit*, we should recall that the latter came out of Bunyan's trial. Justice Kelynge argued that Christ provided a form of prayer when "he taught his disciples to pray, as John also taught his disciples" (*GA* 107). Kelynge echoes scripture to challenge Bunyan's confidence. Bunyan replied with Romans 8:26. The Spirit, not the Prayer Book, guides the praying subject. He then addresses the Lord's Prayer:

> And as to the Lord's Prayer, although it be an easy thing to say *Our Father, &c.* with the mouth; yet there is very few that can, in the spirit, say the first two words of that Prayer; that is, that can call God their Father, as knowing what it is to be born again, and as having experience, that they are begotten of the spirit of God: Which if they do not, all is but babbling, &c. (*GA* 107)

Naming the Father is the test of individual sincerity, not corporate worship, and few meet the standard. Bunyan prefers Paul's "father" to the prayer book's: "For ye have not received the spirit of bondage again to fear; but ye have received the Spirit of adoption, whereby we cry, Abba, Father" (Rom. 8:15). The duality of bondage and adoption works better with predestination than the charitable "Our Father" of Andrewes.

Bunyan was under verbal siege at his trial, and so this exchange could have influenced his invention of the "nameless terrible instrument" in *The Holy War*. He debates the prayer to resist bondage, just as Mansoul resists the Diabolonians.

Short comments on the Lord's Prayer in *I Will Pray with the Spirit* distinguish liturgy from scripture. Bunyan persists with the polemical question: is the prayer a prescribed form? Naming it would validate it as a set form. Naming is a sensitive theme in *I Will Pray with the Spirit*. He distances himself from naming, calling the Lord's Prayer the "so-called" Lord's Prayer:

> And when I say believingly, I mean, for the soul to believe, and that from good experience, that the work of Grace is wrought in him. This is the right calling of God Father; and not as many do, to say in a babling way, the Lord's prayer (so called) by heart, as it lyeth in the words of the book. No, here is the life of prayer, when in or with the Spirit, a man being made sensible of sin, and how to come to the Lord for mercy; he comes, I say, in the strength of the Spirit, and cryeth Father. (*MW* 2: 252)

Bunyan also says "that form called" the Lord's Prayer to deny that Christ intended a set form:

> But we find that the disciples desired that Christ would teach them to pray, as John also taught his disciples; and that thereupon he taught them that form called the LORD'S PRAYER. Answ. 1. To be taught by Christ, is that which not only they, but we desire; and seeing he is not here in his person to teach us, the Lord teach us by his Word and Spirit; for the Spirit it is which he hath said he would send to supply in his room when he went away, as it is (John 14:16; 16:7). 2. As to that called a form, I cannot think that Christ intended it as a stinted form of prayer. (1.) Because he himself layeth it down diversely, as is to be seen, if you compare Matthew 6 and Luke 11. Whereas if he intended it as a set form, it must not have been so laid down, for a set form is so many words and no more. (2.) We do not find that the apostles did ever observe it as such; neither did they admonish others so to do. (*MW* 2: 269)

Bunyan sees blasphemy in the pretense of sanctity: "[H]ow sadly would even those men look, and with what terror would they walk up and down the world, if they did but know the lying and blaspheming that proceedeth out of their mouth, even in their most pretended sanctity?" (*MW* 2: 255). He dismisses shows of piety: "[T]hey will come to Church and say, Our Father. Nay further, these men, though every time they say to God, our Father, do most abominably blaspheme, yet they must be compelled thus to do." Bunyan exposes the irony of a nation in which persecutors are seen as "good Churchmen," while "God's People" are "looked upon to be a turbulent, seditious and factious people" (*MW* 2: 253).

Bunyan's treatment of names in *I Will Pray with the Spirit* illuminates the nameless instrument in *The Holy War*. He includes the Lord's Prayer as Emanuel's invention on his own terms, expecting his readers to make the right identification without compromising with the prayer book. He harmonizes his Pauline emphasis on the Spirit with Christ's edicts: "Christ bids, Pray for the Spirit" (*MW* 2: 269). Finally, he provides an explanation for the role of Captain Credence, who operates the nameless instrument: "[O]ne word spoken in Faith, is better than a thousand prayers, as men call them, written and read, in a formal, cold, luke-warm way" (*MW* 2: 252). This aligns the nameless instrument with Matthew's framing of the Lord's Prayer, which dismisses excessive oratory.

In *The Holy War,* Bunyan satirizes common prayer in the figures of Mr Tradition, Mr Human-wisdom, and Mr Man's-invention (58). These are "proper men" of "courage and skill, to appearance" (58). They enlist with Captain Boanerges or "sons of thunder," a name Jesus confers on James and John (Mark 3:17). Lord Willbewill, or willpower corrupted by the Fall, captures them in their first skirmish and takes them to Diabolus, who asks them to change sides. They comply in a gesture of conformity, telling Diabolus that "they did not so much live by religion, as by the fates of fortune. And that since his lordship was willing to entertain them, they should be willing to serve him" (59). Diabolus assigns them to "Captain Anything," who makes Mr Man's-invention his "ancient-bearer" (60). These figures show Bunyan's skepticism of the "human" elements of tradition, wisdom, and invention, which are more coercive than creative in the prayer book.

Bunyan depicts free prayer in a conference of Captains who seek to regain Mansoul for Emanuel. After Diabolus hardens Manoul's heart against Shaddai, the Captains "gather themselves together, to have free conference among themselves, to know what was yet to be done to gain the town, and to deliver it from the tyranny of Diabolus; and one said after this manner, and another after that." The marginal gloss reads, "The Captains leave off to summons, and betake themselves to prayer" (73). Their "free conference" and different styles or "manners" illustrate freedom of prayer in their respective "regiments" or congregations. The phrase "after this manner," however, strongly echoes Matthew's presentation of the Lord's Prayer: "after this manner therefore pray ye" (6:9). Unlike Luke's "When ye pray, say," Matthew's phrase assures Bunyan that the Lord's Prayer is not a prescribed form. The different manners the Captains use express confidence in extemporaneous prayer.

When Shaddai sends Emanuel to retake Mansoul, Bunyan again parodies set forms in petitions for peace sent by Diabolus. Mr Loth-to-stoop is the envoy of Diabolus, who puts "into his mouth what he should say" (89). Emanuel rejects his propositions for compromise: Diabolus can no longer advise Mansoul, since its citizens "are bid before, in everything by prayer and supplication to let their requests be made known to my Father" (HW, 91). This exhortation is formal but scriptural: the source is Phillipians 4:6: "in every thing by prayer and supplication with thanksgiving let your requests be made known unto God." A similar exhortation occurs in the Book of Common Prayer: "Almighty God, who hast given us grace at this time with one accord to make our common supplications unto thee; and dost promise that when two or three are gathered together in thy Name thou wilt grant their requests" (Order for Morning Prayer). This is, in fact, a prayer of Saint Chrysostom, though it echoes Philippians 4:6 and Matthew 18:20.

Certain episodes in *The Holy War* show Bunyan's ideal of spontaneous prayer, often in petitions that are accepted, rejected, or revised. The trope of prayer as spiritual weapon is not, however, limited to the nameless instrument. Mouthgate, where the "nameless terrible instrument" stands, becomes a sally-port "out at which the townsfolk did send their petitions to Emmanuel, their Prince." It is also "the gate from the top of which the captains did play their slings at the enemies" to such effect that Diabolus "sought, if possible, to land up Mouthgate with dirt." The dual function of Mouthgate as a place for petitions and weapons develops the metaphor of prayer as spiritual weapon. The effectiveness of the slings affirms extemporaneous prayer.

Descriptions of the Diabolonian and Mansoulian camps develops the trope of prayer as weapon: "Then they which were of the camp of Diabolus came down to the town to take it, and the captains in the castle, with the slingers at Mouthgate played upon them amain." While the townspeople pray and sing psalms, "the enemy replied with horrible objections, and the terribleness of their drum; but the town made answer with the slapping for their slings, and the melodious noise of their trumpets" (HW 224–5). The prayers that fly from the slings of the Mansoulians provoke rage in the Diabolonians. They reply with "horrible objections," meaning polemical writings that demonize dissent, and the "terribleness of their drum," or the military power that enforces law.

In a climactic episode, Mansoul frames a new petition to Emanuel, and the Lord Secretary is now willing to cooperate. On this occasion, Mansoul has persevered in battle to the limits of its own strength: "Our wisdom is gone, our power is gone, because thou art departed from us" (*HW* 237). The Lord Secretary agrees to sign, but with these conditions: "Yourselves must be present at the doing of it. Yea, you must put your desires to it. True, the hand and pen shall be mine, but the ink and paper must be yours; else how can you say it is your petition? Nor have I need to petition for myself, because I have not offended" (*HW* 236). Ink and paper are key symbols. The Lord Secretary agrees to "draw up" the petition, just as the Spirit intercedes in Romans 8:26. Bunyan defers to the Spirit and remains cautious of human invention, identifying it more with effort than imagination. The Lord Secretary appoints Captain Credence, who manned the "nameless terrible instrument," to carry the petition through Mouthgate because Credence is "a well-spoken man" (*HW* 236).

Captain Credence's embassy to Emanuel is the allegory of the "prayer of faith," not the "nameless terrible instrument." He returns carrying personal notes of encouragement from Emanuel to the leaders of Mansoul, including the Lord Mayor, Lord Willbewill, the Subordinate Preacher, Mr Godlyfear, and Mansoul itself. The Lord Secretary (Holy Spirit) appoints Captain Credence as the commander of all the forces in Mansoul (*HW* 242). Emanuel arrives to defend Mansoul on the "third day," prefiguring the Resurrection as a victory over Satan. The battle ends with the defeat of doubters and "bloodmen," and the trial of figures of sin. At the end, Emanuel promises to pray continually for Mansoul, telling him to hold fast till his return.

As a specific scriptural prayer, the nameless instrument differs from Bunyan's typical representations of prayers as written petitions. Given the epic scale of the story, it makes sense that Bunyan would be inclusive on prayer and address a prayer debated at his trial. By rejecting human invention, Bunyan faced an artistic problem: how to invent the Lord's Prayer as allegory. Namelessness solves this problem. It offers insights into the formation of Bunyan's dissenting conscience. It shows a defensive posture of strategic circumspection, and relies on the reader to discern his meaning. The emblem uses enigma to separate godly readers from persecutors. It is another place where Bunyan could say, the "Philistians understand me not."

Afterword

Scholars and teachers ask the past to illuminate some part of our present. At present, in the first two decades of the twenty-first century, attacks on religious communities are increasing. Many attacks happen at prayer meetings. On 17 June 2015, for example, a white supremacist murdered nine African Americans during their prayer meeting at the Emanuel African Methodist Episcopal Church in Charleston, South Carolina. Other victims include six Muslim men at prayer at the Islamic Cultural Centre in Quebec City (29 January 2017), thirty people at prayer in the Sahib-ul-Zaman Mosque in Gardez, Afghanistan (3 August 2018), and eleven during Shabbat morning service at the Tree of Life Synagogue in Pittsburgh (27 October 2018). Prayer meetings may draw extremists because they occur at set times with the certainty of finding innocent people in attendance.

On 15 March 2019, a white supremacist killed fifty-one people and injured forty-nine while attacking two mosques in Christchurch, New Zealand. One week later, a photograph with this description went "viral" on the Internet "Holding a Bushmaster semi-automatic rifle, Constable Michelle Evans donned a black scarf on her head and a rose on her chest. The young police officer stood guard outside the Christchurch Memorial Park Cemetery today, a week after last Friday's mosque shootings."[1] A Muslim mother carries one small child and leads another by the hand through a gate. The picture shares qualities with early modern emblems that combine symbolic images with brief didactic texts. Women personify virtues in many emblem books. George Wither, for example, depicted hope and labour as a "Woman with an Anchor, and a Spade."[2] I see Constable Evans as a twenty-first-century emblem of empathy and protection.

Her hijab and rose express empathy. Without those objects, the image would not have gained any attention. The weapon and the gate convey a duty to protect and invite comparison with the frontispiece to Bunyan's *The Holy War*, an emblem of the embattled Town of Mansoul. Bunyan stands outside the high stone wall of the gated town of Mansoul. Constable Evans stands guard at a low stone wall outside a cemetery. Bunyan depicts the metaphoric violence of allegory; Constable Evans depicts the literal violence of history. I juxtapose these images to encourage dialogue between our post-secular present and the pre-secular otherness of the past. Bunyan's pre-secular moment was pervasively religious and religiously contentious, giving rise to ideas of toleration and rights. Constable Evans is post-secular: her uniform represents the protection of life and liberties in a secular state, whereas her hijab and rose acknowledge of her own volition Islam and Muslim women as part of a diverse society.

"Pre-secular" and "post-secular" imply changing relationships among religions and secular societies. Milton championed the secular principle of the separation of church and state, but he did so as a religious writer in the service of God. In *A Treatise of Civil Power in Ecclesiastical Causes* (1659), he argued that the state must not coerce individual conscience in matters of religion. Milton saw the restraint of the state, not as secularism, but as essential to the Protestant Reformation. His ideal Reformation was as an endless pursuit of truth through the exercise of reason. Later national revolutions mindful of the English revolution took care to separate organized religion and government. The first article of the U.S. Constitution states: "Congress shall make no law respecting an establishment of religion, or prohibiting the free exercise thereof; or abridging the freedom of speech, or of the press." Free prayer is arguably part of the pre-history of secular free speech. In Canada, a Charter of Rights and Freedoms proclaimed in 1982 also aligns freedom of religion and conscience with freedom of belief, opinion, and expression, and freedom of the press, reaffirming common secular principles.[3]

Secularism demands tolerance to religions so long as they break no civil laws, a key point in John Locke's argument for toleration in 1689. Feisal Mohamed observes that tolerance is contradicted when the state regulates religion on the basis of its "claim to a monopoly on reason." As he argues, when "that claim occurs at the level of politics, it can be an instrument of power deployed to harass religious minorities."[4] Constitutional rights are tested when governments target minority religions with selective laws in the name of secularism. These tests invite comparison to laws that marginalized Anglicans in the 1640s and 1650s and persecuted Dissenters in the 1660s. Laws for censorship (1643) or against blasphemy (1650) came from Parliaments seeking political credibility. Much of the story this book tells concerns the state's regulation of religion from the proscription of the prayer book in 1645 to the

Acts of Uniformity in 1662. State regulation of religious expression may illustrate our post-secular moment.

Like readers in the early modern period, we often experience polemic as divisive. Invective often degrades our public discourse. Similarly, Bunyan complained that honest Dissenters were called "turbulent, seditious and factious" people. His phrase describes invective of such intensity that he, like Milton, had to teach Dissenters to discern true voices of conscience using discretion. In our time, "tweets" fuse printed texts with extemporaneous speech, but fragment our experience of both in their brevity. Taylor lamented the reduction of prayers to "atomes" in his defence of common prayer. He created a coherent scholarly record of history, memory, and tradition to educate his readers in a time of political and religious conflict. Milton offered equally great scholarship from an opposed perspective. Then and now, in agreement or disagreement, scholarship implies genuine respect for readers.

Eamon Duffy calls prayer "the most fundamental religious activity."[5] Poetry is also a fundamental human activity. How they can or should combine exercised the writers in this study. The Canadian philosopher James Mensch uses Christian theology and phenomenology to describe prayer as a fundamental activity. The description is unavoidably poetic. In "Prayer as Kenosis," an essay that has greatly encouraged my work, Mensch presents prayer as an interaction of kenosis and incarnation. Christ undertakes kenosis by setting aside his divinity and taking human form in the Incarnation. Kenosis is a mode of receptivity that makes space for the movement of the Spirit. Empathy is a mode of Incarnation: we allow the sufferings of others to come into our consciousness, or "a feeling (a suffering or undergoing) of the world in and through another person."[6] Together they become a *mythos* of prayer deeper than words and broader than dogmas, as Paul asserts in Romans 8:26.

The invocation to Book 1 of *Paradise Lost* captures this mythos as Milton recasts a convention of classical epic into a Christian prayer for connection to the Spirit that broods over the kenotic "vast Abyss" (1: 21) and shapes a poem of cosmic scope. Bunyan's *I Will Pray with the Spirit* is a zealous insistence on connection to the Spirit before all other considerations, whether personal, legal, or political. Jeremy Taylor, in contrast, recalls the Spirit's formation of the Church on the Day of Pentecost and places human art and imagination as talents in the service of the Spirit. Like Andrewes, he sees unbroken apostolic succession and the presence of a king as elements of an incarnate church. All four writers, whether they favour scripted or spontaneous prayers, value poetry as a civilizing influence in society, and a humanizing polemic when religions forsake or forget their poetic foundations.

Notes

Introduction

1 As Brian Cummings notes, "Two alternative title pages were made for the 1662 edition; some copies contain both. The engraving is by David Loggan (1634–1692), after an original by J.B. Gaspars (1620–1691). *The Book of Common Prayer: The Texts of 1549, 1559, and 1662,* ed. Cummings, 183.

2 Jesse Lander, *Inventing Polemic: Religion, Print, and Literary Culture in Early Modern England,* 1.

3 Ibid., 11.

4 I agree with Sharon Achinstein's criteria for the term "Dissenter." Notwithstanding sectarian differences, all Dissenters shared a "Protestant belief in the immediate apprehension of the divine; and a refusal to partake in compelled religious ceremonialism exemplified by unwillingness to join the English state-sponsored church after the Restoration government's legislation of 1662." See *Literature and Dissent in Milton's England,* 10.

5 Sir Philip Sidney, *A Defence of Poetry,* 54.

6 An early appearance is found in Anne Bacon's 1548 translated work, *Sermons of Barnardine Ochine of Sena*: the subject is sufferings that "haue bene and shalbe hys gyftes and graces, geuen and graunted of a great loue for my welthe and profit" (A5v–A6r). These gifts nurture spiritual virtues of faith, patience, wisdom. My focus is on the gift and responsibility of writing poetry. I thank an anonymous reader at the Press for this reference.

7 Ian Robinson, "The Prose and Poetry of the Book of Common Prayer," *The Book of Common Prayer: Past, Present and Future,* ed. Prudence Dailey, 70–81. 75.

8 David Curry, "Something Understood," *The Book of Common Prayer,* 52–69. 55.

9 Stella Brook, *The Language of the Book of Common Prayer,* 22. Brook notes that the names of Cranmer's collaborators and assistants are not recorded,

though some can be inferred, including his fellow martyr, Bishop Ridley of Rochester (25).

10 P.D. James, "Through all the Changing Scenes of Life: Living with the Prayer Book," *The Book of Common Prayer*, 48.

11 Daniel R. Gibbons, *Conflicts of Devotion: Liturgical Poetics in Sixteenth- and Seventeenth-Century England*, 43.

12 Ibid., 35.

13 Anne Ferry, *The Art of Naming*, 130.

14 Private prayers in English also gained in confidence. See Amie Shirkie, "Marketing Salvation: Devotional Handbooks for Early Modern Householders," doctoral dissertation.

15 "Something Understood," 60.

16 Book of Common Prayer (1549), *Book of Common Prayer: The Texts of 1549, 1559 and 1662*, ed. Brian Cummings, 109. All references to the Book of Common Prayer are to this edition.

17 Ibid., 43.

1 Lancelot Andrewes and George Herbert: The Word of Charity

1 Brooke Conti, *Confessions of Faith in Early Modern England*, 7.

2 P.E. McCullough, "Lancelot Andrewes's Transforming Passions," *Huntington Library Quarterly* 71 no. 4 (2008): 573–89. 573.

3 Anthony Milton, *Catholic and Reformed: The Roman and Protestant Churches in English Protestant Thought: 1600–1640*, 7.

4 Patrick Collinson, *The Birthpangs of Protestant England: Religious and Cultural Change in the Sixteenth and Seventeenth Centuries*, 12.

5 For important distinctions between a naive or predictive apocalypse and a literary or "readerly" apocalypse, see Northrop Frye, "Typology II: Apocalypse" in *The Great Code: The Bible and Literature* and Frank Kermode, *The Sense of an Ending: Studies in the Theory of Fiction*.

6 Collinson, *The Birthpangs of Protestant England*, 14.

7 Charles Prior, *Defining the Jacobean Church: The Politics of Religious Controversy, 1603–1625*, 4.

8 Ibid., 5.

9 Lake, "Lancelot Andrewes, John Buckeridge, and Avant-Garde Conformity at the Court of James I," 113.

10 Ibid., 114.

11 Diarmaid MacCulloch, *The Reformation*, 487.

12 Ibid., 490–1.

13 Deborah Shuger, *Habits of Thought in the English Renaissance*, 136.

14 Ibid., 145.

15 MacCulloch, *The Reformation*, 498.

16 Collinson, *The Birthpangs of Protestant England*, 141.

17 Ibid., 144

18 Lake, "Lancelot Andrewes, John Buckeridge, and Avant-Garde Conformity at the Court of James I," 117.

19 Ibid.

20 Ibid., 116.

21 Luke develops his theme of importunity in prayer in the Parable of the Unrighteous Judge (Luke 18:1–7). The Parable of the Pharisee and the Publican that follows (Luke 18:9–14) came to illustrate extemporaneous prayer for many Puritan writers; however, Luke presents the parable to caution some "which trusted in themselves that they were righteous, and despised others," rather than to polarize groups in the manner of Matthew.

22 Thomas Manton, *A Practical Exposition of the Lord's Prayer*, 14.

23 Ibid., 74.

24 Henry Hammond, *A View of the New Directory and A Vindication of the Ancient Liturgy of the Church of England*, 11.

25 Abrahamus Scultetus, *A Defence of the Humble Remonstrance Against the frivolous and false exceptions of Smectymnuus*, 17.

26 Thomas Long, *An Excercitation concerning the use of the Lords Prayer in Public Worship*, 16.

27 Jewish and Christian scholars note that certain elements of the prayer incorporate texts from the Hebrew Bible and other ancient sources. 1 Chronicles 29:10–11 show parallels. See Kaufmann Kohler, "The Lord's Prayer," *Jewish Encyclopedia: The Unedited Full text of the 1906 Jewish Encyclopedia*, jewishencyclopedia.com.

28 For other commentaries see Brian Najapfour, "After This Manner Therefore Pray Ye": Puritan Perspectives On The Lord's Prayer," *Puritan Reformed Journal* 4 no. 4 (2012), 158–69.

29 See Roy Hammerling, *The Lord's Prayer in the Early Church*, 27.

30 Tertullian, *De Oratione*, ed. and trans. Ernest Evans, § 1.

31 *A vindication of the answer to the humble Remonstrance*, 17.

32 Tertullian, *De Oratione*, § 1.

33 Ibid., § 1.

34 Ibid., § 1.

35 *The Private Devotions of Lancelot Andrewes*, trans. F.E. Brightman, 7.

36 See P.E. McCullough, "Henry Isaacson," *Oxford Dictionary of National Biography*. "In 1630 appeared *Institutiones piae*, attributed to 'H.I.' but in fact a rough compilation of extracts from Andrewes' devotional and catechetical writings, probably not assigned to their true author in deference to William Laud's exclusive copyright to Andrewes' works."

37 Lancelot Andrewes, *Institutiones Piae or directions to pray*, 17–18.

38 Ibid., 18.

39 Ibid., 35.

40 Ibid., 30.

41 Andrewes examines the Apostle's Creed, a main component of formal liturgy, after the Lord's Prayer. Following Augustine, Andrewes calls the creed a "Symbolum Fidei," with "symbol" denoting integration of the orthodox articles of faith.

42 P.E. McCullough, "Making Dead Men Speak: Laudianism, Print, and the Works of Lancelot Andrewes, 1626–1642." *The Historical Journal* 41 no. 2 (1998): 401–24. 410–11.

43 See P.E. McCullough, "Lancelot Andrewes," *ODNB*.

44 P.E. McCullough, "Henry Isaacson," *ODNB*.

45 *The Reformation*, 494.

46 *Glory, Laud and Honour*, 113.

47 Elizabeth McCutcheon, "*Preces Privatae*: A Journey through Time," *Studies in Philology*. 65 no. 2 (1968): 223–41. 223.

48 Ibid., 226.

49 Brightman, "Preface," *Private Devotions*, li.

50 Ibid., lvii.

51 *Private Devotions*, 25.

52 Lancelot Andrewes, *Preces Privatae Graece & Latine*, 17.

53 Ibid., 17.

54 Ibid., 25.

55 Ibid., 40.

56 Book of Common Prayer (1559), 109.

57 *Private Devotions*, 40–1.

58 Ibid., 89.

59 "*Preces Privatae*: A Journey through Time," 239.

60 Richard Drake, ed., *A manual of the private devotions and meditations of The Right Reverend Father in God Lancelot Andrewes*, A9v–A10r.

61 Ibid., A10v.

62 *Glory, Laud and Honour*, 132.

63 *The Latin Poetry of George Herbert: A Bilingual Edition*, transl. Mark McCloskey and Paul Murphy, 5.

64 *Glory, Laud and Honour*, 132.

65 Rowan Williams, "George Herbert and Henry Vaughan," Address Delivered to the Temenos Society, 28 March 2007.

66 Sharon Achinstein, "Reading George Herbert in the Restoration," *English Literary Renaissance*, 36 no. 3 (2006): 430–65. 430.

67 Gary Kuchar, *George Herbert and the Mystery of the Word: Poetry and Scripture in Seventeenth-Century England*, 21.

68 Ibid., 22.

69 Ibid., 58.

70 Kuchar, *George Herbert and the Mystery of the Word,* 16.

71 *Common Prayer,* 96.

72 Kate Narveson, "Herbert and Early Stuart Psalm Culture: Beyond Translation and Meditation," in *George Herbert's Pastoral: New Essays on the Poet and Priest of Bemerton.* Christopher Hodgkins, 211–34, 218.

73 Paul Dyck, "George Herbert and the Liturgical Experience of Scripture," *George Herbert's Pastoral,* 198.

74 Gibbons states persuasively that Herbert is not an overt polemicist in his study of Herbert's liturgical poetics. See *Conflicts of Devotion,* 203.

75 Walton, *Lives,* 74.

76 Terry Sherwood, *Herbert's Prayerful Art,* 7.

77 Ibid., 4.

78 Ibid., 5.

79 Achinstein notes that many dissenting writers emulated Herbert. See *Literature and Dissent in Milton's England,* 183. Kuchar observes: "If critiques of dogmatic certainties are audible in "avant-garde" churchmen such as Andrewes and Hooker and if they register in moderate puritans such as Sibbes and Preston, then they are also characteristic of Dissenters such as Richard Baxter and Francis Rous. Despite many important differences, all of these writers recognized the spiritual and social dangers of religious polarity and exaggerated certitude." See *George Herbert and the Mystery of the Word,* 16.

80 *The English Poems of George Herbert,* ed. Helen Wilcox (st. 67, ll. 397–402). All references are to this edition.

81 Michael Schoenfeldt, *Prayer and Power: George Herbert and Renaissance Courtship,* 162.

82 Ibid., 163.

83 *Picturing Religious Experience,* 131.

84 Cynthia Garrett, "The Rhetoric of Supplication: Prayer Theory in Seventeenth-Century England," *Renaissance Quarterly* 46 no. 2 (1993), 328–57. 339.

85 Holy Sonnet 5, *John Donne's Poetry,* ed. Donald R. Dickson.

86 *Private Devotions,* 7.

87 *De Oratione,* ch. 39, § 29.

88 *Works,* 288.

89 Ibid., 288.

90 Ibid., 289.

91 Book of Common Prayer (1559), 138.

92 Ibid., 289.

93 *Prayer and Power,* 156.

2 Jeremy Taylor and Henry Vaughan: The Stock of Nature and Art

1 *Apology,* 59.
2 Taylor was a descendant of Rowland Taylor, a chaplain to Thomas Cranmer and, in 1555, a martyr. See C.J. Stranks, *The Life and Writings of Jeremy Taylor,* 29.
3 *Life and Writings,* 113.
4 *XXV sermons preached at Golden-Grove,* 45. A second sermon on this subject offers a train of metaphors: "Prayer is the issue of a quiet mind, of untroubled thoughts, it is the daughter of charity, and the sister of meekness" (60).
5 Ibid., 58.
6 *A Discourse of Praying with the Spirit,* a2r.
7 *Of the sacred order and offices of episcopacy,* 27.
8 Ibid., "Epistle Dedicatory," a4r.
9 *Liberty of Prophesying,* B3r.
10 Ibid., 9.
11 Ibid., 10.
12 See Stranks, *The Life and Writings of Jeremy Taylor,* 73.
13 Ibid., 516.
14 H. Boone Porter, *Jeremy Taylor: Liturgist,* 46.
15 Calvin on the Psalms, quoted in Patrick Miller, *Interpreting the Psalms,* 19. See also "John Calvin to the Reader," *The Psalmes of David and others. With M. John Calvins Commentaries,* A5.v.
16 Ibid., 19–20. See also *Preface to the Psalter* in *Luther's Works, Vol. 35: Word and Sacrament I,* ed. E. Theodor Bachman, 253–7.
17 *The Psalter of David,* A3r. The 1644 edition was published anonymously. The 1647 edition I cite here bears Taylor's name.
18 Ibid., A3v.
19 Ibid., A3r.
20 Ibid.
21 Ibid., A3v.
22 Ibid., A3v–A4r.
23 George Wither remarks, "As the Psalmes are excellent in regard of the Author and Matter of them; so, are they also in respect of their Forme. For, they are in Verse, & Verse of sundry kinds; wherein there is also greater varietie of expression, then can be found in any one volume of Poesie." The Psalms illustrate the categories of petition in David's "manner of setting forth those things he purposeth: which is sometime by way of complaint, some time petitionarily, some time in one fashion, and some time in another." Importantly, they collapse the distinction between extemporaneous speech and printed text endemic to the polemics of

prayer and liturgy in the period: "And, in my opinion, it addeth somewhat to their dignitie, that they doe by a sweete and extraordinary kind of speaking, seeke to ravish the mind with the love of God." *A Preparation to the Psalter*, 127.

24 Ibid., A7r–A7v.
25 Ibid., A6r.
26 Ibid., A5v.
27 *Jeremy Taylor: Liturgist*, 46.
28 *Psalter of David*, A4v.
29 Ibid., A6v–A7r.
30 *Defence of Poetry*, 22.
31 *Liturgy and Literature in the Making of Protestant England*, 136.
32 Horton Davies, *Worship and Theology in England from Cranmer to Baxter and Fox, 1534–1690*, 344.
33 Geoffrey Nuttall, *The Holy Spirit in Puritan Faith and Experience*, 67.
34 *A Directory for the Publique Worship of God*, 5.
35 Ibid., 2.
36 Ibid., 3.
37 "The Liturgical Experience of Scripture," *George Herbert's Pastoral: New Essays on the Poet and Priest of Bemerton*, ed. Christopher Hodgkins, 200. Emphasis mine.
38 *Directory*, 1–2.
39 Ibid., 3.
40 *The Power of the Holy Ghost*, a2r.
41 Ibid., 34.
42 Ibid., 35.
43 Ibid., 36.
44 *Apology*, 8. The section of the quotation in Latin comes from Saint Ambrose's commentary on Luke 1:39: "And Mary arose in those days, and went into the hill country with haste." Taylor generally renders quotations from patristic or classical sources in Greek or Latin and presents Bible passages in English.
45 *Apology*, 14–15. The Vulgate Romans 8:26 is as follows: "*similiter autem et Spiritus adiuvat infirmitatem nostram nam quid oremus sicut oportet nescimus sed ipse Spiritus postulat pro nobis gemitibus inenarrabilibus.*"
46 *Literature and Religious Culture in Seventeenth-Century England*, 105.
47 *Defence of Poetry*, 54.
48 Spinks writes, "A fine of forty shillings was to be imposed for failure to use the Directory, and for using the prohibited Prayer Book, a fine of £5 for the first offence, £10 for the second, and a year in prison for a third." See "From Elizabeth I to Charles II," *The Oxford Guide to the Book of Common Prayer: A Worldwide Survey*, ed. Charles Hefling and Cynthia Shattuck, 51.

49 Ibid., 51.

50 *Jeremy Taylor: Liturgist*, 8.

51 *The Golden Grove*, A7v.

52 *XXV sermons preached at Golden-Grove*, 13.

53 Ibid., 15.

54 Ibid., 16.

55 In this same period, Taylor produced *The Great Exemplar* (1649), a biography of Christ combined with meditations, *Holy Living and Holy Dying* (1651), and *The Guide of Infant Devotion*, later called *A Choice Manual Containing What is to be Believed, Practiced, and Desired or Praied for; the Praiers being fitted to the several Daies of the Week*.

56 *The Golden Grove*, A3r–A3v.

57 Ibid., A4r.

58 Ibid., A4v.

59 "The dangers of prudence: salus populi suprema lex, Robert Sanderson, and the 'Case of the Liturgy,'" *Renaissance Studies*, 23 no. 4 (2009), 536.

60 *An Ordinance for the ejecting of Scandalous, Ignorant and Insufficient Ministers and School-Masters*, 612.

61 Ibid., 613.

62 Cummings, *The Book of Common Prayer*, xxxix.

63 *The Reformation*, 510.

64 *A petition for the vindication of the publique use of the Book of Common-Prayer*, A1v.

65 *Euchologia*, A5r.

66 *A Plea of the Book of Common Prayer*, A4r.

67 *A Rationale Upon the Book of Common Prayer*, A3r.

68 *Collection of Offices*, A3v, § 2.

69 *Collection of Offices*, A4r, § 3.

70 Ibid., A4v, § 4.

71 Ibid., A6r, § 6.

72 Ibid., § 18.

73 Ibid., §46.

74 *A Discourse of the Liberty of Prophesying*, 251.

75 Ibid., 252–3.

76 Ibid., 252.

77 See Anne James, *Poets, Players, and Preachers: Remembering the Gunpowder Plot in Seventeenth-Century England*.

78 David Daniel Rees, "Augustine Baker," *Oxford Dictionary of National Biography*.

79 Serenus Cressy, O.S.B, *Fanaticism Fanatically Imputed to the Catholick Church by Doctour Stillingfleet and the Imputation refuted and retorted by S.C. A Catholick O.S.B.* (1670).

80 *Sancta Sophia or Directions for the Prayer of Contemplation* (Douai, 1657), British Library Copy. The frontispiece and poem do not appear in some copies.

81 See Nandra Perry, "'Tis Heav'n She Speakes': Lady Religion, Saint Teresa, and the Politics of Ceremony in the Poetry of Richard Crashaw," *Religion & Literature*, 38 no. 2 (Summer, 2006), 3.

82 "A Hymn to the Name and Honor of the Admirable Saint Teresa," *George Herbert and the Seventeenth-Century Religious Poets*, ed. Mario A. Di Cesare, 84.

83 "Of the Spirit of Grace," 15.

84 See "The Temple in 'The Night': Henry Vaughan and the Collapse of the Established Church," *Modern Philology*, 84 no. 2 (1986), 146.

85 Rees "Augustine Baker," *ODNB*.

86 *Sancta Sophia*, ii–iii.

87 Ibid., iii.

88 Ibid., xii.

89 Ibid., iv.

90 Ibid., xii.

91 Ibid., viii.

92 Ibid., ix.

93 Ibid., xiv–xv.

94 Ibid., xxv.

95 Ibid., Treatise II: 4.

96 Ibid., II: 64.

97 "Rules and Lessons": *Henry Vaughan: The Complete Poetry*, ed. Alan Rudrum, ll. 139–41.

98 *Liberty of Prophesying*, A1r.

99 *The Works of Henry Vaughan*, ed. L.C. Martin, 2nd ed., 391.

100 *The Collected Works of Katherine Philips, The Matchless Orinda*, vol. 1 The Poems, ed. Patrick Cross, 97, ll. 25–8.

101 Lorna Hutson notes, for example, that Philips corresponded with Taylor on the subject of friendship. See "The Body of the Friend and the Woman Writer: Katherine Philips's Absence from Alan Bray's *The Friend*," *The Noble Flame of Katherine Philips: A Poetics of Culture, Politics, and Friendship*, ed. David L. Orvis and Ryan Singh, 281–5.

102 Alan Rudrum, "Paradoxical Persona: Henry Vaughan's Self-Fashioning Author(s)," *Huntington Library Quarterly* 62 (1999), 365.

103 *Vaughan's Works*, 138.

104 Ibid., 138.

105 "Rules and Lessons": *Henry Vaughan: The Complete Poetry*, ed. Alan Rudrum, ll. 139–41.

106 *Vaughan's Works*, 140.

107 Ibid., 140.

108 *Henry Vaughan: The Achievement of Silex Scintillans*.

109 "'Grace Beyond a Curl'd Lock': Further Thoughts on Henry Vaughan's 'Isaac's Marriage,'" *Connotations* 12 nos. 2–3 (2002/3), 169.

110 *Complete Poems*, 160, ll. 1–4.
111 "Narrative, Typology and Politics in Henry Vaughan's 'Isaac's Marriage,'" *Connotations* 11 no. 1 (2001/2), 78–90. 84.
112 Ibid., 88.
113 Philip West, *Henry Vaughan's Silex Scintillans: Scripture Uses*, 144.
114 See Imilda Tuttle, *Concordance to Vaughan's Silex Scintillans*, 161.
115 *Vaughan's Works*, 144.
116 Ibid., 476. This is the second of two lyrics under this title in *Silex Scintillans*, part 1, added after the publication of *Mount of Olives*.
117 *Complete Poems*, 160, ll. 7–8.
118 See James F. Forrest, "Mercy and her Mirror," *Philological Quarterly* 42 (1963), 121–5.
119 *Milton's Burden of Interpetation*, 131 ff.
120 *Complete Poems*, 311, ll. 17–22.
121 Ibid., 485, ll. 17–24.
122 *Scripture Uses*, 171.
123 *Vaughan's Works*, 147.
124 "Thou didst betray me to a lingering book": Discovering Affliction in *The Temple*," *George Herbert Journal* 28 1 and 2 (2004–5), 28–46.
125 *Complete Poems*, 155, ll. 1–4.
126 *Holy Rules and Helps to Devotion* (London, 1675), 51–2.
127 *Complete Poems*, 156, ll. 45–8.
128 Ibid., 169, ll. 8–9.
129 Ibid., 178, ll. 17–18.
130 Ibid., 179, ll. 18–24.
131 Ibid., 191, ll. 13–15.
132 Ibid., 192, ll. 7–9.
133 Ibid., 193, ll. 19–24.
134 Ibid., 238, ll. 13, 16.
135 Ibid., 167, ll. 20–4.

3 John Milton (1634–1650): The Spirit of Utterance

1 *The Shape of the Liturgy*, 1.
2 Ibid., 2.
3 In 1626, Milton wrote "Elegy III" to commemorate the death of Lancelot Andrewes. Written in Latin, it exercises Milton's skill in Latin meter and classical allusions. The poem welcomes Andrewes into "the delights of [his] father's kingdom" (*Complete Poems*, 23).
4 *Ceremony and Community*, 157.
5 *Milton's Aristocratic Entertainments*, 2.
6 *John Milton: Life, Work and Thought*, 84.

7 William B. Hunter, *Milton's Comus: Family Piece*, 30. Texts for Michaelmas Eve included 1 Corinthians 13; the readings for Michaelmas included Revelation 12. As Hunter states, Milton would "expect the audience to make the immediate association with the reading of the night before."

8 Andrew Foster writes: "Richard Neile was the political and practical patron of the Arminian group within the Church of England that took Lancelot Andrewes and John Overall as intellectual mentors and sought some return to reverence, dignity, and decorum in worship – lost, they felt, at the Reformation. They opposed the fashionable stress on preaching and reaffirmed their belief in the importance of prayer and the sacraments, which in turn led them to emphasize strict adherence to the Book of Common Prayer" (*Oxford Dictionary of National Biography*, "Durham House Group").

9 *A Collection of Private Devotions*, A3v–A42.

10 The Mask exists in five forms: the Trinity Manuscript (dated 1634); the Bridgewater Manuscript; the print publications of 1737, 1645, and 1673. See S.E. Sprott, *A Maske: The earlier Versions*, 4. The Lady's short prayer is common to all.

11 *A Collection of Private Devotions*, A3v.

12 *A Brief Survay and Censure*, 41.

13 Ibid., 62.

14 Attacks came at great risk. Peter Smart faced degradation from his ministry for attacking Cosin. See *The vanitie & downe-fall of superstitious popish ceremonies: or, A sermon preached in the cathedrall church of Durham by one Mr. Peter Smart, a praebend there.*

15 *A Tryall of Private Devotions*, E4r.

16 *A Defense of the Liturgie*, 12.

17 *Triall of the English Liturgie*, 4–5.

18 Ibid., 15.

19 Ibid., 16.

20 Ibid., 19.

21 Ibid., 18.

22 Ibid., 16.

23 *A friendly trial*, 17.

24 John Sutton, "John Ball," *Oxford Dictionary of National Biography*.

25 Smectymnuus is formed from the names of five anti-episcopal writers: Stephen Marshall, Edward Calamy, Thomas Young, Matthew Newcomen and Edward Spustow.

26 *An Humble Remonstrance*, 10–11.

27 *A Defence of the Humble Remonstrance*, 16.

28 Ibid., 17. Hall here refers to George Cassander, a sixteenth-century theologian and liturgist.

29 Ibid., 12.

30 *An Answer to a Booke Entituled, An Humble Remonstrance*, 8.

31 "Dissociation and Decapitation," *Trauma and Transformation: The Political Progress of John Bunyan*, 16.

32 According to James Clifford, a printer who worked on the first edition, Taylor "accidentally" entered the shop of the Royalist publisher Richard Royston, and saw the proofs of the *Eikon Basilike* under the title "The Royal Plea." Alarmed that so obvious a title "would betray the Book," Taylor wrote to the King to urge a change in title, suggesting that the Greek title *Eikon Basilike* would not draw the attention of anti-Royalists, and would also, as a tribute, evoke James I's *Basilikon Doron*. The Royalist writer Richard Hollingworth collected Clifford's testimony in order to attribute the *Eikon Basilike* solely to Charles I. See *Dr. Hollingworth's Defence of K. Charles the Firsts Holy and Divine Book, called Eikon Basilike* (London, 1692), 14. Hollingworth secured Clifford's testimony and included it as an affidavit in order to maintain Charles as sole author against claims that John Gauden was the real author. See also *A New Bibliography of the Eikon Basilike* by Francis F. Madan, 131. As Madan notes, Taylor, though living in Wales, is thought to have been in London in 1648. Taylor knew Royston, who published Taylor's and Sir Christopher Hatton's *Psalter of David* in 1646 (see H.R. Tedder, rev. William Proctor Williams, "Richard Royston" *ODNB*).

33 *Eikon Basilike with Selections from Eikonoklastes*, 25.

34 The King holds a crown of thorns in his right hand. A ray of heavenly light bears the words "*clarior e tenebris.*" The King's upward gaze bears the words "*caela specto.*" The key to the emblems turns these Latin phrases to verse: "So triumph I, And shine more bright / In sad Affliction's Darksom night" (*clarior e tenebris*); "That heav'nlie Crowne, already mine / I view with eyes of Faith divine" (*caela specto*).

35 Laura Lunger Knoppers, *Politicizing Domesticity from Henrietta Maria to Milton's Eve*, 73.

36 Ibid., 75.

37 One version, written by the Royalist writer David Lloyd, served to support the restoration of monarchy its original helped to ensure: *Eikon basilike: or, The true pourtraiture of His Sacred Majestie Charls the II, in three books, beginning from his birth 1630 unto this present year, 1660.*

38 *Eikon Basilike* and the rhetoric of self-representation," *The Royal Image: Representations of Charles I*, ed. Thomas Corns, 122.

39 *Eikon Basilike with Selections from Eikonoklastes*, 16.

40 Ibid., 51.

41 Ibid., 53.

42 Ibid., 87.

43 Ibid., 139.

44 Adam and Eve's morning "Orisons" echo this passage, but their prayers model spontaneous expression in "various style" (*Paradise Lost* 5. 145–6).

45 *Literature and Dissent in Milton's England*, 163.

46 See David Loewenstein, "Milton's Nationalism and the English Revolution: Strains and Contradictions," *Early Modern Nationalism and Milton's England*, 25–50.

47 *Milton and the Revolutionary Reader*, 162.

48 *Milton and the Spiritual Reader: Reading and Religion in Seventeenth-Century England*, 35.

49 Ibid., 58.

50 *Iconoclasm and Poetry in the Englihs Revolution*, 154.

51 *Milton and the Reformation Aesthetics of the Passion. Studies in the History of Christian Traditions*, 47–8.

52 *Milton and the Drama of History: Historical Vision, Iconoclasm, and the Literary Imagination*, 63.

53 Ibid., 54.

54 *Eikon Basilike* 111 qtd. in *Drama of History*, 54.

55 "Prayer as Kenosis," *The Phenomenology of Prayer*, ed. Bruce Benson and Norman Wirzna, 68.

56 *Eikon Basilike*, 132.

57 Ibid., 131.

58 Achsah Guibbory, "Charles's Prayers, Idolatrous Images, and True Creation in Milton's *Eikonoklastes*," in *Of Poetry and Politics: New Essays on Milton and His World*, ed. P.G. Stanwood, 283–94.

59 Hughes cites the birth of Typhoeus in Hesiod's *Theogony* (*Milton: Complete Poems and Major Prose* 216, n. 197). "The hands and arms of him are mighty, / and have work in them, / and the feet of the powerful go / were tireless, and up from his shoulders / there grew a hundred snake heads, / those of a dreaded dragon, /and the heads licked with dark tongues" (*Theogony* 826–32). Hughes notes Renaissance allegories of Typhoeus as "ambition that assails even heaven itself."

60 Milton also cites Matt. 18:19–20, "where two or three gather'd together in his name shall agree to ask him anything, it shall be granted" (*CPW* 3: 507).

61 Lana Cable, *Carnal Rhetoric: Milton's Iconoclasm and the Poetics of Desire*, 163.

4 John Milton (1650–1674): The Spirit of Prayer

1 Angela Esterhammer notes the etymology of divide in this word as Milton understood it. See *Creating States: Studies in the Performative Language of John Milton and William Blake*, 106–7.

2 "'Till one greater man/ Restore us … ': Restoration Images in Milton and Bunyan," *Bunyan Studies* 6 (1995–6), 25.

3 I owe this memorable distinction to hearing it in a Milton seminar Professor Keeble led in October 1995.
4 "A Life of Milton" in *John Milton*, ed. Merritt Y. Hughes, 1034.
5 See David Norbrook, *Writing the English Republic: Poetry, Rhetoric and Politics, 1627–1660*, 433.
6 See Peter Kaufman, *Prayer, Despair and Drama: Elizabethan Introspection*, 33.
7 "*Paradise Lost* and the Apotheosis of the Suppliant," *Arion: A Journal of Humanities and the Classics*, 6 no. 2 (1998), 91.
8 Qtd. In Huntley, *Bishop Hall and Protestant Meditation in Seventeenth-Century England*, 85. Hall's Protestant meditations are more sermonic than prayerful as they reflect on virtues and vices. Ignatian meditation selects specific events in the life of Christ.
9 Ibid., 86.
10 *Milton's Places of Hope: Spiritual and Political Connections of Hope with Land*, 155.
11 Ibid., 157.
12 *The Paradise Within: Studies in Vaughan, Traherne and Milton*, 23.
13 Michael Travers suggests that Milton is "closer in his later poetry to Augustinian or Reformed devotion," but he does not design his poetry according to any one method. See *The Devotional Experience in the Poetry of John Milton*, 6.
14 Ibid., xiv.
15 *Bishop Hall and Protestant Meditation*, 3.
16 *A Pretious Book of Heavenly Meditation*, A7v.
17 "Joseph Hall and Protestant Meditation," *Texas Studies in Literature and Language*, 20 no. 3 (1978), 374.
18 "Milton's Satanic Parable," *English Literary History* 50 no. 2 (1983), 282.
19 See Barbara Lewalksi, *The Rhetoric of Literary Forms in Paradise Lost*.
20 "Through the Telescope of Typology: What Adam Should Have Done," *Milton Quarterly* 23 (1989), 121–7.
21 See *The morall law expounded*.
22 See Barbara Lewalski, *Milton's Brief Epic: The Genre, Meaning, and Art of Paradise Regained*.
23 *Seven Sermons*, 1–2.
24 Ibid., 8.
25 Ibid., 10.
26 Ibid.
27 *Spiritual Architecture*, 124–5.
28 Ibid., 125.
29 Elizabeth Pope, *Paradise Regained: The Tradition and the Poem*, 54.
30 *Nationalism: Five Roads to Modernity*, 76.
31 Ibid., 77.

32 Greenfeld notes, "there are no exact equivalents of the word 'nation' (especially in the modern sense) in either Biblical Hebrew or Greek." Yet, the word "nation" occurs 454 times in the Authorized Version. See *Nationalism: Five Roads to Modernity*, 52.

33 Ibid., 19.

34 See Russell Hillier, *Milton's Messiah: The Son of God in the Works of John Milton*, 217. See also Erin Henrikson, *Milton and the Reformation Aesthetics of the Passion, Studies in the History of Christian Traditions*.

35 "*Samson Agonistes*: The Deliverer as Judge," *Milton Studies* 23 (1987), 259–90.

36 Bal proposes the idea of "counter-coherence" as a strategy for feminist readings of Judges. See *Death and Dissymmetry: The Politics of Coherence in the Book of Judges* (Chicago: University of Chicago Press, 1988), 20–1.

37 See James G. Williams, *Women Recounted: Narrative Thinking and the God of Israel* (Sheffield: Almond Press, 1982), 21.

38 *Praise and Lament in the Psalms*, 170.

39 See *The Rambler*, 16 July 1751 in *Milton: Comus and Samson Agonistes: A Casebook*, 163.

40 Anthony Low, *The Blaze of Noon: A Reading of Samson Agonistes* (New York: Columbia University Press, 1974), 4.

41 Moreover, the integration of the Book of Job, where three friends question Job, enhances the poem's relation to *Paradise Regained*, and could indicate Milton's positive, if ironic, comparison of Samson and Job. See Barbara Lewalksi's *Milton's Brief Epic*.

42 Revisionist critics revitalized debate over *Samson Agonistes* and the entire 1671 volume in productive ways, leading to new appraisals of what John Shawcross calls the "uncertain world" of the poem, and the development of a "new" Milton criticism that acknowledges conflict as well as consensus in Milton's poetry. In addition to Low, examples of "regenerationist" readings include Don Cameron Allen, "The Idea as Pattern: Despair and *Samson Agonistes*" and Mary-Ann Radzinowicz, *Towards Samson Agonistes*. For Joseph Wittreich, Jesus embodies and perfects the "better fortitude of patience" which is the "higher argument" of Milton's entire poetic corpus; Samson's martial heroism provides an ironic foil to the true messiah of *Paradise Regained*.

43 *The Uncertain World of Samson Agonistes*.

44 *Time and Narrative*, vol. 1, 5–51. Ricoeur selects Augustine's *Confessions* as the exemplar of discordant, experiential temporality, and Aristotle's concept of emplotment in the *Poetics* as the epitome of the poetic control of time. *Samson Agonistes* explores a similar convergence of biblical and classical temporalities.

45 *The Sense of an Ending: Studies in the Theory of Fiction*, 59.

46 See *Poetics*, 75.

47 *Literature and Dissent*, 147.

48 *Common Prayer*, 37.

49 "The meaning of the Joint Publication of *Paradise Regained* and *Samson Agonistes*," in *Originality and Adventure: Essays on English Language and Literature in Honour of Msahiko Kanno*, ed. Yoshiyuki Nakao and Akiyuki Jimura, 138.

50 *Exiled from Light: Divine Law, Morality, and Violence in Milton's Samson Agonistes*, 52.

51 *Literature and Dissent*, 150.

52 Ibid., 152.

53 *Worship and Theology in England*, vol. 2, 230.

54 Ibid., 232.

55 Ibid., 335.

56 *The Righteous Ruler, A Sermon Preached at St. Maries in Cambridge*, June 28, 1660, 15–16.

57 Ibid., 43.

58 "Israel and English Protestant Nationalism," *Early Modern Nationalism and Milton's England*, 116.

59 *Divine efficacy without humane power. Opened in a sermon preached at St. Margarets Church in Westminster before the Right Honourable the House of Commons, June 28. 1660. Being the day of solemne thanksgiving for the happy return of the Kings Majesty*, A2r.

60 *Davids deliverance and thanksgiving*.

61 *A Proclamation For the Observation of the Nine and twentieth day of May instant, as a day of Publick Thanksgiving, according to the late Act of Parliament for that purpose* (London, May 20, 1661).

62 Ibid.

63 *Worship and Theology in England*, vol. 2, 383.

64 *A Form of Prayer with Thanksgiving, To be Used of All the Kings Majesties Loving Subjects the 29th of May Yearly, For His Majesties Happy Return to His Kingdoms: It being also the Day of His Birth. Set forth by His Majesties Authority*, B1r.

65 Ibid., C4v.

66 Ibid.

67 *Praise and Lament in the Psalms*, 198, 8.

5 John Bunyan: The Nameless Terrible Instrument

1 *The Declaration of Breda, The Stuart Constitution: Documents and Commentary*, ed. J.P. Kenyon, 358.

2 Ibid., 362–3.

3 *Historicizing Milton: Spectacle, Power, and Poetry in Restoration England*, 126.

4 Kenyon, *The Stuart Constitution*, 363.
5 See David Appleby, *Black Bartholomew's Day: Preaching, Polemic and Restoration Nonconformity.*
6 Revision of the Prayer Book began on November 21. The Convention Parliament compelled the use of the revision in the Act of Uniformity passed on December 21. See Spinks, "From Elizabeth I to Charles II," 53–4.
7 Geoffrey Nuttall, *Richard Baxter*, 86.
8 *Protestant Autobiography in the Seventeenth-Century Anglophone World*, 235.
9 *Richard Baxter*, 86.
10 *Five Disputations of Church Government and Worship* (1659), 378, qtd. in *Worship and Theology*, II: 429.
11 Dr. Williams's Library, London, Ms 5: 9, qtd. in Davies, *Worship and Theology*, II: 427.
12 *Richard Baxter: Puritan Man of Letters*, 17.
13 *A Petition for Peace* (London, 1661), 145.
14 Ibid., 16.
15 *Considerations Touching the Liturgy of the Church of England*, 1.
16 Ibid., 9.
17 Ibid., 12.
18 Ibid., 7.
19 Richard Greaves, *Glimpses of Glory: John Bunyan and English Dissent*, 131–2.
20 See Greaves, *Glimpses of Glory*, 133–4. I am grateful to W.R. Owens for adding more information to this sequence of events.
21 1593: 25 Eliz. I, c. 1, *The Tudor Constitution: Documents and Commentary*, 2nd ed., ed. C.R. Elton, 458.
22 Ibid., 459.
23 *John Bunyan in Context*, 75.
24 Greaves, *Glimpses of Glory*, 133.
25 *A Relation of the Imprisonment of Mr. John Bunyan*, in *Grace Abounding with other Spiritual Autobiographies*, ed. John Stacchniewski with Anna Pacheco, 105. As Stachniewski notes this text consisted of "five reports or letters from the imprisoned Bunyan to the church" concerning his "arrest, prosecution, and imprisonment." It is not part of *Grace Abounding*, and was "unpublishable in the time when it was written." Preserved by his descendants, it first appeared in print in 1765.
26 *The Restoration: England in the 1660's*, 134–5.
27 Ibid., 135.
28 Ibid., 48.
29 Ibid., 45.
30 *Confessions of Faith*, 149.
31 Camden, "Blasphemy and the Problem of the Self in Grace Abounding," *Bunyan Studies* 1 no. 2 (Spring 1989), 6.
32 Ibid., 6.

33 Ibid., 5.
34 In contrast, Conti argues that Bunyan formulates the sin as "selling Christ" in the manner of Esau (typologically) and Judas (literally). See *Confessions of Faith*, 156–8.
35 "A Dark Side of Seventeenth-Century English Protestantism: The Sin Against the Holy Spirit," *The Harvard Theological Review* 77 nos. 3–4 (July–October 1984), 305.
36 "'Most Fit for a Wounded Conscience": The Place of Luther's *Commentary on Galatians* in *Grace Abounding*," *Renaissance Quarterly*, 50 no. 3 (Autumn, 1997), 826.
37 "A Dark Side of Seventeenth-Century English Protestantism: The Sin Against the Holy Spirit," 311.
38 *Persecution and Toleration in Protestant England: 1558–1689*, 167.
39 See Mark Goldie. "The Search for Religious Liberty," *The Oxford Illustrated History of Tudor and Stuart Britain*, ed. John Morrill, Tudor and Stuart Britain, 301.
40 *George Fox and Early Quaker Culture*, 8.
41 Ibid., 27–30.
42 *The Quaker's Catechism*, B32.
43 Corns, "No Man's Copy," 99.
44 See *Early Quaker Writings*, 501, 152.
45 *Let Your Words Be Few: Symbolism of Speaking and Silence among Seventeenth-Century Quakers*, 11.
46 Ibid., 127.
47 Ibid., 23.
48 *A brief relation of the irreligion of the northern Quakers* in *Early Quaker Writings: 1650–1700*, ed. Hugh Barbour and Arthur O. Roberts, 70.
49 Ibid., 70–1.
50 The critical problem concerns the Quakers' practice of speaking only when the Spirit moves them to speak. If, in consequence, silence is a major part of their worship, then prayer is most often silent and inward. Silence is not an absence, but the very ground of worship. Corns notes that Fox "makes no attempt to describe the working of the spirit" in prose, something Bunyan does at great length. Fox would have "regarded such an attempt as beyond the range of what human language can achieve" ("'No Man's Copy,'" 100).
51 As Bauman notes, the Quaker doctrine of inspired speaking eliminated the need to study original biblical languages, which they considered to be natural languages. Quakers idealized the inspiration of the primitive church and the speech of God as an Ur-language or "Adamic language." See *Let Your Words be Few*, 38.
52 *A Declaration concerning fasting and prayer*, 8.
53 Ibid., 8.

54 Bauman, 77.
55 *George Fox and Early Quaker Culture*, 44.
56 *George Fox: The Journal*, ed. Nigel Smith, 35.
57 *The Sorrows of the Quaker Jesus*, 206.
58 *George Fox: The Journal*, 201.
59 Ibid., 202.
60 *The Grand Imposter*, qtd. in *The Sorrows of the Quaker Jesus*, 148.
61 *George Fox and Early Quaker Culture*, 52.
62 *The Grand Imposter*, qtd. in *The Sorrows of the Quaker Jesus*, 131.
63 "'For then I should be a Ranter or a Quaker': John Bunyan and Radical Religion," *Awakening Words: John Bunyan and the Language of Community*, ed. David Gay, James G. Randall, Arlette Zinck, 127.
64 Douglas Gwyn, "James Nayler and the Lamb's War," *Quaker Studies* 12 no. 2 (2008), 175.
65 Ibid., 175.
66 *Something in answer to that book called The church-faith*, 19.
67 Ibid., 20.
68 Ibid., 4.
69 Ibid., 7.
70 Ibid., 36.
71 Ibid., 34.
72 *Quakerism no Paganism*, 12.
73 Ibid., 13.
74 Letter quoted by David Neelon in "James Nayler in the English Civil War," *Quaker Studies* 6 no. 1 (2002), 11.
75 *Quakerism no Paganism*, 338.
76 Ibid., 338.
77 Ibid., 50.
78 Ibid., 56.
79 Greaves, *Glimpses of Glory*, 79.
80 Ibid., 81.
81 "The Unbearable Inner Light: John Bunyan's Controversy with the Quakers," *Bunyan Studies* 10 (2010), 34.
82 Ibid., 40.
83 *George Fox and Early Quaker Culture*, 52.
84 "'For then I should be a Ranter or a Quaker': John Bunyan and Radical Religion," *Awakening Words: John Bunyan and the Language of Community*, ed. David Gay, James G. Randall, Arlette Zinck, 127.
85 *Women's Speaking*, 10.
86 Ibid., 14.
87 "'Baffled and Befooled': Misogyny in the Work of John Bunyan," *Awakening Words*, 155.

88 *The Narrative of the Persecution of Agnes Beaumont. The Narrative of the Persecution of Agnes Beaumont*, ed. Vera Camden, 2002.

89 *Glimpses of Glory*, 411.

90 Benjamin Keach, *Troposchemalogia: Tropes and Figures; or, a treatise of the Metaphors, Allegories, and express Similitudes &c. contained n the Bible of the Old and New Testament* (London, 1682), 161. Also quoted in Forrest and Sharrock (*HW*, 265).

91 Forrest went on to describe the broader tradition equating prayer with divine weaponry. He offers the "nameless terrible instrument" as a solution to the more famous crux in Milton's "Lycidas," written in 1637: "But that two-handed engine at the door / Stands ready to smite once, and smite no more." See "Milton and the Divine Art of Weaponry," *Milton Studies* 16 (1982), 131–40.

92 *John Bunyan's Master Story: The Holy War as Battle Allegory in Religious and Biblical Context*, 178.

93 Ibid., 178–9.

94 Bunyan poses a riddle in the preface to *Grace Abounding to the Chief of Sinners:* "I have sent you here enclosed a drop of that honey, that I have taken out of the Carcase of a Lyon, Judg. 14. 5, 6, 7, 8. I have eaten thereof my self also, and am much refreshed thereby. (Temptations when we meet them at first, are as the Lyon that roared upon Sampson: but if we overcome them, the next time we see them, we shall finde a Nest of Honey within them.) The Philistians understand me not" (*GA*, 1).

95 Hebrews 11 is a scriptural source for exploits of faith, and could have influenced Tertullian.

96 Bunyan uses the name "Lord's Prayer" positively on one occasion: his meditation "Upon the Lord's Prayer" in his *Book for Boys and Girls,* published in 1686. This is a paraphrase of the prayer, not a transcription. The "Lord's Prayer" was certainly a familiar name to the dissenting community. This does not contradict my argument. I contend that Bunyan rejects the name in the context that generated Dissent.

97 Ibid., ch. 39, § 29.

98 Benjamin Keach explicates this idea, arguing that prayer has "stopp'd the Lion's Mouth" and "opened Prison-Door." There "is none of the battering Rams, or Artillery of Hell can stand against it.'Tis like an Engine (as one observes) that makes the Persecutors tremble; and wo to them that are the Buts and Marks that it is levell'd at, when it is fired with the Fire of the Spirit, and discharged in the Strength of Faith" (*Troposchemalogia*, 161).

99 Hebrews 11 provides a partial list of these many exploits. Heroes of faith "subdued kingdoms, wrought righteousness, obtained promises, stopped the mouths of lions … waxed valiant in fight, turned to flight the armies of the aliens" (11:33–4) and endured persecution and imprisonment."

But what of Tertullian's claim that prayer alone "conquers God"? This establishes the tradition of prayer as the believer's assault, not on adversaries, but on heaven itself. Dependence on grace requires a spiritual attack on the throne of grace. Jesus commends this kind of spiritual violence: "And from the days of John the Baptist until now the kingdom of heaven suffereth violence, and the violent take it by force" (Matt. 11:12).

Afterword

1 *NZ Herald*, 20–12–19. The photographer is Vincent Yu of the Associated Press.
2 *A Collection of Emblemes* (London 1635), 81.
3 Government of Canada, *Constitution Act, 1982*, section 2.
4 *Milton and the Post-secular Present: Ethics, Politics, Terrorism*, 7.
5 *The Stripping of the Altars: Traditional Religion in England c. 1400–c. 1580*, 7.
6 "Prayer as Kenosis," 68.

Bibliography

Primary Sources

Andrewes, Lancelot. *XCVI Sermons by the Right Honorable and Reverend Father in God, Lancelot Andrewes, late Lord Bishop of Winchester.* London, 1629.
– *The Private Devotions of Lancelot Andrewes.* [1647]. Translated by F.E. Brightman. New York: Meridian, 1961.
– *Scala Coeli: Nineteen Sermons Concerning Prayer.* London, 1611.
– *Institutiones Piae or Directions to Pray.* London, 1640.
– *The morall law expounded.* London, 1642.
– *Preces Privatae Graece & Latine.* Oxford: 1675.
– *Seven sermons on, the wonderfull combate (for Gods glorie and mans salvation) betweene Christ and Sathan Delivered by the Reverend Father in God, Doct. Andrewes, Bishop of Winchester, lately deceased.* London, 1627.
Anon. *Triall of the English Liturgie.* London, 1637.
Aristotle. *Poetics. Literary Criticism from Plato to Dryden.* Edited by Alan H. Gilbert. Detroit: Wayne State University Press, 1982.
Bacon, Anne. *Sermons of Barnardine Ochine of Sena.* London, 1548.
Baker, Augustine O.S.B. *Sancta Sophia or Directions for the Prayer of Contemplation.* Translated by Serenus Cressy O.S.B. Douai, 1657.
Ball, John. *A friendly triall of the grounds tending to separation in a plain and modest dispute touching the lawfulnesse of a stinted liturgie and set form of prayer.* London, 1640.
Barclay, Robert and George Keith. *Quakerism confirmed, or, A vindication of the chief doctrines and principles of the people called Quakers from the arguments and objections of the students of divinity (so called) of Aberdeen in their book entituled Quakerism convassed.* London, 1676.
Baxter, Richard. *A Petition for Peace with the Reformation of the Liturgy.* London, 1661.
– *Five Disputations of Church Government and Worship.* London, 1659.
– *The Quaker's Catechism.* London, 1657.

Beaumont, Agnes. *The Narrative of the Persecution of Agnes Beaumont*. Edited by Vera Camden. East Lansing: Michigan State University Press, 2002.

Book of Common Prayer: The Texts of 1549, 1559 and 1662. Edited by Brian Cummings. Oxford: Oxford University Press, 2011.

Bunyan, John. *The Holy War*. Edited by James F. Forrest and Roger Sharrock. Oxford: Clarendon Press, 1982.

– *Grace Abounding to the Chief of Sinners*, in *Grace Abounding with other Spiritual Autobiographies*. Edited by John Stachniewski with Anita Pacheco. Oxford: Oxford University Press, 1998.

– *Pilgrim's Progress*. Edited by W.R. Owens. Oxford: Oxford University Press, 2003.

– *I Will Pray with the Spirit*. The Miscellaneous Works of John Bunyan. Vol. 2. Edited by Richard Greaves. Oxford: Clarendon Press, 1976.

– *A Case of Conscience Resolved*. The Miscellaneous Works of John Bunyan. Vol. 4. Edited by T.L. Underwood. Oxford: Clarendon Press, 1989.

Burton, Henry. *A Tryall of Private Devotions*. London, 1628.

Calvin, John. *The Psalmes of David and others. With M. John Calvins Commentaries*. London, 1571.

– *A commentarie upon S. Paules epistles to the Corinthians*. Translated by T. Timme. London, 1577.

Charles II. *The Declaration of Breda. The Stuart Constitution: Documents and Commentary*. Edited by J.P. Kenyon, 357–8. Cambridge: Cambridge University Press, 1966.

Cosin, John. *A Collection of Private Devotions*. London, 1627.

Crashaw, Richard. "A Hymn to the Name and Honor of the Admirable Saint Teresa." In *George Herbert and the Seventeenth-Century Religious Poets*, edited by Mario A. Di Cesare, 84–8. New York: Norton, 1978.

Cressy, Serenus, O.S.B. *Fanaticism Fanatically Imputed to the Catholick Church by Doctour Stillingfleet and the Imputation refuted and retorted by S.C. A Catholick O.S.B.* 1670.

Deacon, John. *The Grand Imposter: Or, The Life, Tryal, and Examination of James Nayler, the Seduced and Seducing Quaker With the Manner of his Riding into Bristol. Whereunto is added, the sentence passed upon him by the High Court of Parliament*. London, 1657.

Dell, William. *The Power of the Holy Ghost Dispersed through the Whole Body of Christ*. London, 1645.

Donne, John. *John Donne's Poetry*. Edited by Donald R. Dickson. New York: Norton, 2007.

Drake, Richard, ed. *A manual of the private devotions and meditations of The Right Reverend Father in God Lancelot Andrews*. London, 1648.

Duppa, Bryan. *Holy Rules and Helps to Devotion*. London, 1675.

Edwards, Thomas. *Gangraena, or a Catalogue and Discovery of many of the Errours, Heresies, Blasphemies and pernicious Practices of the Sectaries of this Time*. London, 1646.

Fell, Margaret. *Women's Speaking Justified*. London, 1667.

Fisher, Ambrose. *A Defense of the Liturgie of the Church of England*. London, 1630.

Fox, George. *The Journal*. [1694]. Edited by Nigel Smith. London: Penguin, 1998.

– *Something in answer to that book called the church-faith*. London, 1660.

– *Something in answer to the old Common-prayer-book*. London, 1660.

Gatford, Lionel. *A petition for the vindication of the publique use of the Book of Common-Prayer*. London, 1654.

Gauden, John. *Considerations Touching the Liturgy of the Church of England*. London: 1661.

Government of Canada. *Constitution Act, 1982*. http://laws-lois.justice.gc.ca/eng/Const/page-15.html.

Government of England. *An Ordinance for the ejecting of Scandalous, Ignorant and Insufficient Ministers and School-Masters*. London, 1654.

Hall, Joseph. *An Humble Remonstrance to the High Court of Parliament*. London, 1640.

– *A Defence of the Humble Remonstrance*. London, 1641.

– *Meditations and Vowes, Divine and Morall*. London, 1606.

Hammond, Henry. *A View of the New Directory and A Vindication of the Ancient Liturgy of the Church of England*. Oxford, 1646.

Harwood, John. *A Plea of the Book of Common Prayer*. London, 1657.

Herbert, George. *The English Poems of George Herbert*. Edited by Helen Wilcox. Cambridge: Cambridge University Press, 2007.

– *The Latin Poetry of George Herbert: A Bilingual Edition*. Translated by Mark McCloskey and Paul Murphy. Athens: Ohio University Press, 1965.

– *The Country Parson*. [1652]. *The Works of George Herbert*. Edited by F.E. Hutchinson. Oxford: Clarendon Press, 1941.

Higginson, Francis. *A brief relation of the irreligion of the northern Quakers*. London: 1653. In *Early Quaker Writings: 1650–1700*. Edited by Hugh Barbour and Arthur O. Roberts, 64–78. Wallingford PA: Pendle Hill Publications, 2004.

Hollingworth, Richard. *Dr. Hollingworth's Defence of K. Charles the Firsts Holy and Divine Book, called Eikon Basilike*. London, 1692.

Keach, Benjamin. *Troposchemalogia: Tropes and Figures; or, a treatise of the Metaphors, Allegories, and express Similitudes &c. contained n the Bible of the Old and New Testament*. London, 1682.

Leslie, Henry. *A Discourse of Praying with the Spirit*. London, 1660.

Lloyd, David. *Eikon basilike: or, The true pourtraiture of His Sacred Majestie Charls the II, in three books, beginning from his birth 1630 unto this present year, 1660*. London, 1660.

Loddington, William. *Quakerism No Paganism*. London, 1674.

Long, Thomas. *An Excercitation concerning the use of the Lords Prayer in Public Worship*. London, 1658.

Luther, Martin. *Preface to the Psalter*. In *Luther's Works, Vol. 35: Word and Sacrament I*. Edited by Theodor Bachman, 253–7. Philadelphia: Muhlenberg Press, 1960.

Manton, Thomas. *A Practical Exposition of the Lord's Prayer*. London, 1684.

Milton, John. *John Milton: Complete Poems and Major Prose*. Edited by M.Y. Hughes. Indianapolis: Bobbs-Merrill, 1984.

– *Complete Prose Works of John Milton*. 8 vols. Edited by Don Wolfe et al. New Haven: Yale University Press, 1953–82.

Parliament of England. *A Directory for the Publique Worship of God, throughout the three Kingdoms of England, Scotland, and Ireland. Together with an Ordinance of Parliament for the taking away of the Book of Common-Prayer: Ordered by the Lords and Commons assembled in Parliament*. London, 1644.

– *A Proclamation For the Observation of the Nine and twentieth day of May instant, as a day of Publick Thanksgiving, according to the late Act of Parliament for that purpose*. London, May 20, 1661.

– 1593: 25 Eliz. I, c. 1. *The Tudor Constitution: Documents and Commentary*. 2nd ed. Edited by C.R. Elton, 458–61. Cambridge: Cambridge University Press, 1960, rpt. 1982.

Philips, Katherine. *The Collected Works of Katherine Philips, The Matchless Orinda*. Vol. 1: The Poems. Edited by Patrick Cross. Stump Cross, Essex: Stump Cross Books, 1990.

Powell, Vavasor. *Common Prayer Book No Divine Service*. London, 1660.

Prideaux, John. *Euchologia, or, The doctrine of practical praying*. London, 1656.

Prynne, William. *A Brief Survay and Censure of Mr. Cosins his couzening devotions*. London, 1628.

Reynolds, Edward. *Divine efficacy without humane power. Opened in a sermon preached at St. Margarets Church in Westminster before the Right Honourable the House of Commons, June 28. 1660. Being the day of solemne thanksgiving for the happy return of the Kings Majesty*. London, 1660.

Rogers, Thomas. *A Pretious Booke of Heavenlie meditations, called A private talk of the soul with God*. London, 1616.

Scultetus, D. Abrahamus. *A Defence of the Humble Remonstrance Against the frivolous and false exceptions of Smectymnuus, translated from Latin*. London, 1641.

Sheldon, Gilbert. *Davids deliverance and thanksgiving*. London, 1660.

Sidney, Sir Philip. *A Defence of Poetry*. Edited by J.A. Van Dorsten. Oxford: Oxford University Press, 1984.

Smart, Peter. *The vanitie & downe-fall of superstitious popish ceremonies: or, A sermon preached in the cathedrall church of Durham by one Mr. Peter Smart, a praebend there*. London, 1628.

Smectymnuus. *An Answer to a Booke Entituled, An Humble Remonstrance*. London, 1641.

Sparrow, Anthony. *A Rationale Upon the Book of Common Prayer of the Church of England*. London, 1657.

Spencer, John. *The Righteous Ruler, A Sermon Preached at St. Maries in Cambridge*, June 28, 1660. Cambridge: 1660.

Taylor, Jeremy. *An Apology for Authorized and Set Forms of Liturgie against the Pretence of the Spirit*. London, 1649.

– *A discourse concerning prayer ex tempore, or, by pretence of the spirit. In justification of authorized and set-formes of lyturgie*. London, 1646.

– *XXV sermons preached at Golden-Grove*. London, 1653.

– *Of the sacred order and offices of episcopacy*. Oxford, 1642.

– *A Discourse of the Liberty of Prophesying*. London, 1647.

– *The Psalter of David*. London, 1647.

– *An Apology for Authorized and Set Forms of Liturgie against the Pretence of the Spirit*. London, 1649.

– *XXVIII Sermons preached at Golden Grove*. London, 1654.

– *The Rule and Exercises of Holy Living*. London, 1650.

– *A collection of offices or forms of prayer in cases ordinary and extraordinary*. London, 1657.

– *The golden grove, or, A manuall of daily prayers and letanies, fitted to the dayes of the week*. London, 1654.

– *Symbolon theologikon*. London, 1674.

Tertullian, Septimus. *De Oratione* (Tertullian on the Prayer). Edited and translated by Ernest Evans. London: S.P.C.K., 1953. http://www.tertullian.org/articles/evans_orat/evans_orat_04english.htm.

– *On Prescription against Heretics, The Writings of Quintus Sept. Flor. Tertullianus*. 3 vols. Vol. 2. Translated by Peter Holmes. Edinburgh: T.T. Clark, 1884.

Vaughan, Henry. *The Works of Henry Vaughan*. Edited by L.C. Martin. Second edition. Oxford: Oxford University Press, 1957.

– *Henry Vaughan: The Complete Poems*. Edited by Alan Rudrum. Harmondsworth: Penguin, 1983.

Walton, Izaak. *The lives of Dr. John Donne, Sir Henry Wotton, Mr. Richard Hooker, Mr. George Herbert written by Izaak Walton*. London, 1670.

Williams, Roger. *The Bloudy Tenent of Persecution, for cause of Conscience, discussed, in a conference betweene Truth and Peace*. London, 1644.

Wither, George. *A Preparation to the Psalter*. London, 1619.

– *A Collection of Emblemes, ancient and moderne quickened with metricall illustrations, both morall and divines*. London, 1635.

Wren, Matthew. *A Form of Prayer with Thanksgiving, To be Used of All the Kings Majesties Loving Subjects the 29th of May Yearly, For His Majesties Happy Return to His Kingdoms: It being also the Day of His Birth. Set forth by His Majesties Authority*. London, 1662.

Secondary Sources

Achinstein, Sharon. *Literature and Dissent in Milton's England*. Cambridge: Cambridge University Press, 2003.

– *Milton and the Revolutionary Reader*. Princeton: Princeton University Press, 1994.

– "Reading George Herbert in the Restoration." *English Literary Renaissance* 36 no. 3 (2006): 430–65.

Ainsworth, David. *Milton and the Spiritual Reader: Reading and Religion in Seventeenth-Century England*. New York: Routledge, 2008.

Allen, Don Cameron. "The Idea as Pattern: Despair and *Samson Agonistes*." In *Twentieth Century Interpretations of Samson Agonistes*, edited by Galbraith Crump, 51–62. Englewood Cliffs: Prentice-Hall, 1968.

Appleby, David. *Black Bartholomew's Day: Preaching, Polemic and Restoration Nonconformity*. Manchester: Manchester University Press, 2012.

Bal, Mieke. *Death and Dissymmetry: The Politics of Coherence in the Book of Judges*. Chicago: University of Chicago Press, 1988.

Barbour, Reid. *Literature and Religious Culture in Seventeenth-Century England*. Cambridge: Cambridge University Press, 2002.

Bauman, Richard. *Let Your Words Be Few: Symbolism of Speaking and Silence among Seventeenth-Century Quakers*. London: Quaker Home Service, 1998.

Blessington, Francis. "*Paradise Lost* and the Apotheosis of the Suppliant." *Arion: A Journal of Humanities and the Classics* 6 no. 2 (1998): 83–97.

Branch, Lori. *Rituals of Spontaneity: Sentiment and Secularism from Free Prayer to Wordsworth*. Waco: Baylor University Press, 2006.

Brook, Stella. *The Language of the Book of Common Prayer*. London: Andre Deustsch, 1965.

Brown, Cedric. *Milton's Aristocratic Entertainments*. Cambridge: Cambridge University Press, 1985.

Brueggemann, Walter. "Psalms and the Life of Faith: A Suggested Typology of Function." *Journal for the Study of the Old Testament* 17 (1980): 3–30.

– *Praise and Lament in the Psalms*. Edinburgh: T & T Clark Ltd., 1981.

Cable, Lana. *Carnal Rhetoric: Milton's Iconoclasm and the Poetics of Desire*. Durham: Duke University Press, 1995.

Calhoun, Thomas. *Henry Vaughan: The Achievement of Silex Scintillans*. Newark: University of Delaware Press, 1981.

Camden, Vera. "Blasphemy and the Problem of the Self in *Grace Abounding*," *Bunyan Studies* 1 no. 2 (Spring 1989): 5–21.

– ""Most Fit for a Wounded Conscience": The Place of Luther's *Commentary on Galatians* in *Grace Abounding*," *Renaissance Quarterly* 50 no.3 (Autumn, 1997): 819–49.

– "The Unbearable Inner Light: John Bunyan's Controversy with the Quakers." *Bunyan Studies* 10 (2010): 34–55.

Campbell, Gordon, and Thomas Corns. *John Milton: Life, Work, and Thought.* Oxford: Oxford University Press, 2008.

Coffey, John. *Persecution and Toleration in Protestant England: 1558–1689.* Harlow, England: Pearson, 2000.

Collinson, Patrick. *The Birthpangs of Protestant England: Religious and Cultural Change in the Sixteenth and Seventeenth Centuries.* London: Macmillan 1988.

Conti, Brooke. *Confessions of Faith in Early Modern England.* Philadelphia: University of Pennsylvania Press, 2014.

Corns, Thomas. "'No Man's Copy': The Critical Problem of Fox's *Journal.*" In *The Emergence of Quaker Writing: Dissenting Literature in Seventeenth-Century England,* 99–111. London: Frank Cass and Company, 1995.

Corthell, Ron. "Joseph Hall and Protestant Meditation." *Texas Studies in Literature and Language* 20 no. 3 (1978): 367–85.

Cummings, Brian. "Introduction." In *The Book of Common Prayer,* ix–lii. Oxford: Oxford University Press, 2011.

– *The Literary Culture of Reformation: Grammar and Grace.* Oxford: Oxford University Press, 2002.

Curry, David. "Something Understood." In *The Book of Common Prayer: Past, Present and Future,* edited by Prudence Dailey, 52–69. London: Continuum, 2011.

Daems, Jim, and Holly Faith Nelson, eds. *Eikon Basilike with Selections from Eikonoklastes.* Peterborough: Broadview, 2006.

Damrosch, Leo. "James Nayler." *Oxford Dictionary of National Biography.*

– *The Sorrows of the Quaker Jesus: James Nayler and the Puritan Crackdown on the Free Spirit.* Cambridge, Massachusetts: Harvard University Press, 1996.

Danielson, Dennis. "Through the Telescope of Typology: What Adam Should Have Done." *Milton Quarterly* 23 (1989): 121–7.

Davies, Horton. *Worship and Theology in England from Cranmer to Baxter and Fox, 1534–1690.* Grand Rapids: Eerdmans, 1975.

Dix, Dom Gregory. *The Shape of the Liturgy.* Westminster: Dacre Press, 1945.

Doerksen, Daniel. *Picturing Religious Experience: George Herbert, Calvin, and the Scriptures.* Newark: University of Delaware Press, 2011.

Duffy, Eamon. *The Stripping of the Altars: Traditional Religion in England c. 1400–c. 1580.* New Haven and London: Yale University Press, 1992.

Dyck, Paul. "George Herbert and the Liturgical Experience of Scripture." In *George Herbert's Pastoral: New Essays on the Poet and Priest of Bemerton,* edited by Christopher Hodgkins, 197–210. Newark: University of Delaware Press, 2010.

– "Thou didst betray me to a lingering book": Discovering Affliction in *The Temple.*" *George Herbert Journal* 28 nos. 1 and 2 (2004–5): 28–46.

Esterhammer, Angela. *Creating States: Studies in the Performative Language of John Milton and William Blake.* Toronto: University of Toronto Press, 1994.

Ferry, Anne Davidson. *The Art of Naming.* Chicago: University of Chicago Press, 1988.

Forrest, James F. "Milton and the Divine Art of Weaponry." *Milton Studies* 16 (1982): 131–40.

– "Mercy and her Mirror." *Philological Quarterly* 42 (1963): 121–5.

Fenton, Mary. *Milton's Places of Hope: Spiritual and Political Connections of Hope with Land.* Aldershot UK and Burlington VT: Ashgate Publishing, 2006.

Foster, Andrew. "Durham House Group." *Oxford Dictionary of National Biography.*

Frye, Northrop. *The Great Code: The Bible and Literature.* Toronto: Academic Press, 1982.

Garrett, Cynthia. "The Rhetoric of Supplication: Prayer Theory in Seventeenth-Century England." *Renaissance Quarterly* 46 no. 2 (1993): 328–57.

Gibbons, Daniel R. *Conflicts of Devotion: Liturgical Poetics in Sixteenth and Seventeenth-Century England.* South Bend: University of Notre Dame Press, 2017.

Gilman, Ernest. *Iconoclasm and Poetry in the English Reformation.* Chicago: University of Chicago Press, 1986.

Goldie, Mark. "The Search for Religious Liberty." *The Oxford Illustrated History of Tudor and Stuart Britain,* edited by John Morrill, 293–309. Oxford: Oxford University Press, 1996.

Greaves, Richard L. *Glimpses of Glory: John Bunyan and English Dissent.* Stanford: Stanford University Press, 2002.

Greenfeld, Liah. *Nationalism: Five Roads to Modernity.* Boston: Harvard University Press, 1992.

Guibbory, Achsah. "Charles's Prayers, Idolatrous Images, and True Creation in Milton's *Eikonoklastes.*" In *Of Poetry and Politics: New Essays on Milton and His World,* edited by P.G. Stanwood, 283–94. Binghamton, NY: Medieval and Renaissance Texts and Studies, 1995.

– *Ceremony and Community from Herbert to Milton.* Cambridge: Cambridge University Press, 1998.

– "Israel and English Protestant Nationalism: 'Fast Sermons' during the English Revolution." In *Early Modern Nationalism and Milton's England,* edited by David Loewenstein and Paul Stevens, 115–38. Toronto: University of Toronto Press, 2008.

Gwyn, Douglas. "James Nayler and the Lamb's War." *Quaker Studies* 12 no. 2 (2008): 171–88.

Hammerling, Roy. *The Lord's Prayer in the Early Church.* New York: Palgrave Macmillan, 2010.

Haskin, Dayton. *Milton's Burden of Interpetation.* Phildelphia: University of Pennsylvania Press, 1994.

Henrikson, Erin. *Milton and the Reformation Aesthetics of the Passion. Studies in the History of Christian Traditions.* Boston: Brill, 2010.

Hinds, Hilary. *George Fox and Early Quaker Culture.* Manchester: Manchester University Press, 2011.

Hillier, Russell. *Milton's Messiah: The Son of God in the Works of John Milton.* Oxford: Oxford University Press, 2011.

Hunter, William B. *Milton's Comus: Family Piece.* Whitston Publishing Co., 1983.

Huntley, Frank Livingstone. *Bishop Hall and Protestant Meditation in Seventeenth-Century England.* Binghamton NY: Centre for Medieval and Renaissance Studies, 1981.

Hutson, Lorna. "The Body of the Friend and the Woman Writer: Katherine Philips's Absence from Alan Bray's *The Friend.*" In *The Noble Flame of Katherine Philips: A Poetics of Culture, Politics, and Friendship,* edited by David L. Orvis and Ryan Singh Paul, 267–90. Pittsburgh: Duquesne University Press, 2015.

James, Anne. *Poets, Players, and Preachers: Remembering the Gunpowder Plot in Seventeenth-Century England.* Toronto: University of Toronto Press, 2016.

James, P.D. "Through all the Changing Scenes of Life: Living with the Prayer Book." *The Book of Common Prayer: Past, Present and Future,* edited by Prudence Dailey, 45–51. London: Continuum, 2011.

Kaufman, Peter. *Prayer, Despair and Drama: Elizabethan Introspection.* Urbana and Chicago: University of Illinois Press, 1996.

Keeble, N.H. "'Till one greater man/ Restore us … ': Restoration Images in Milton and Bunyan." *Bunyan Studies* 6 (1995–6): 6–33.

– *Richard Baxter: Puritan Man of Letters.* Oxford: Oxford University Press, 1982.

– *The Restoration: England in the 1660's.* Oxford: Blackwell, 2002.

Kenyon, J.P., ed. *The Stuart Constitution: Documents and Commentary.* Cambridge: Cambridge University Press, 1966.

Kermode, Frank. *The Sense of an Ending: Studies in the Theory of Fiction.* London: Oxford University Press, 1966.

Knoppers, Laura Lunger. *Politicizing Domesticity from Henrietta Maria to Milton's Eve.* Cambridge: Cambridge University Press, 2014.

– *Historicizing Milton: Spectacle, Power, and Poetry in Restoration England.* Athens, Georgia: University of Georgia Press, 1994.

Kohler, Kaufmann. "The Lord's Prayer." *Jewish Encyclopedia,* Jewishencyclopedia.com.

Kuchar, Gary. *George Herbert and the Mystery of the Word: Poetry and Scripture in Seventeenth-Century England.* Cham, Switzerland: Palgrave Macmillan, 2017.

Lake, Peter. "Lancelot Andrewes, John Buckeridge, and Avant-Garde Conformity at the Court of James I." In *The Mental World of the Jacobean Court,* edited by Linda Levy Peck, 113–33. Cambridge: Cambridge University Press, 1991.

Lander, Jesse M. *Inventing Polemic: Religion, Print, and Literary Culture in Early Modern England.* Cambridge: Cambridge University Press, 2006.

Lewalski, Barbara. *The Rhetoric of Literary Forms in Paradise Lost*. Princeton: Princeton University Press, 1985.

– *Milton's Brief Epic: The Genre, Meaning, and Art of Paradise Regained*. Providence: Brown University Press, 1966.

Loewenstein, David. "Milton's Nationalism and the English Revolution: Strains and Contradictions." *Early Modern Nationalism and Milton's England*, 25–50. Toronto: University of Toronto Press, 2008.

– *Milton and the Drama of History: Historical Vision, Iconoclasm, and the Literary Imagination*. Cambridge: Cambridge University Press, 1990.

– "Treason against God and State: Blasphemy in Milton's Culture and *Paradise Lost*." In *Milton and Heresy*, edited by Stephen Dobranski and John Rumrich, 176–98. Cambridge: Cambridge University Press, 1998.

Loscocco, Paula. "Royalist Reclamation of Psalmic Song in 1650's England." *Renaissance Quarterly*, 64 (2011), 500–43.

Low, Anthony. *The Blaze of Noon: A Reading of Samson Agonistes*. New York: Columbia University Press, 1974.

Lovelock, Julian, ed. *Milton: Comus and Samson Agonistes: A Casebook*. London: Macmillan, 1975.

Lynch, Kathleen. *Protestant Autobiography in the Seventeenth-Century Anglophone World*. Oxford: Oxford University Press, 2012.

MacCallum, Hugh. "*Samson Agonistes*: The Deliverer as Judge," *Milton Studies* 23 (1987): 259–90.

MacCulloch, Diarmaid. *The Reformation*. New York: Viking, 2003.

Madan, Francis F. *A New Bibliography of the Eikon Basilike*. Oxford: Oxford University Press, 1950.

Martz. Louis. L. *The Paradise Within: Studies in Vaughan, Traherne and Milton*. New Haven and London: Yale University Press, 1964.

McCullough, P.E. "Lancelot Andrewes's Transforming Passions." *Huntington Library Quarterly* 71 no. 4 (2008): 573–89.

– "Lancelot Andrewes." *Oxford Dictionary of National Biography*.

– "Henry Isaacson." *Oxford Dictionary of National Biography*.

– ed. *Lancelot Andrewes: Selected Sermons and Lectures*. Cambridge: Cambridge University Press, 2005.

– "Making Dead Men Speak: Laudianism, Print, and the Works of Lancelot Andrewes, 1626–1642." *The Historical Journal* 41 no. 2 (1998): 401–24.

McCutcheon, Elizabeth. "Preces Privatae: A Journey through Time." *Studies in Philology* 65 no. 2 (1968): 223–41.

Mensch, James. "Prayer as Kenosis." *The Phenomenology of Prayer*. Edited by Bruce Benson and Norman Wirzna, 63–74. New York: Fordham, 1995.

Merrill, Thomas F. "Milton's Satanic Parable." *English Literary History* 50 no. 2 (1983): 279–95.

Miller, Patrick. *Interpreting the Psalms*. Philadelphia: Fortress Press, 1986.

Milton, Anthony. *Catholic and Reformed: The Roman and Protestant Churches in English Protestant Thought: 1600–1640*. Cambridge: Cambridge University Press, 1995.

Mohamed, Feisal. *Milton and the Post-secular Present: Ethics, Politics, Terrorism.* Stanford: Stanford University Press, 2011.

Mullett, Michael. *John Bunyan in Context.* Pittsburgh: Duquesne University Press, 1997.

Najapfour, Brian G. "After This Manner Therefore Pray Ye": Puritan Perspectives on The Lord's Prayer." *Puritan Reformed Journal* 4 no. 4 (2012): 158–69.

Narveson, Kate. "Herbert and early Stuart Psalm Culture: Beyond Translation and Meditation." In *George Herbert's Pastoral: New Essays on the Poet and Priest of Bemerton.* Edited by Christopher Hodgkins, 211–34. Newark: University of Delaware Press, 2010.

Neelon, David. "James Nayler in the English Civil War." *Quaker Studies* 6 no. 1 (2002): 8–36.

Norbrook, David. *Writing the English Republic: Poetry, Rhetoric and Politics, 1627–1660.* Cambridge: Cambridge University Press, 1999.

Nuttall, Geoffrey. *The Holy Spirit in Puritan Faith and Experience.* Chicago: University of Chicago Press, 1946, rpt. 1992.

– *Richard Baxter.* London: Nelson, 1965.

Parry, Graham. *Glory, Laud and Honour: The Arts of the Anglican Counter-Reformation.* London: Boydell, 2006.

Perry, Nandra. "'Tis Heav'n She Speakes': Lady Religion, Saint Teresa, and the Politics of Ceremony in the Poetry of Richard Crashaw." *Religion & Literature* 38 no. 2 (Summer 2006): 1–23.

Pope, Elizabeth. *Paradise Regained: The Tradition and the Poem.* New York: Russell and Russell, 1962.

Porter, H. Boone. *Jeremy Taylor: Liturgist.* Alcuin Club; SPCK, 1979.

Prior, Charles. *Defining the Jacobean Church: The Politics of Religious Controversy, 1603–1625.* Cambridge: Cambridge University Press, 2005.

Pursglove, Glyn. "'Grace Beyond a Curl'd Lock": Further Thoughts on Henry Vaughan's 'Isaac's Marriage.'" *Connotations* 12 no. 2–3 (2002/3): 167–82.

Radzinowicz, Mary-Ann. *Towards Samson Agonistes: The Growth of Milton's Mind.* Princeton: Princeton University Press, 1978.

Rees, David Daniel. "Augustine Baker." *Oxford Dictionary of National Biography.*

Ricoeur, Paul. *Time and Narrative,* vol. 1. Chicago: University of Chicago Press, 1983.

Robinson, Ian. "The Prose and Poetry of the Book of Common Prayer." In *The Book of Common Prayer: Past, Present and Future,* edited by Prudence Dailey, 70–81. London: Continuum, 2011.

Rosendale, Timothy. *Liturgy and Literature in the Making of Protestant England.* Cambridge: Cambridge University Press, 2011.

Ross, Aileen. "'Baffled and Befooled': Misogyny in the Work of John Bunyan." *Awakening Words: John Bunyan and the Language of Community,* edited by David Gay, James G. Randall, Arlette Zinck, 153–68. Newark: University of Delaware Press, London: Associated University Presses, 2000.

Rudnytsky, Peter L. "Dissociation and Decapitation." *Trauma and Transformation: The Political Progress of John Bunyan,* 14–35. Stanford: Stanford University Press, 2008.

Rudrum, Alan. "Paradoxical Persona: Henry Vaughan's Self-Fashioning Author(s)." *Huntington Library Quarterly* 62 (1999): 351–67.

– "Narrative, Typology and Politics in Henry Vaughan's 'Isaac's Marriage.'" *Connotations* 11 no. 1 (2001/2): 78–90. Web.

Runyon, Daniel V. *John Bunyan's Master Story: The Holy War as Battle Allegory in Religious and Biblical Context.* Lewiston: The Edwin Mellen Press, 2007.

Schoenfeldt, Michael. *Prayer and Power: George Herbert and Renaissance Courtship.* Chicago: University of Chicago Press, 1991.

Shawcross, John. *The Uncertain World of Samson Agonistes.* London: D.S. Brewer, 2001.

Sherwood, Terry. *Herbert's Prayerful Art.* Toronto: University of Toronto Press, 1989.

Shirkie, Amie. "Marketing Salvation: Devotional Handbooks for Early Modern Householders." Doctoral Dissertation. Edmonton: University of Alberta, 2014.

Shitaka, Hideyuki. "The meaning of the Joint Publication of *Paradise Regained* and *Samson Agonistes.*" In *Originality and Adventure: Essays on English Language and Literature in Honour of Msahiko Kanno,* edited by Yoshiyuki Nakao and Akiyuki Jimura. Tokyo: Eihosha, 2002.

Shuger, Deborah, *Habits of Thought in the English Renaissance.* Berkeley: University of California Press, 1990.

Simpson, Ken. *Spiritual Architecture and Paradise Regained: Milton's Literary Ecclesiology.* Pittsburgh: Duquesne University Press, 2007.

Skerpan-Wheeler, Elizabeth. *Eikon Basilike* and the rhetoric of self-representation." *The Royal Image: Representations of Charles I,* edited by Thomas Corns, 122–40. Cambridge: Cambridge University Press, 1999.

Spinks, Bryan. "From Elizabeth I to Charles II." In *The Oxford Guide to the Book of Common Prayer: A Worldwide Survey,* edited by Charles Hefling and Cynthia Shattuck, 44–55. Oxford: Oxford University Press, 2006.

Sprott, S.E. *A Maske: The Earlier Versions.* Toronto: University of Toronto Press, 1973.

Stranks, C.J. *The Life and Writings of Jeremy Taylor.* London: SPCK, 1952.

Sutton, John. "John Ball." *Oxford Dictionary of National Biography.*

Targoff, Ramie. *Common Prayer: The Language of Public Devotion in Early Modern England.* Chicago: University of Chicago Press, 2001.

Tedder, H.R. Revised. William Proctor Williams. "Richard Royston." *Oxford Dictionary of National Biography.*

Tipson, Baird. "A Dark Side of Seventeenth-Century English Protestantism: The Sin Against the Holy Spirit." *The Harvard Theological Review* 77 nos. 3–4 (July–October 1984): 301–30.

Travers, Michael Ernest. *The Devotional Experience in the Poetry of John Milton.* Lewiston: Edwin Mellon Press, 1988.

Tuttle, Imilda. *Concordance to Vaughan's Silex Scintillan.* University Park and London: The Pennsylvania State University Press, 1969.

Underwood, T.L. "'For then I should be a Ranter or a Quaker': John Bunyan and Radical Religion." In *Awakening Words: John Bunyan and the Language of Community*, edited by David Gay, James G. Randall, Arlette Zinck, 127–40. Newark: University of Delaware Press, London: Associated University Presses, 2000.

Vallance, Edward. "The dangers of prudence: salus populi suprema lex, Robert Sanderson, and the 'Case of the Liturgy.'" *Renaissance Studies* 23 no. 4 (2009): 534–51.

Watson, Graeme. "The Temple in 'The Night': Henry Vaughan and the Collapse of the Established Church." *Modern Philology* 84 no. 2 (1986): 144–61.

West, Philip. *Henry Vaughan's Silex Scintillans: Scripture Uses.* Oxford: Oxford University Press, 2001.

Williams, James G. *Women Recounted: Narrative Thinking and the God of Israel.* Sheffield: Almond Press, 1982.

Williams, Rowan. "George Herbert and Henry Vaughan." Address Delivered to the Temenos Society, March 28, 2007. rowanwilliams.archbishopofcanterbury .org/articles.php/2004/the-archbishop-on-george-herbert-and-henry-vaughan.

Wittreich, Joseph. *Interpreting Samson Agonistes.* Princeton: Princeton University Press, 1986.

Wood, Derek. *Exiled from Light: Divine Law, Morality, and Violence in Milton's Samson Agonistes.* Toronto: University of Toronto Press, 2001.

Index

Achinstein, Sharon, 12, 36, 95, 122, 167n4, 171n79
Act of Uniformity, 20, 131, 133, 135, 165, 183n6
Ainsworth, David, 95
Allen, Don Cameron, 181n42
Alter, Robert, 77, 119
Ambrose, 173n44
Anabaptist, 52
Andrewes, Lancelot, 10–12, 14–50, 55, 57, 61–2, 64, 81–2, 85–6, 88–9, 95–6, 98, 109, 112–16, 136, 141, 145, 158, 165, 168–71, 176n3, 177n8; works: *Institutiones Piae*, 14, 22, 26–8, 169n36; *The morall law expounded*, 180n21; *Nineteen Sermons Concerning Prayer*, 22–3, 26–7; "Of Imaginings," 17–19, 58, 84; *Preces Privatae* (or private devotions), 11, 22, 29–30, 32, 34, 43, 62; *XCVI Sermons*, 18, 26–7; *Seven sermons on, the wonderfull combate (for Gods glorie and mans salvation) between Christ and Sathan*, 112–13
Anselm, 74
Apocalypse, 15, 70, 90, 168n5
Appleby, David, 183n5
Aubrey, John, 103

Augustine of Canterbury 69
Augustine of Hippo, 15, 30, 71, 104, 106, 118, 121, 170n4, 180n13, 181n44
Aristotle, 120–1, 181n44
Arminianism, 15–17, 85, 177n8

Bacon, Anne, 167n6
Baker, Augustine, O.S.B., 11, 68–72
Bal, Mieke, 119
Ball, John, 88
baptism, 8, 20, 37, 52, 113, 152, 156
Baptist, 133, 141, 152
Barbour, Hugh, 142
Barbour, Reid, 61
Barclay, Robert, 149–50
Bastwick, John, 87
Bauman, Richard, 142, 184n51
Baxter, Richard, 11, 131–2, 141, 171
Beaumont, Agnes, 153
Bedford, 129–30, 133, 151
Bible, Old Testament: Genesis, 29–31, 36, 74, 76, 79, 101, 128, 151, 154; Exodus, 40, 119; Deuteronomy, 117; Joshua, 66; Judges, 13, 66, 116, 118–19, 122–3, 127–8, 130, 133, 145, 147, 181n36; 2 Samuel, 66, 126; 2 Kings, 36; 1 Chronicles, 169n27; Job, 113, 120, 181n41; Psalms, 6, 11–12, 22, 31, 37, 53–6, 62, 92,

117–19, 125, 127–8, 139, 142, 161,
    172; Ecclesiastes, 58; Isaiah, 9, 84,
    94, 125; Daniel, 131; Jonah, 95
Bible, New Testament: Matthew,
    19–20, 22, 41, 115–16, 125–6, 156,
    159–61, 169n21; Mark, 118, 139,
    160; Luke, 5, 19–21, 24, 30–1, 40,
    74, 115–16, 118, 134, 138, 159, 161,
    169n21, 173n44; John, 30, 43, 76, 87,
    159; Acts, 7–8, 18, 62, 139, 147, 151;
    Romans, 8, 22, 24, 43, 46–7, 58–62,
    72, 80, 98, 104, 126, 135, 137, 143,
    153, 158, 162, 165, 173n45; 1
    Corinthians, 5, 44, 75, 85–6, 88–9,
    98, 112, 130, 143, 151, 177n7; 2
    Corinthians, 23, 75; 1 Timothy, 32;
    Hebrews, 114, 186n95; 1 Peter, 31,
    130; Revelation, 15, 32, 70, 76, 85,
    88, 151, 154, 157, 177n7
Black Bartholomew's Day, 118, 131,
    183n5
blasphemy, 12–13, 63, 109–11, 126,
    129, 132, 136, 138–41, 144–7, 151,
    159–60, 164
Blessington, Francis, 103
Book of Common Prayer (or prayer
    book), 3–13, 16, 23, 30–1, 36–7, 40,
    49, 53–4, 56–7, 61, 63–4, 67, 75, 77–
    9, 81, 83–5, 87, 91, 94, 96–7, 117–18,
    122–3, 127, 130–3, 135–7, 142–3,
    147–9, 152, 157, 160–1, 164, 177n8
Branch, Lori, 135
Brightman, F.E., 30–1
Brook, Stella, 9, 167n9
Brown, Cedric, 85
Brueggeman, Walter, 119, 128
Buckeridge, John, 16–17, 32
Bunyan, John, 12–13, 15, 17, 38, 64, 96,
    127, 129–65, 184nn34, 50, 186nn94,
    96; works: A Case of Conscience
    Resolved, 13, 151, 153; Grace
    Abounding, 13, 127, 130, 138–41,

151, 183n25; The Holy War, 13, 72,
    129, 139, 153–62, 164; I Will Pray
    with the Spirit, 13, 127, 130, 133,
    135–6, 138, 157–60, 165; Pilgrim's
    Progress part one, 13, 138–9, 153
Burrough Edward, 141, 150
Burton, Henry, 87

Cable, Lana, 100
Calhoun, Thomas, 75
Calvinism (or Calvin) 11, 13, 15–17,
    23, 38, 40, 56–7, 88–9, 141, 150
Cambridge, 8, 38, 50
Camden, Vera, 138, 140, 151
Campbell, Gordon, 85
charity, 14, 18–19, 23, 25, 29, 39–42,
    44–5, 48, 51, 53, 55–6, 70, 72, 85,
    88–9, 96, 110, 112, 132, 139, 172n4
Charles I, 11–12, 16–17, 29, 50, 54,
    63–4, 91–2, 94–9, 123, 133, 178n32,
    179n58
Charles II, 10, 16, 91–2, 102, 124, 126,
    130–1, 133, 157, 173n48, 178n37,
    183n6
Civil War, 16, 50, 54, 56–7, 69–70, 96,
    102, 130, 164, 185n74
Clifford, James, 178n32
Coffey, John, 141
Collinson, Patrick, 15, 17
communion, 5, 17, 19, 36–7, 40, 45, 47,
    55, 66–7, 71, 88, 96, 135, 151. See also
    Eucharist
Conformity (Conformists), 11–13,
    15–17, 19, 44, 83–4, 89, 111, 116, 118,
    130–4, 136, 160
contemplative prayer, 69, 71–2, 104,
    106–7
Conti, Brooke, 14, 137, 184n34
Corns, Thomas, 85, 142
Corporation Act, 154
Corthell, Ron, 107
Cosin, John, 16, 55, 62, 86–7, 177n14

Cranmer, Thomas, 3, 10, 29, 49, 57, 157, 167n9, 172n2
Crashaw, Richard, 69
Creed, 22, 26, 45, 51–2, 55, 68, 87, 124, 170n41
Cressy, Serenus, O.S.B., 11, 69, 71–2
Cromwell, Oliver, 62–3, 72, 149
Cummings, Brian, 167n1
Curry, David, 9–10

Daems, Jim, and Holly Faith Nelson, 92
Damrosch, Leo, 145–6
Danielson, Dennis, 111
Davies, Horton, 123
Declaration of Breda, 130–2
Dell, William, 57–8
despair, 108, 180n6, 181n42
Directory of Public Worship 3, 11, 55–8, 60–1, 63–4, 67, 97, 148
Dissent (and Dissenters), 6, 11–13, 15, 63–4, 84, 88, 91, 102, 110–11, 119, 121–3, 127, 129, 131, 135, 137–8, 146, 148, 153, 156–8, 162, 164–5, 167n4, 171n75, 186n96
Dix, Dom Gregory, 83
Doerksen, Daniel, 40
Donne, John, 32, 41, 44, 106, 108
Drake, Richard, 32–4
Duffy, Eamon, 165
Duppa, Bryan, 79
Dyck, Paul, 37, 57, 78

Egerton, Sir Charles, 70
Egerton, John, Earl of Bridgewater, 85
Eikon Basilike, 12, 29, 50, 64, 84, 91–8, 100, 102–3, 108, 118, 178n32
Elizabeth I, 3, 10, 11, 16, 68, 70, 133, 173n48
episcopacy, 17, 32, 49, 51, 53, 67
Esterhammer, Angela, 179n1
Eucharist, 20, 25, 43, 45–6, 48, 54, 58–9, 61, 67, 83–5, 94, 111, 126. See also communion
Evans, Michelle, 163–4

fancy, 17–18, 33, 61, 69–70, 86, 99, 108
Fell, Margaret, 12, 151
Fenton, Mary, 104, 139
Ferrar, Nicholas, 37
Ferry, Anne Davidson, 10
Fisher, Ambrose, 87
Forrest, James F., 156–7, 186n90
Foster, Andrew, 177n8
Foster, William, 133, 177n8
Fox, George, 12–13, 142–5, 147–9, 151
Foxe, John, 15, 67
Frye, Northrop, 168n5

Garrett, Cynthia, 40
Gatford, Lionel, 63
Gauden, John, 91, 132–3, 178n32
genre, 15, 30, 85, 109, 119
Gibbons, Daniel R., 10
Gifford, John, 130
Gilman, Ernest, 95
Goldie, Mark, 184n39
Goodwin, John, 52, 72
Gowry Plot, 123
Great Tew Circle, 69
Greaves, Richard L., 133, 150, 154
Greenfeld, Liah, 116
Guibbory, Achsah, 124
Gunpowder Plot, 68, 123, 125
Gwyn, Douglas, 147

Hall, Joseph, 89, 104, 180n8
Hammond, Henry, 20
Harwood, John, 64
Haskin, Dayton, 77
Henrikson, Erin, 118, 181n34
Henry VIII, 16
Herbert, George, 10–12, 14, 29, 32–3, 36–48, 70, 73, 78–81, 85, 109, 156,

158; poems from *The Temple*: "The
Altar," 37, 39–40; "The Church
Floor," 41; "The Church Porch," 38;
"The Collar," 46; Latin epigram,
33; "Love (2)," 14, 41–2; "Prayer
(1)," 43–4, 47, 80, 156, 158; "Prayer
(2)," 45, 47; "Superluminare," 40–1;
prose: *The Country Parson*, 44–5
Herbert, Magdalen, 41
heresy, 7, 66, 68, 84, 87, 109, 137, 146
Hesiod, 179n59
Higginson, Francis, 142
Hillier, Russell, 118, 181n34
Hinds, Hilary, 141, 144, 146, 151
Hollingworth, Richard, 178n32
Holy Trinity, 21, 26, 45–6, 84, 106
Homer, 103
Hooker, Richard, 16–17, 49, 171n79
hope, 22–3, 29, 42–3, 53–4, 68, 85, 88,
    112, 118–20, 122, 127, 131–2, 134, 163
Hughes, Merritt, 99, 179n59
Hunter, William B., 177n7
Huntley, Frank Livingstone, 106, 180n8
Hutson, Lorna, 175n101

Ignatius Loyola, 104, 106, 180n8
imagination, 4, 6–7, 11, 18, 23, 33, 47,
    61–2, 95–6, 100, 145, 149, 162, 165
imaginings, 6, 14, 17–19, 22–3, 44, 48,
    57, 61–2, 70, 85–8, 95, 136, 146
Incarnation, 26, 45, 81–2, 92, 94, 96,
    117, 165
Independents, 56, 58, 148
inspiration, 4, 7–8, 24 39, 49, 56, 59–
    61, 68, 71–2, 78, 87–8, 101, 122, 142,
    144, 149–50, 157, 184n54
intercession, 8, 12, 24–5, 32, 59, 92, 98,
    103, 109, 111–12, 136, 162
Interregnum, 49, 51, 61, 63, 66–7, 72,
    132
Ireland, 50
Isaacson, Henry, 22, 29, 169n36

James I, 17
James, P.D., 9
Jeremiad, 66–7
Jewish prayers, 20–1, 89–90, 116,
    169n27
Jones, Inigo, 91
Jonson, Ben, 6, 91
Juxon, William, 50, 91

Keach, Benjamin, 156
Keeble, N.H., 102, 132, 135, 180n3
Keith, George, 150
Kelynge, John, 130, 135, 147–8, 158
kenosis, 47, 81, 96, 113–14, 165
Kenyon, J.P., 131
Kermode, Frank, 121, 168n5
Kiffin, William, 152
Knoppers, Laura Lunger, 92, 131
Kohler, Kauffman, 169n27
Kuchar, Gary, 36, 171n79

Lake, Peter, 10, 16–18
Lander, Jesse, 5
Laud, William (and Laudianism),
    11–12, 16–18, 22, 26–7, 29, 32–3, 36,
    50–1, 55, 67, 69, 70, 85, 88, 169n36
Lawes, Henry, 85
Leslie, Henry, 51
Lewalski, Barbara, 180n22
Lindale, William, 133–4
Litany, 9–10, 64
liturgy, 3, 5–6, 9, 11–13, 18, 21, 26,
    29, 36–7, 47, 50, 55–6, 58, 61, 63–4,
    66–7, 75, 78, 80–1, 83–91, 94–8, 111,
    118–21, 123, 125–8, 131–2, 135, 142,
    158–9, 170n41, 172–3n23
Lloyd, David, 178n37
Locke, John, 164
Loddington, William, 149
Loewenstein, David, 95–6
Lord's Prayer, 11–12, 14, 18–26, 29,
    32–3, 37, 41, 43, 45, 53, 86–7, 89, 98,

104, 107, 113–15, 129–30, 132, 135,
144, 146, 148, 157–62, 169nn21, 27,
170n41, 186n96
Loscocco, Paula, 53
Low, Anthony, 120
Luther, Martin, 53–4, 140
Lynch, Kathleen, 131

MacCallum, Hugh, 119
MacCulloch, Diarmaid, 16, 29, 63
Madan, Francis F., 178n32
Manton, Thomas, 20
Marshall, William, 29, 92–3, 97
Martz, Louis L., 104, 106
McCullough, P.E., 11, 26, 29, 32, 63
McCutcheon, Elizabeth, 29, 32
meditation, 11–12, 22–3, 29–30, 32–3,
37–9, 45–6, 50, 55, 59, 61, 64, 69, 75–
9, 82, 84, 92, 95, 103–4, 106–9, 111,
118–19, 128, 138, 180n8, 186n96
Mensch, James, 96, 165
Merrill, Thomas F., 107
Miller, Patrick, 117
Milton, Anthony, 15
Milton, John, 6, 8, 9, 11–13, 15,
49, 52, 59, 76–7, 83–93, 95–103,
107–23, 125–9, 137–8, 146, 164–5,
177n7, 179n60, 181n42, 186n91;
prose works: *Animadversions*,
90–1; *Areopagitica*, 49, 52, 92, 96,
98, 129; *De Doctrina Christiana*, 91;
Eikonoklastes, 12, 83–4, 91, 95, 97,
103; *Reason of Church Government*,
8, 101, 117; *Of Reformation*, 90–1;
Of True Religion, 109, 109 114–15;
*Ready and Easy Way to Establish a
Free Commonwealth*, 84, 91; *Treatise
of Civil Power*, 84, 91, 146, 164;
poems: *Comus* (A Mask presented
at Ludlow Castle), 11–12, 83–6,
88–9, 99, 111, 177nn7, 10; Elegy III,
176n3; "Lycidas," 8, 188n91; "On

the Morning of Christ's Nativity,"
84; *Paradise Lost*, 15, 76, 84, 90–1,
98–9, 101–2, 105–7, 109–10, 118,
122, 165, 179n45; *Paradise Regained*,
12, 89–90, 98, 112–15, 118, 120,
122, 181n41; *Samson Agonistes*, 84,
118–23, 127–8; Sonnet 7, 84; Sonnet
9, 109; Sonnet 19, 59, 107
Mohamed, Feisal, 164
Mullett, Michael, 133

Najapfour, Brian G., 169n28
Narveson, Kate, 37
Neelon, David, 185n74
Nonconformity, 3, 12, 36, 102, 131–2
Norminton, Leander, 69–70
Nuttall, Geoffrey, 56, 58

Oxford, 50, 73

parables: Pharisee and Publican, 31,
33, 169n21; Prodigal Son, 107; Talents, 59, 106–7; Unrighteous Judge,
169n21
Parliament of England, 3, 11–12, 56–7,
63, 89, 94, 124, 129, 131, 138, 145,
164, 183n6
Parry, Graham, 29, 33
patience, 41, 75, 84, 102, 107, 111–13,
121, 167n6
Paul, Apostle, 7, 23, 37, 42, 44, 47, 53,
57, 59, 69, 72, 75, 78, 85–6, 88–9,
121, 130, 136–7, 143–4, 158, 160, 165
Pearson, Anthony, 147
persecution, 13, 52–3, 72, 97, 121, 132,
137, 146–9, 156–7, 160, 162, 164,
186nn98, 99
Philips, Katherine, 73–4, 76
Phillips, Edward, 103
Popish Plot, 154
Porter, H. Boone, 53, 55, 61
predestination, 15–17, 23, 141, 158

Presbyterians, 16, 56, 58, 131, 148
Prideaux, John, 64
Prior, Charles, 16
prison, 13, 15, 51, 66, 83, 99, 127, 130,
     132–4, 138, 141, 145, 147–8, 150,
     158, 173, 183n25, 186nn98, 99
Prynne, William, 87
Pursglove, Glyn, 76

Quakers, 13, 15, 129, 138, 141–52,
     184nn50, 51
Quintilian, 58

Radzinowicz, Mary-Ann, 181n42
Ranters, 138, 142, 146, 151
recusants, 68, 70
Rees, David Daniel, 68
Reformation, 5–6, 9–10, 16, 53, 57, 67,
     71, 90–1, 110, 132, 134, 164, 177n8
regicide, 11–12, 49, 53, 84, 91, 123–4,
     127, 138
Restoration, 12, 16, 36, 50, 64, 72, 84,
     91–2, 100, 102, 110, 116, 118, 120,
     122–4, 126–7, 129–30, 132–3, 141,
     146, 167n4, 178n37
Reynolds, Edward, 124
Ricoeur, Paul, 121, 181n44
Robartes, Foulke, 70
Roberts, Arthur O., 142
Robinson, Ian, 9
Rogers, Thomas, 104, 106
Rosendale, Timothy, 56
Ross, Aileen, 152
Royston, Richard, 50, 64, 178n32
Rudnytsky, Peter L., 91
Rudrum, Alan, 74, 76
Runyon, Daniel V., 156–7

Savoy Conference, 64, 124, 131
Schoenfeldt, Michael, 39, 46
Scotland, 16, 56
Scultetus, D. Abrahamus, 20

sects (or sectarian), 51–3, 63, 69, 70–2,
     112, 132–3, 138, 141, 149, 151, 167n4
Septuagint, 9
Sharrock, Roger, 156–7
Shawcross, John, 120, 181n42
Sheldon, Gilbert, 131
Sherwood, Terry, 38
Shirkie, Amie, 168n14
Shitaka, Hideyuki, 122
Shuger, Deborah, 17
Sidney, Mary, 54
Sidney, Philip, 6, 54–6, 61, 98
Simpson, Ken, 115
Skerpan-Wheeler, Elizabeth, 92
Smart, Peter, 87, 177n14
Smectymnuus, 21, 89–90, 169, 177n25
Sparrow, Anthony, 64
Spencer, John, 123
Spenser, Edmund, 6
Spinks, Bryan, 173n48
Sprott, S.E., 177n10
Stranks, C.J., 50

Targoff, Ramie, 37, 122
Taylor, Jeremy, 6–9, 11–12, 18, 49–64,
     66–73, 75, 77–9, 81–3, 91–2, 95–7,
     99–100, 136, 165, 174n55, 175n101,
     178n32; prose works: *Apology
     for Authorized and Set forms of
     Liturgie*, 6–9, 49–50, 55–61, 68,
     94–7; *A Collection of Offices or Forms
     of Prayer*, 53, 64–8; *A Discourse
     concerning prayer ex tempore*, 50, 52,
     94; *Discourse of the nature, offices,
     and measures of friendship*, 73; *The
     Great Exemplar*, 61; *The Golden
     Grove*, 62; *XXVIII Sermons Preached
     at Golden Grove*, 62; *XXV Sermons
     Preached at Golden-Grove*, 172n4;
     The Liberty of Prophesying, 50–3,
     68; *Of the sacred order and offices of
     episcopacy*, 51–2; *Psalter of David*,

53–5, 92; *The Rules and Exercises of Holy Dying*, 61; *The Rules and Exercises of Holy Living*, 61; *Symbolon theologikon*, 50

Tedder, H.R., 178n32

Teresa of Avila, 69

terror, 117, 120, 140, 159

Tertullian, Septimus, 20–2, 43–4, 45, 86, 88, 90, 148, 158, 169, 186n95, 186–7n99

Tipson, Baird, 140–1

toleration, 49–53, 55, 63, 69, 72, 84, 116, 130–2, 150, 164

tragedy, 12, 66, 103, 119–21, 128

Travers, Michael Ernest, 180n13

Tyndale, William, 9–10

Underwood, T.L., 141, 146, 150–1

Vallance, Edward, 63

Vaughan, Henry, 11, 72–82; poems: "The Call," 80; "Isaac's Marriage," 76–7; "The Match," 80; "The Morning-watch," 80; "Mount of Olives (I)," 81–2; "Mount of Olives (2)," 8; "Regeneration," 79; "Religion, 79–80; "Rules and Lessons," 72, 80–1; "The Storm," 80; "To the Holy Bible," 77–8; "White Sunday," 78–9; prose works: *The Mount of Olives, or Solitary Devotions*, 74–5, 77–9, 81; *The Praise and Happiness of the Country Life*, 73

Venner, Thomas, 131

violence, 46, 110, 119–22, 126, 131, 146, 148, 164, 186–7n99

Virgil, 103

Vulgate, 31, 173n45

Wales, 50, 61, 73–4, 85, 178n32

Walton, Izaak, 36

Walwyn, William, 52

Watson, Graeme, 70

Wedlock, Thomas, 146

West, Philip, 77, 79

Whitehall, 91, 98, 124

Whittingham, William, 56

Williams, Roger, 52

Williams, Rowan, 33, 38

Wingate, Francis, 133

Wither, George, 163, 172–3n23

Wittreich, Joseph, 181n42

Wood, Derek, 122

Wren, Matthew, 16, 125

zeal, 12, 14, 18, 22, 40–2, 44, 48, 50–1, 70–1, 89, 92, 96, 109–10, 112, 115, 138–9, 163, 165